RACISM:
THE AUSTRALIAN EXPERIENCE
A STUDY OF RACE PREJUDICE IN AUSTRALIA

VOLUME 1
PREJUDICE AND XENOPHOBIA

VOLUME 2
BLACK versus WHITE

VOLUME 3
COLONIALISM

RACISM:
The Australian Experience

A STUDY OF RACE PREJUDICE IN AUSTRALIA

Edited by

F. S. STEVENS

VOLUME 1

PREJUDICE AND XENOPHOBIA

TAPLINGER PUBLISHING CO. INC.

NEW YORK

First published in the United States in 1972 by
TAPLINGER PUBLISHING CO, INC
New York, New York

Published simultaneously in the Dominion of Canada by
Burns & MacEachern Ltd, Ontario

Library of Congress Catalog Card Number: 70-179992

ISBN 0-8008-6580-4

PREFACE

With the object of assisting in the celebration of the United Nations International Year for Action to Combat Racism and Racial Discrimination, an *ad hoc* committee of interested individuals was formed in Sydney in October, 1970. Under the chairmanship of Hyam Brezniak, Editor of *The Bridge*, journal of the Australian Jewish Quarterly Foundation, the committee was limited to a small, but balanced representation of university and community leaders. These included:

> Sol Encel, Professor of Sociology, University of New South Wales
> Frank Engel, Secretary of the Australian Council of Churches
> Peter McGregor, Secretary, The Australian Citizens Campaign to Overcome Racial Discrimination (A.C.C.O.R.D.)
> Frank Stevens, Senior Lecturer in Industrial Relations, University of New South Wales

After consideration of various ways in which the most direct contribution to discussion of the subject of race prejudice might be made, the committee decided to produce an anthology on the subject, contributed to by people working in the field of race relations.

As a statement of policy, the committee determined that the question of the existence of racism in Australia was to be an open matter and that contributors invited to participate in the series should be selected, not for their opinions on the matter, but on their standing in the field. In all, some ninety invitations to contribute were extended, and approximately one third of the recipients accepted the opportunity. Their contributions are published in full, without any attempt to achieve a strict editorial format tied to the general terms of reference of the main or subsidiary titles of the volumes.

F.S.S.

Kensington

June 71

The publication of this book has been sponsored by the
United Nations Association of Australia
and the
Australian Committee to Combat Racism
and
Racial Discrimination

CONTENTS

AUTHORS

M. BITTMAN, B.A.(U.S.N.W.)

> Tutor, School of Sociology
> University of New South Wales, Kensington, N.S.W.
> *(Chapter 1)*

I. H. BURNLEY, M.A.(Cantab.), Ph.D.

> Research Fellow, Department of Demography,
> Research School of Social Sciences, Australian National University,
> Canberra, A.C.T.
> *(Chapter 5)*

S. O. D'ALTON, M.Ec.(Syd.)

> Lecturer, School of Sociology
> University of New South Wales, Kensington, N.S.W.
> *(Chapter 1)*

A. G. DOCZY, B.A., Ph.D., Dip.Ed.(W. Aust.), M.A.Ps.S., A.B.Ps.S.

> Senior Lecturer, Department of Education
> University of Newcastle, Newcastle, N.S.W.
> *(Chapter 4)*

S. ENCEL, M.A., Ph.D.(Melb.)

> Professor, Department of Sociology
> University of New South Wales, Kensington, N.S.W.
> *(Chapter 3)*

REVEREND F. ENGEL, B.A., B.D.(Melb.)

> Secretary, Australian Council of Churches
> 511 Kent Street, Sydney, N.S.W.
> *(Chapter 16)*

M. C. FRAME, M.B., B.Ch., M.A.N.Z.P., D.P.M.

> Medical Superintendent, Gladesville Hospital and Admission Centre
> Victoria Road, Gladesville, N.S.W.
> *(Chapter 2)*

R. V. HALL, B.A.(Syd.)

> Private Secretary, Leader of the Opposition
> Parliament House, Canberra, A.C.T.
> *(Chapter 12)*

J. HEISS, B.A., M.A.(N.Y.), Ph.D.(Ind.)

> Professor, School of Sociology
> University of Connecticut, Connecticut, U.S.A.
> *(Chapter 9)*

A. HUCK, M.A.(Melb.)

> Reader, Department of Political Science
> University of Melbourne, Melbourne, Vic.
> *(Chapter 10)*

C. B. KERR, D.Phil.(Oxford), M.B., B.S.

Professor of Preventive and Social Medicine, School of Public Health and Tropical Medicine
University of Sydney, Sydney, N.S.W.
(Chapter 7)

H. O. McQUEEN, M.A.(Qld.)

Lecturer, Department of History, School of General Studies
Australian National University, Canberra, A.C.T.
(Chapter 11)

P. Y. MEDDING, M.A.(Melb.), Ph.D.(Harvard)

Reader in Politics, Faculty of Economics and Politics
Monash University, Clayton, Vic.
(Chapter 8)

MOST REVEREND R. A. MULKEARNS, D.D., D.C.L.

Bishop of Ballarat
P.O. Box 121, Ballarat, Vic.
(Chapter 17)

R. G. NETTHEIM, A.M.(Tufts), LL.B.(Syd.)

Professor, Faculty of Law
University of New South Wales, Kensington, N.S.W.
(Chapter 15)

A. C. PALFREEMAN, Licès Ses. Pol.(Gen.)

Senior Lecturer, School of Political Science
University of New South Wales, Kensington, N.S.W.
(Chapter 13)

MOIRA SALTER, M.Ec.(Syd.)

Research Fellow, Research School of Pacific Studies,
Institute of Advanced Studies, Australian National University, Canberra, A.C.T.
(Chapter 6)

W. E. H. STANNER, M.A.(Syd.), Ph.D.(Lon.)

Emeritus Professor of Anthropology, Research School of Pacific Studies
Institute of Advanced Studies, Australian National University, Canberra, A.C.T.
(Introduction)

F. S. STEVENS, B.A.(Syd.), M.A.(Stan.)

Senior Lecturer, Department of Industrial Relations
School of Economics, University of New South Wales, Kensington, N.S.W.
(Editor, Foreword)

A. T. YARWOOD, M.A., Dip.Ed.(Syd.)

Associate Professor, Department of History
University of New England, Armidale, N.S.W.
(Chapter 14)

FOREWORD

F. S. Stevens

The question of whether or not Australia is a 'racist' country has been freely mooted since the early days of settlement. Because of the changing patterns of social analysis and the varying standards of sophistication of the social sciences, the debate has lacked vigour, as even the standards of the most articulate have a tendency to conform with the accepted mores of any one age. The question, however, has become more critical in recent years.

Geographical and political isolation presented Australia with a unique social and cultural heritage. The Australian continent has developed, in many ways, as the backwater to the affluent societies of the Western world, but events are edging it towards the areas of turbulence which are transforming world politics in the closing decades of the twentieth century.

Australia, as a trading nation, has been forced to take these changing power relationships into account in adapting itself to the pragmatic opportunities of international commerce. There are some who would say that this adjustment has been too slow and, to date, virtually inconsequential; hence the nation has forfeited its right to commercial leadership in the new world because of its excesses in the old. Certainly the processes of change have been painful.

The involvement of Australia in the total conflagration against racism in Nazi Germany revealed to many the insecurity of their own position when judged by standards acceptable to an increasingly tolerant world. To others, of course, it simply meant an additional opportunity whereby the evasions and prejudices of the past could be erected into a new form of nationalist bias. Victory, unfortunately, has meant the continuation and rejuvenation of old attitudes, making the process of adjustment even more difficult.

But the majority of Australians, today, are sensitive to the charge of racial intolerance. However, their reactions, as might be expected in conditions of change, have been confused and contradictory. On the one hand, policy has moved forward to an accommodation with the complexities of existence which present themselves to an insular people; on the other, resentment and resistance to criticism have reflected the persistence of long established assumptions and ideologies.

Australians are slowly becoming aware of the opportunities they have forgone because of isolation and a singular cultural and racial inheritance. Today, they are groping to understand the circumstances which have deprived them of the unique social experiences of the original inhabitants of the continent. Similarly, they are searching for an accommodation with their immediate neighbours, without ever coming to grips with their position. An enlargement of Australia's cultural and political horizons requires the Australian community to understand the complexities of race relations, both internally and externally, and to move away from the complacent isolation of the past. This complacency is reflected in the

1

lopsided teaching of history, both at schools and universities, and the hesitant growth of anthropology and sociology as academic subjects. Instead of critical thought and scholarship, there has been the shibboleth of the 'White Australia' policy to fall back on.

The area of public debate, itself, seems to be cloudy and muddled. The study of race relations is an infant subject. Are not the very premises on which social reformers call for reconsideration and restraint, themselves but newly and poorly formed? Has it been proven beyond all scientific doubt that no racial group has a preserve of intelligence and drive? These are questions of moment which even the most ungenerous critics might concede. Are we, in fact, really sure of the grounds on which the debate over racial prejudice is waged? What are the fundamental bases of the charge? It is here that difficulty ensues.

Like the debate on social policy, in most countries the urgency of race relations frequently depends on the economic realities of life. Australia, in the past, has been able to afford such luxuries as a selective immigration policy and in doing so has conducted itself, in fact, very little differently from the majority of countries which have formulated restrictive entry policies. However, Australia's needs and political affiliations have changed, bringing the necessity to adjust its policies in accord with the new standards of international morality. The whole world, in fact, may be considered to have grown to its present level of technical and industrial sophistication within a framework of racial discrimination. The disparities of international growth have provided a format within which racial groups could operate with greatly varying advantages. However, with the rapid expansion of the new nation states of Africa and Asia, the technological superiority of any one group is no longer paramount in the settlement of world affairs.

These thoughts were in the minds of the group which came together to plan these three volumes. The problem appeared, initially, as a simple one. It became more complicated when it was found impossible to restrict the enquiry to overt examples of discrimination or brutality. Race conflict, like cancer, seems to feed on itself and use even the most unsuspecting groups as the vehicle for its contagion. But again, like clinical analysis, it became difficult at the extremes of the condition to define the malaise and to distinguish the healthy portion of the body politic. What, in fact, was evidence of racism, and what were the characteristics of other aspects of social disorder, malfunction or inequality?

To add to this problem there was a semantic question of what was meant by race prejudice and precisely when it became racism. Indeed, what was meant by the latter in any case?

Two readily available definitions of racism came to mind and they bear repeating in the introduction to these two volumes so that the reader may develop his own order of priorities in an endeavour to solve some of the problems faced by research workers on the subject. The Uppsala Assembly of the World Council of Churches approached the problem in the following way:—

>By *racism* we mean ethnocentric pride in one's own racial group and preference for the distinctive characteristics of that group; belief that these characteristics are fundamentally biological in nature and are thus transmitted to succeeding generations; strong

negative feelings towards other groups who do not share those characteristics, coupled with the trust to discriminate against and exclude the out-group from full participation in the life of the community.[1]

A committee of experts drafted the following definition for U.N.E.S.C.O. in 1967:—

> *Racism,* namely anti-social beliefs and acts which are based on the fallacy that discriminatory inter-group relations are justifiable on biological grounds . . . . Racism falsely claims that there is a scientific basis for arranging groups hierarchically in terms of psychological and cultural characteristics that are immutable and innate. In this way it seeks to make existing differences appear inviolable as a means of permanently maintaining current relations between groups.[2]

Superimposed on these definitions of attitudes are the less clearly defined limits of practice; of the intermingling of human thought and reaction which might give rise to any particular course of events in a given set of conditions. It is here that the real difficulty in understanding the problem began to show.

Encel, in his paper in Volume 1 clearly points out the need to differentiate between *racism* and *racialism,* the first being ideology and the second practice. He then states that the difference is of no practical bearing as it is virtually impossible to find one without the other. But this might be said about most facets of social relations. They are an amalgam of many competing and often conflicting and illogical responses on the part of people under stress or endeavouring to improve their own position or comfort in life. When can one claim, with adequate proof, that the reactions of people to any given situation are the result of one singular logical, or indeed, illogical, standard of the mind? Reactions in all situations are woven from the total consciousness and philosophy of the individual. As Frame indicates, in this volume, the real causes might be buried deep in the sub-conscious and not immediately known to the individual at all. In this light, responses to any complex social situation might be equally the result of social forces other than the consideration of racial difference, it being virtually impossible at any one time to determine the prime cause.

The problems of abstraction, however, are not sufficient to prevent, in themselves, the development of constructive method in an endeavour to isolate one postulate. Using it as a central theme, it becomes possible to note the varying influences of the other areas of human experience. Indeed, having determined one, the other factors of social conditioning take on a different bloom, and contribute to fuller understanding of the whole.

The problems we found, however, were most difficult where biological differences were least. It is here that *passing* becomes greatest. Burnley, in his paper in Volume 1, notes, for example, that Northern European migrants to Australia stand a better chance of complete assimilation in a short time than those from Southern Europe. In this light, it must also be noted that the biological and social transfer opportunities are greatest for similar people. This is no great revelation. However, the isolation of the race/accommodation split in understanding problems of social adjust-

ment of new arrivals in Australia could have important bearing on such
diverse matters as town planning and the provision of health and
educational facilities. Doczy and Kerr seem to deal with the polar
extremes of this problem. Kerr sees it as a pattern of adjustment affecting
access to health services, and Doczy as a pattern of behaviour affecting
inter-personal relationships, or access of people and groups to the
intellectual and social opportunities available to the whole community.
Salter, carrying the theme a little further sees it as laying a barrier to
improving the health services themselves.

The pattern of constraint that prejudice creates reinforces the
structural differences of social groups. This, whilst giving the *out-group*
certain advantages of cohesion in meeting the challenges of prejudice with
which they are faced, reinforces the differences, making identification of
the problem easier for the bigoted and less tolerant. Huck, Medding and
Heiss look at the group aspects of constraint and welcome the protection
it provides to cultural diversity.

Although mental attitudes are founded, initially, on experience learning, the intellectual development of intolerance rests heavily on the public
educational media. It is here that the written word as well as the more
vocal social activists play an important part. The role of the popular press
and the trade union movement in accomplishing Australia's most notorious
act of race prejudice, 'The White Australia Policy', is so well documen-
ted as hardly to need treatment in a volume such as this. However,
Palfreeman and Yarwood clearly establish the root sources of the objection
to broadening the racial basis of Australian society. McQueen and Hall
bring to light a new, possibly more challenging, area of understanding of
the Australian national character and the personality building role of the
press and literature in this lengthy process.

In Western democracies some institutions are more critically placed
to soften the worst aspects of social disparities. The development of the
welfare state in the twentieth century has been achieved through common
recognition that the state has certain obligations to its citizens rising above
the normal framework of government. However, many private organizations have laid claim to moral leadership, and the Christian Church is
undoubtedly the most important of these. Accordingly, it was necessary
to investigate its response to, and responsibility for, the level of racial
intolerance in Australia.

Not unlike the difficulties of diagnosis experienced in defining the
problem, any attempt to attach the blame to lack of religious leadership
also falls short of a satisfactory explanation. For, not unlike the
community itself, the Church has been at once the vanguard of ameliora-
tion of racial intolerance, but also its cause. The cause, however, would
seem to be more in its appreciation of the urgency of its task in the
broader community when all of the competing demands for its assistance
were experienced. But the Church remains in a strategic place to contribute to the necessary reorientation of Australian national and personal
values. All branches of the faith have now clearly stated their position
and this is adequately covered in the contributions of Engel and
Mulkearns. Nettheim, on the other hand, considers an area of current
debate in Christian circles, through the positive alignment of the World
Council of Churches with activist organizations throughout the world
fighting race prejudice. As a layman, his contribution should assist con-

siderably in the Christian understanding of this decision and help in applying the agreements internally in Australia.

Finally, it is the editor's opinion that the papers contained in this volume do not necessarily achieve the prime concern of the series ... that is, proof of racism in Australia. They do, however, clearly indicate that racialism is of some consequence in, at least, the interpersonal relationships between its endogenous and exogenous citizens. Volume 2 deals with a different aspect of race prejudice in Australia, the nation's treatment of the original inhabitants of the continent, the Aborigines. It is believed that, in that volume, ample evidence of racism, the combination of ideology and system, is clearly established. This, however, is for the reader to judge.

Volume 3 takes the reader into a broader appreciation of Australia's international role and the effect of domestic conditioning on the nation's foreign responsibilities. Again, one finds the pattern becomes confused and hard to delineate, although providing an overlay of intolerance within which policy is made and action takes place. But, as has already been pointed out, social and political relationships are frequently founded on a complex of bases. To prove that one exists is not necessarily to measure its influence. It does, however, allow one to more adequately comprehend the operation of the whole.

REFERENCES

1 Fourth Assembly of the World Council of Churches, Uppsala, Sweden, 1968, The Uppsala '68 Report, p. 241.

2 Statement on Race and Racial Prejudice, U.N.E.S.C.O., Paris 26, 1967.

INTRODUCTION
AUSTRALIA AND RACIALISM

W. E. H. *Stanner*

As an anthropologist, I may be expected to have a special interest in the facts of race and in the social problems arising—or supposed to arise—from them. That qualification 'supposed to arise' is the essence of what I have to say.

There are observable physical differences between the races, as well as hidden physical differences. These differences are heritable. We do not know positively that they are, but they could turn out to be connected with obscure mental, temperamental and personality characteristics. While the races have performed unequally in history, as yet there is no experimental, or even quasi-experimental evidence that really warrants leaping from the plane of physical differences to the plane of mental capacity, or capacity for civilization, or performance in history. In all the alleged facts and arguments so far put forward to support the contention that there are some inferior and some superior races, there seems always to have been a flaw or fallacy, something unconvincing or wrong from a scientific point of view. A test has to distinguish, truly distinguish, between innate powers and powers affected by environment, training and motivation, in short, by 'culture'. We are still looking for one that will do so and not be merely trivial.

It is important that the general public should understand that, in other aspects too, we are only beginning to know what we are talking about when we talk of human 'race'. A number of specialized disciplines are now concerning themselves with it—not only physical and social or cultural anthropology, ethnology and archaeological prehistory, but several branches of human biology and genetics, geography, ecology, population theory, and other specialisms. Not one of them, as far as I know, would claim to have made more than a beginning. The 'every man his own expert' approach is no longer possible. The study is shifting from the rostrum to the laboratory. What this means is clear enough. It is a warning to beware of popular theories about what 'race' is and signifies. They stand to scientific and demonstrable knowledge as astrology stands to astronomy.

There is apparently no need to postulate a specific and universal instinct of racial antipathy. 'An adequate explanation of racial antagonisms can be found in impulses and motives that are independent of race'[1] and the intimate experience of living with people of other race certainly gives no reason to suppose that on the level of human nature people anywhere are very different from people everywhere. Because of that experience, anthropologists have become more or less colour-blind, so to speak, towards racial differences. They forget to notice the tint of someone's skin, or the shape of his head, or whether his hair has a kink or a curl. Most of them have come to agree with Confucius that 'men's natures are alike:

7

it is their habits that carry them far apart', habits, in this case, meaning beliefs, customs, standards and ways of life. Here, in their opinion, is the source of conflict and the ground of prejudice.

In understanding what is going on in the world in the name of race, some distinctions are useful. One of them concerns what is now widely called 'racism'. A 'racist' is one who propagates the dogma that some races are, and will be perpetually, inferior to others for innate or congenital reasons, and 'racism' is the advocacy or practice of a policy expressing that dogma. A thoroughgoing or general racism is rare; we are more familiar with less extreme policies directed against particular races, e.g. the African negro. More widespread is an ideological racism, strong but not strong enough to be able to dominate national policies, although it may handicap them. Most persuasive of all, is a vague but unshakeable suspicion that there probably is something in the inferiority argument in relation to particular races. I suppose that this suspicion has been expressed most often and most persistently about the Aborigines, although the African negroes would probably run them a close second. 'Racism' is too strong a word to apply to it. I think it serves no purpose, other than the purposes of political controversy, to label the more diffuse attitudes, beliefs and policies in this way. It is hard to know how best to describe them, but I think that we might speak of degrees of 'racialism' rather than 'racism'. The great test, in my opinion, is whether a national policy and practice defends discrimination by a creed or dogma of general or specific inferiority. If it does, then I would apply the description 'racism' to it.

There would be problem enough if this were all. But in recent years we have discovered, with some consternation, that racial affairs after all are two-sided. In many countries there are peoples who, when they were under some kind of alien rule, had the experience of feeling judged, and sometimes of being told they were, inferior because of race. Many of them are now in a position, or approaching a position, in which they in turn can tie unpleasant and damaging qualities to the fact of having a white skin, and, much as we used to, justify themselves in this way for whatever acts of prejudice, discrimination and violence *they* want to direct against *our* interests. I will call this 'reciprocal racism'. The Samoans have a saying that 'power is like a fish: it is slippery and hard to hold'. History, by redistributing power, has turned the tables on the discrimina-tors. I can see no reason for supposing that the process of redistribution is near its peak, let alone its end. While the process works itself out, reciprocal racism is likely to be a favoured technique in both national and international politics. It is a 'natural' for those who may think there could be advantage for them in escalating racial ill-will to the continental scale. In their day, the catch-cries that went with racism were very useful politically. They satisfied uneasy consciences, promoted unity, and made many an enormity seem morally justified. The catch-cries of reciprocal racism will probably prove as useful; they have, indeed, already proven so. The mere accusation of 'racism' in recent years has been sufficient in itself to unnerve many authorities. In the present climate of opinion it can thus have easy victories. One does not need much foresight to see that the political prospect will be fully explored.

For the sake of perspective, let us remember that racial likes and dislikes are as old as history, and have probably been true of all peoples.

In very ancient monuments, you may see race indicated in the relationships of conqueror and conquered, and master and slave. Cicero advised Atticus not to obtain his slaves from Britain 'because they are so stupid and so utterly incapable of being taught that they are not fit to form part of the household of Athens.' In parts of Africa where I worked, there was an aristocracy of Hamites or Nilo-Hamites and a subservient class of negroes. I heard Masai, the Nilo-Hamitic cattle-herders, speak with contempt of the Bantu-speaking Kikuyu, the people who produced Jomo Kenyatta, the present President of Kenya. African students have been disparaged in Indian universities. I have heard golden-brown Samoans speak of the Fijians as 'those black-things'. Some aborigines I know used to affix to the words 'white fellow' a language particle implying 'wild beasts'.

The very universality of racialism makes one hesitate to put much trust in the assurances which some people of goodwill are ready to give, that, to modify in a major way, the racial aspect of Australian immigration policy need have no unhappy sequel. Experience and commonsense suggest rather the contrary. The argument is inherently undemonstrable; at least, only the event could demonstrate it. The same applies to many other arguments one hears. For example, it is widely asserted, perhaps even truly believed, that just as we know how to build, say, computers we also 'know' how to 'plan' to avoid racial tensions, frictions and conflicts, so that they need never happen here.[2] This is a statement of faith, not of demonstrated or demonstrable truth. The rather crazy dialectic which has now set in with reciprocal racism is a strong reason for caution. A simple fallacy—that communities and nations can deal with each other as if they were individual persons of goodwill—has also blurred the public grasp of the great struggles which can be, are being, and may yet be waged under the banner of race. The conclusion seems inescapable that the time for change is not yet.

Racial conflict begins with the human impulse to clannishness, to set bounds to a group within which something is to be shared. Sociologists speak of it as the forming of 'in-groups' and 'out-groups'. It is a necessary condition of human group-life, but it can take on narrow and hurtful forms. Locality, class, education, income, politics, religious belief, and habits of life give it much to work on. So does race, especially when looked at through eyes both clannish and ignorant. The physical differences, especially if they are radical—as between ourselves and the Aborigines and negroes—seem outward and visible signs of thoroughgoing inward differences. The motive to exclude, because of difference, turns the signs into symbols by building up more vivid ideas about them, and charging them with emotion. Through the symbols, we project all manner of fears, dislikes and self-protective impulses. These are not 'racial' in origin, but by a trick of the mind, they can become connected with the idea of a particular race or race in general. 'When this association takes place the feelings may be aroused by contact with any member of that race and operate with all the force of an instinctive antipathy.'[3]

In racial problems, seen from the clannish side, there are always three things—a threat, whether real or imagined or simply cooked-up; a reaction to the threat; and a way of justifying the reaction so that it has a good moral appearance. Or, putting it another way, there is always something people want—so they say—to 'defend'; something they attack in order to 'defend' it; and an excuse for attacking. In the history of racial conflicts, many things have been 'defended' because of real, imagined or cooked-up threats—life, land and possessions, women and family, religion and religious liberty, freedom, the glory of the nation, even the simple right to live with people of one's own kind only. Few of them have been bad things, as human purposes go. They are the kind of things for which people want security, even in the conscious knowledge that they are disregarding wider interests and bringing loss or even misery to others. If we are going to quarrel with that, our quarrel is with men's social nature. Where true badness enters is in the means used to win or preserve that security; in racial matters, where a dogma of race becomes a weapon of militant political force, justifying the means by the end. I suppose that the extreme example of modern times was the Nazi plan of genocide—the extermination of the Jews in order to preserve the security of the Reich, and through it, the non-existent purity of the Nordics, the supposed master-race. We are familiar with lesser examples of attempts to exclude people of this race or that from a full share in the possibilities of a social life which is dominated by people of another race. It is with the third element, the excuse, that badness and casuistry can make ugly compact. Every excusatory device the human mind can invent finds a place here. One need not go to other continents for examples. I could quote passages from the writings of men of religion, letters and politics offering extraordinary excuses for our early policy towards the aborigines. Here I may well quote a distinguished recent visitor to Canberra, Sir Stephen Runciman, who said in one of his books: 'It is part of human nature to like to appeal to some tribunal whose moral authority is recognized, even if the appellant had no intention of abiding by an adverse verdict.'[4] Over the last century, the racially prejudiced have sought more and more to appeal to the tribunal of scientific authority. The reasoning has been that, if the superiority and inferiority of particular races can be demonstrated scientifically, then it is not unethical for a superior race to discriminate against an inferior race. People who hope for such a proof do not seem to grasp how disastrous it would be to their posture. When moral justifications are sought or found for damaging the already weak because they are also inferior, then candid felony becomes almost admirable by comparison. But I have said that, in the present state of anthropology, there would be great difficulty in setting up such a tribunal. Few judges would be willing to sit on it, because they regard the practicable evidence as too obscure, and the probable testimony as twisted. Nor would there be any good constructive law to guide them.

To ignore race will not drive it away. We have to live with it as a permanent if changeable aspect of man. Nevertheless, if people stopped chattering about it as if they knew what it signifies, or as if there were nothing more to learn, we would have a better chance to look soberly at what seems an elementary truth. We are usually prejudiced *about race* because of *other things*. If I am correct in saying so, then it seems to follow that, to try to remove the symptom, prejudice, without admitting and understanding the complaint, the other things cannot be very effective. Some aspects of Australian racialism are worth looking at from this point of view.

No one here thought much about race as such before the 1830s. After the first phase of idealistic policy, the Aborigines, to quote one historian, became a 'melancholy footnote to Australian history'. They were widely regarded as scarcely human, and were left to the fitful paternalism of government, the hard mercy of pastoralists, and the charity of Christian missions. There was no line of battle, as with the Maori or Redskins; no true conquest, because the truth of it is that we inched and filched a continent into our possession. The Aborigines were not organized to resist. A few spears, a few shots, a few punitive parties, and locality by locality it was over to all intents and purposes. Nothing in the whole affair made us deeply conscious of the Aborigines as a people or a race, but nevertheless I think that the emptiness of conscience and compassion that made the melancholy business tolerable had something to do with our racial views later. The subject of race first came into prominence because of worries over proposals to indenture Indian, Chinese and other non-European labour. There was a serious clash of interests between those who wanted that labour and those who did not. One section of the community forced an issue on to another. True, a few people spoke about 'colour' and 'race purity'—W. C. Wentworth was one of them—but it was the cheap-labour threat to wage, employment and social standards that really mattered. The riots against the Chinese on the goldfields in 1857 and 1861 were the start of racialism in that sense. The tension built up over time, but it broke only *after* the fields began to dwindle and fail. Envy, jealousy and fear were among the root causes. At one time there were nearly 50,000 Chinese on the Victorian fields. The European population of the continent before the rush had been about half a million. One wonders how different our response would be now if, over the next five years, a million Chinese—that would be about the proportion—arrived among us and congregated in a locality. The numbers in themselves must have seemed a threat. There they were—hardworking, efficient, content with small returns, and willing to put up with privations that a European would not tolerate. Here, for the first time in Australian history, was the actualization of a threat that had aroused some anxiety in the 1830s and 1840s: competition by another race on terms unfavourable to Europeans. The Chinese were radically alien, not only in physical appearance, but in speech, custom and outlook. Even 'in the debates in the Federal Parliament on the 1901 Immigration Restriction Act, economic criticism was mingled with attacks on their servility, their alien dress and customs, their frugality, their gambling, and their alleged immorality.'[5] In the 1850s and 60s the situation was made to order for a blind, unreasoning outburst of a kind that has happened a thousand times in racial encounters.

Historians trace the development of the White Australia policy to those beginnings. We must leave it to them to say how much race, as such, had to do with it. I do not find the answer as easy as some of them have. Something can be said for a view that they may have made too much of the symptom, race, and too little of the underlying complaint. The cry of 'race' was the mob's cry. It pointed to, but did not identify or exhaust, the real trouble. Once raised, it became a symbol, and thereafter it stayed a half-furled banner for many grievances and fears. When it was used a generation later, this time in Queensland in the 1870s and later, it was again to rally opinion against a flooding in of not only Chinese, but also Melanesians or Kanakas. It was not simply the son's generation arousing a flag, a fear and cry from the father's time. This was now a different Australia. In 1880, there was real strength behind the idea of 'a nation for a continent and a continent for a nation'—now of nearly 2.25 million. Here, as elsewhere at the time, there was an idea that three things which are independent of each other—race, language and culture—could somehow make a unity expressible in nationhood. The events in Queensland were more than mundane local affairs; they touched a now many-sided ideal. There were private interests, as there had been earlier in New South Wales, that were prepared to push the cheap-labour policy to extremes, with indifference to the effects on wage and social standards or the effects on the coming nation. The traffic in Kanaka labour was a continuing earnest and proof of the intent. To interpret the progressive restrictions on immigration, and the final emergence of the White Australia policy, as simple pointers to a natural streak of xenophobia in the Australian outlook seems to me shallow and wrong. I think that our racialism began as a shadow on the wall, a shadow cast by very real struggles expressing themselves in part, and in part only, by discrimination and exclusion.

Jacques Barzun once pointed out that race-thinking 'diverts our attention from the social and intellectual factors that make up personality.'[6] I would extend that criticism to explanations by racialism. Sociologically speaking, they belong to the 'good king' and 'bad king' version of history. They divert our attention from the social structure of racial conflicts. One of the really serious consequences is that they give aid and comfort to the fallacy that communities and nations of different race are never divided by real and grave interests, which are not identical and perhaps cannot be made so in this kind of world. There is, at present, a deluge of literature of the pamphlet or tractarian order which put many current racial problems in the same preposterously over-simplified way.

Our racialism may have begun as a shadow on the wall, but it soon became more than that. I think we have to look outside Australia for a not unimportant part of the explanation. Up to the end of the 19th century, our racial experience had been highly specific—Aborigines, Chinese, Melanesians, all radically unlike ourselves in outlook and custom as well as in race. The relationships were ungenial in every way. In the end, racialism and nationalism ran together in tandem. That was true not only of Australia. In Europe, roughly at the time of our goldfield riots, some bad history, nonsensical anthropology, and reactionary politics led to the idea of an aristocratic lineage or species or race which, through different branches, had ruled all the civilized countries, and must continue to do so if the future were to have any nobility. These 'natural' rulers were identified with the Aryan or, as we should now say, Nordic stratum of the European population, which were represented as a superior biological class fitted by that fact to be a princely social class. All others were unprincely, of mixed and inferior racial stocks, and arranged by nature to be ruled. These ideas had all been heard of before, but at that particular time they struck a spark which still glows in Europe. Racialist thought then took the form of a class-ideology, but the class-basis was soon overborne. Communities within nations, and nations as political entities, began using racialist arguments. There was a great confusion between race, nationality, language and culture. Even men of education spoke seriously about 'the English race' or 'the German race', which was about as sensible as speaking of 'Anglican genetics' or 'Teutonic geometry'. A new variety of scholars, who called themselves 'anthroposociologists', developed something like an obsession with the metrical study of the physical stigmata of race. In the 1880s, one of the more obsessed said: 'I am convinced that in the next century millions will cut each other's throats because of one or two degrees more or less of cephalic index',[7] the cephalic index being the ratio between the breadth and length of the head, seen from on top, and expressed as a percentage. What was, in many ways, the most significant development was the growth of the conviction that physical externals pointed to deep internal differences, including mental differences, between races, mysteriously going back to the dim antiquity of mankind. It was supposed that therein lay the explanation of the historical fact that different races had developed different grades of civilization. The corollary was that among living races were some which were biologically inferior. These convictions were made possible by a sketchy understanding of the new Darwinism and by the then rudimentary state of genetical studies. While the confusions were rampant, racial theory became more extensive by making alliance with political nationalism and imperialism. Simultaneously, it became more intensive, as a result of increasing discrimination in countries in which there were particular racial minorities.

It was, of course, coincidence that, at the very time European racialism was on the make, anti-Chinese feeling was on the make here. But was it entirely coincidence? Why was it that in the second half of the century the Aborigines were vilified rather than ignored? I suspect that it was because we were breathing not only Australian air but 19th century air also. Both nationalism and imperialism dined out on racial symbolism. By the end of the century our school-children were singing —

Rule Britannia, Britannia rule the waves,
No more Chinamen are allowed in New South Wales.

The racialist ideology was in high vogue. The Sydney *Bulletin* of the 1880s and 90s contained good examples—especially in the cartoons—of the frenetic extremes to which it could be pushed. Even when I was an undergraduate in the late 1920s, the classics of modern racism—Madison Grant's *The Passing of the Great Race*, and Lothrop Stoddard's *The Revolt Against Civilization: the Menace of the Under Man*—were still influential.

The whole question of race has bulked large on the horizon for a century. For that reason it is difficult to discuss the subject without using the very categories in which the conflicts themselves are being conducted. Publicists and scholars have a special responsibility to try to break out of these coils. As I remarked earlier, a whole group of sciences broadly concerned with the anthropology of race are trying to do so. In the scholarly sense their work eventually could have something of the proportions of a Copernican revolution.

There are two points I wish to make, hopefully rather than confidently. Australian racialism could, perhaps, have shallower roots than some of us may have supposed. Where peoples other than the Aborigines were concerned, it seems to have been a thing of occasion or situation. In the absence of cause, it lapsed or hung on only in fringe-mentalities. To bring it to the fore, a manifest threat to domestic or national securities seemed needed. It could then take on an intense and even violent quality. That, I suspect, or at least hope, was more a measure of the value we put on things to be 'defended' than a true ideology of race. The second point is that we have escaped the worst excesses of racialist thinking in the last two generations. We have few, if any, organizations making it their business to build or nurture an extreme ideology of race. The massive changes which took place in our policy and practice towards the

Aborigines after the 1930s had very little opposition. I would not attribute this, at least without better evidence, to natural virtue. I suspect it had more to do with the small scale of the problems and the fact that no European interests of importance were much affected. The 'convential wisdom' of our times is that racialism here is a dying, not just a dwindling, force. The proof will be forthcoming when big and powerful interests again become involved. At the moment, however, we have some reason to congratulate ourselves on what we may call—to put it safely—good fortune.

Two things have happened recently in South Australia that seem to me very significant. The first Aboriginal rights in land have been created, and the policy of assimilation has been replaced by one which allows the Aborigines the right to determine their own social future. If they wish, they may make themselves into a racial community within the Australian nation with the State's blessing. This is a mountainous change of front and, because of it, much may now be possible for some Aborigines that hitherto had been impossible. In a hundred senses it gives them firm ground for their feet.

Comparing the Australian scene with what it was a generation ago, we have no right to be discouraged. In our universities, for example, an Asian student or teacher was a phenomenon in the true sense. We now have thousands of students and scores of teachers—welcome, congenial, respected, taken for granted. But universities are a special segment of the community. I doubt if we can rightly generalize from them to the nation —not yet, anyway. There can be a considerable difference from being an honoured guest in a sheltered home and a permanent lodger down the street. I think that much will be determined by the extent to which we ourselves are now made the targets of reciprocal racism in international politics. One's head has to be very deep in the sand not to see that the racialist attack on Europeans has become a band-wagon that is rolling strongly. How long and far it rolls will have a lot to do with the future of this Montagu and Capulet affair.

ACKNOWLEDGEMENT

This chapter is derived from a paper delivered at St. Mark's Library, Canberra, 21st October, 1965, and published in St. Mark's Review No. 43, February, 1966, pp. 1-11.

REFERENCES

1 OLDHAM, J. H. *Christianity and the Race Problem*, 1924, p. 43.

2 The Immigration Reform Group. *Control or Colour Bar*, 1960, p. vi.

3 OLDHAM, J. H., *loc. cit.*

4 *The Sicilian Vespers*, p. 260.

5 The Immigration Reform Group. *Control or Colour Bar*, 1960, p. 2.

6 *Race: A Study in Modern Superstition*, 1938, p. 282.

7 Quoted in RUTH BENEDICT, *Race and Racism*, 1942, p. 1.

RACE AND SOCIETY

1

THE SOCIOLOGY OF RACE PREJUDICE

S. O. D'Alton, M. Bittman

At the time of Wilberforce there was no such thing as race prejudice—other races simply were inferior. There was no doubt of this; it was an objective condition of existence. Superiority and inferiority were given and the proof was in the dominance of one culture over others. That the other cultures provided alternative methods of social organization was not considered, and superiority was defined in terms of power, both economic and military. Gradually this fact of superiority was eroded, and despite the assumptions and the 'proofs' of early evolutionary anthropologists and Social Darwinists, the notion of Western cultural superiority broke down. By the thirties, interest in race prejudice was focussed around understanding how people came to hold such irrational beliefs, and why they held them. Race prejudice came to be approached as a psycho-social, pathological problem, as a disease, a malady of rational man.

At this time Freud's psychopathology was applied to race prejudice by Fromm[1] and Dollard,[2] Lippman[3] developed his general concept of stereotypes, and this was used in the analysis of race prejudice. Bogardus[4] developed his social distance scale based on the work of Park,[5] and concepts from the rapidly expanding discipline of sociology were brought to bear on what was now the 'problem' of race prejudice.

Dollard, building on Freud, saw race prejudice as an irrational expression of childhood frustration. The hostility and the violence of prejudiced individuals was regarded as the result of individual repression leading to displaced aggression and scapegoating. Lippman's broad concept of stereotyping was taken up by Bettelheim and put to a more specialized use. Bettelheim[6] saw stereotyping as a reaction to helplessness which was essentially a defense mechanism, but which was introjected and acted on even if wrong. Thus Bettelheim takes the concept from a different theoretical strand but uses it in a framework similar to that of Dollard.

The parallel development in sociology was that of social distance. Essentially the aim of this approach was descriptive, although the interest in race prejudice as an example of social distance hinted at an assumption that this phenomenon was a 'problem'. Where this theory attempted to explain the phenomena it described, it did so in terms of 'social laws', that is, in terms of supra-individual forces based on an organismic model of society. Therefore, race prejudice was a problem for the maintenance of harmony and integration in society in so far as conflicts caused by racial tension had to be resolved. Park consequently developed a theory of group relations that involved movement from conflict, competition, accommodation to assimilation.

This theoretical line of argument was unable to synthesise in a single model, both individual and social aspects of race prejudice, and the whole theory emerges as a one-sided analysis of society in which the individual has no personal responsibility for race prejudice. Race prejudice is thus seen by these theorists as a phenomenon over which the individual has no control; it is seen simply as the outcome of autonomous and anonymous social forces.

At the other extreme Adorno *et al* analyse race prejudice from a purely individual point of view. In the *Authoritarian Personality*[7], the authors construct a scale to measure receptivity to Fascist ideology (the 'F' scale) and try to describe general personality characteristics of highly prejudiced people. The study is focused around individual differences within a society and no consistent attempt is made to understand the impact of social conditions on individual behaviour. Consequently, both the social distance theories and the Authoritarian Personality individual focus studies, are not sufficient to explain the phenomenon except within the relatively narrow orientation of their own theoretical referants.

If the Freudism approach is extended, then it is possible to encompass both individual and social manifestations of prejudice and to provide a wider perspective for the understanding of race prejudice on both the individual and social levels. In order to extend the Freudism approach we build on Erich Fromm and Jean-Paul Sartre. Erich Fromm,[8] from a Freudism perspective, shows how the society impinges on the individual and creates in the particular individual the preconditions of aloneness and fear that may express themselves via individual behaviour in race prejudice. While Fromm is not unaware of the extent to which individuals create their own social conditions, Sartre[9] emphasizes this aspect of social life. By synthesising the approaches taken by Fromm and Sartre both sides of social interaction can be illuminated.

Both Fromm and Sartre share a similar set of epistemological assumptions and this facilitates the amalgamation of the points of view. Each considers reality to be a process rather than a static entity. This orientation implies that there are no immanent absolutes that are only waiting to be discovered and it indicates that they operate on a relative view of reality. That is, they are concerned with social truths—with what people believe to be true and act on as truth, e.g. in Wilberforce's time, reality, for people in England was the superiority of their culture. It is obvious that a social reality is not a fixed reality but depends for its existence on the beliefs of the people making up the society, and it is consequently liable to change.

Thus social reality may be seen as a projection; social truth is our own creation, and its existence depends on our affirmation of one state of affairs as truth. The superiority of the West was consequently only a social fact so long as we continued to believe and act on that belief. We believe in our superiority and maintain this belief by organizing incoming data in such a way as to prove it. Stokely Carmichael makes this point when he says:—

> 'Columbus did not discover America. Columbus may have been the first recorded white man to set foot in America. That is all. There were people there before Columbus. Unfortunately, these people were not white—unfortunately for the white West, fortunately for us, they weren't white. But what happens is that white Western

society never recognises the existence of non-white people, either consciously or sub-consciously. So that all around the world, the peoples of the third world never did anything until some white man came along . . .'[10]

From the point of view of social reality there is not a prior intrinsic meaning in the world outside us. It is ourselves who order our sensory input in such a way as to give it meaning to us. We then act on the basis of our own construction of the world, in effect ordering our actions in terms of our attributed meaning. Therefore, in one moment, we project meaning and introject that meaning as the reality in which we act. However, our society provides the context in which we act, and Erich Fromm gives an analysis of the individual and the individual's crisis of identity within a particular social context.

Central to Erich Fromm's concept of the 'self', is that this amorphous and elusive concrete reality is, in effect, a process and not a static thing.[11] The effort to capture 'self', to isolate it as object, is doomed to failure because of the very nature of the process. Consequently, identity as a stable reality is always in danger because it is always becoming something else, constantly in flux, being generated and regenerated. In other words individual identity is constantly being created. This identity so created, is the individual's ongoing answer to the question 'Who am I, what am I like?' With each new act, the individual may either confirm his own stereotypical self, or reveal some new facet which may alter his conception of his total identity. This viewpoint sees Man's identity as a dynamic product which exists only through action. Therefore, the maintenance of a particular identity is an active, not a passive process.

In conjunction with this view of 'self', Fromm emphasizes the aspect of aloneness that is a condition of the becoming self. He states:—

'the other aspect of individualism is growing aloneness. The primary ties offer security and basic unity with the world outside oneself. To the extent to which the child emerges from that world, it becomes aware of being alone, of being an entity separate from all others.'[12]

In order to achieve an individual identity in the face of a huge data input from the environment and to affirm, or be conscious of, a self as agent of action, the creation self must be distanced from the creator. The individual must project an image of self to be contemplated in consciousness in order that he be conscious of his self. He exists, for himself, therefore as an alienated projection, a concretization of a particular set of variables which he has himself ordered so that he may be conscious of a self. This act of conceptualization provides the individual with an identity for himself, ordered as a stereotypical self beyond his unrealized self, the self of his possibilities. It is this basic alienation, the crisis of identity formation, that faces man as a condition of his existence.

Both the creation of a self and the aloneness of the self are unavoidably linked in the process of creating an individual identity. The individual is faced with a massive range of possibilities, an infinite number from among which he must choose alternative identities. From this formless jumble he is forced to select and arrange the constituents, thus creating a form out of the formlessness, meaning out of meaninglessness. The particular form that each individual creates is the expression of his own individuality and affirms his self.

There are two implications from this; first, that the individual creates himself as a matter of free choice and is therefore responsible for the creation, and second, that the individual is alone, since his creation is uniquely his own.

This results in the possibility of being overcome by the vast range of alternatives, of being overpowered by the responsibility of actually making the decision and of being frozen into indecision about the consequences of the choice. Under these conditions the individual's emotional response may be one of anxiety and fear. In order to allay this anxiety and to avoid the responsibility, the individual may abrogate his freedom to choose and, in effect, deny the responsibility for his own actions. This can be done in one of three ways:—

(i) *Authoritarianism*—'a tendency to give up one's own individual self and to fuse oneself with somebody or something outside oneself in order to acquire the strength which the individual self is lacking.'[13]

(ii) *Destructiveness*—'I can escape the feeling of my own powerlessness in comparison with the world outside myself by destroying it.'[14]

(iii) *Automaton conformity*—'the person who gives up his individual self and becomes an automaton, identical with millions of other automatons around him, need not feel alone and anxious any more. But the price that he pays, however, is high; it is the loss of his self.'[15]

The need for these mechanisms of escape is induced by responsibility and aloneness; they are ways of achieving an identity in the face of unbearable external pressures. It is this situation that provides the underlying condition for race prejudice.

In an individual, race prejudice can be regarded as an attempt to create an identity through negative identification. That is, the individual identifies and stereotypes a group to which he does *not* belong, and by implication, a residual group to which he *does* belong. In identifying a group to which he does not belong, the individual attributes negative characteristics to the group members. The negative content of this attribution is not inherent in the qualities themselves but is provided by the in-group. Merton gives a good example of this process when he compares beliefs about Jews and Japanese in the United States with those about Abraham Lincoln. He states:—

'Did Lincoln work far into the night? This testifies that he was industrious, resolute, perseverant and eager to realize his capacities to the full. Do the out-group Jews or Japanese keep these same hours? This only bears witness to their sweatshop mentality, their ruthless undercutting of American standards, their unfair competitive practices. Is the in-group hero frugal, thrifty and sparing? Then the out-group villian is stingy, miserly and penny grinding etc.'[16]

This example indicates the extent to which it is possible to attribute meaning, and to order responses in terms of the attributed meaning, as the individual expresses his construction of reality. This stereotyping, however, goes beyond just the attribution of meaning, and defines both the other and the self. Stereotyping is a formulation of reality that is particularly rigid, and Bettelheim[17] shows how this very stereotyping may prevent individual adjustments to actual circumstances. He describes the relationship between a Gestapo guard and Jewish prisoners at Dachau and shows how the stereotype depersonalizes human interaction forcing it into a fixed mould. The exchange relationship between each individual prisoner and the guard is mediated through the stereotypes they hold of each other. The guard sees each Jew as representative of all Jews, who are seen to be cunning, fawning, unscrupulous and undeserving, in short, less than human. Each prisoner sees the guard as representative of all Gestapomen, as having low intelligence, little education and being of low cultural and social status. Both people in the interaction operate in conformity with their own stereotypes of the other, regardless of the relationship of those to the actual situation—in effect, the introjected stereotype forces the whole interaction into a stereotypical mould which may prevent both from gaining their own ends.

In the process of stereotyping, particularly in relation to race prejudice, the individual defines himself through membership of a residual grouping. In the individual's effort to gain identity for himself, he effectively confers it on the other and his own becomes mere reflection. This gives the other a direct, positive identity while his own identity is indirect, negative, consisting merely of those attributes not possessed by the other. Paradoxically, the individual's effort to affirm his own identity through group membership only succeeds in giving a positive identity to the out-group.

As the definition of the in-group exists only through the identification of the out-group, the result is a particular configuration of negative interrelations which Sartre calls 'seriality'.[18] A good illustration of the relations that hold in a situation of seriality is to be found in a formal examination. In the examination situation, each examinee is in a series defined by the examination, the external reason for their being identified as a group. However, although they are identified as a group, the nature of the reciprocity between each is such that they regard one another as one too many. Each sees every other examinee through his stereotype, each becomes an interchangeable unit, as someone inessential to oneself. Each is uniquely alone and makes a project of his solitude. The way in which reality is constructed by each, reduces all others to objects of competition. The examination orders the internal reciprocal relations of the examinees so that positive human interaction is denied and negative object relations prevail; each becomes an object for the other and is, in turn, an object himself.

A series is characterized by a certain relationship between the people who make up the series; they are unified and identified by virtue of an external object held in common, e.g. an examination or an out-group. It is the external definition and nature of the internal reciprocal relations which distinguish a series from a mere collection of individuals, and gives the series a kind of superficial groupness. In a group, however, the reciprocal relations are positive; there is a real interchange between members that creates the group, as a group, from within. In a series, reciprocity exists only in so far as each relates to each as object, that is, a tacit agreement to treat the other as an interchangeable, identical inessential, single unit.

Laing and Cooper show the relation of the concept 'seriality' to the analysis of race prejudice in the following passage.

'The anti-Semites are a multiplicity of men. What they have in common is a common object—the Jews. "The Jews" for each anti-Jew is his own anti-self. Each anti-Semite recognises his identity with the others who have anti-selves in common with him. This common bad object is a stamp or mark common to all the anti-Semites. This bad object is their badge or symbol of unification. But this unification is the unification of a series; that is, of a multiplicity in which each is identical, interchangeable, inessential, separate, and solitary.'[19]

The expression of race prejudice is an attempt to gain identity through group identification, and it is also an attempt to allay the terror of being alone and to avoid the necessity of choice. It is the attempt to give reality a particular meaning in which the individual has identity. Thus the definition of an out-group may be seen as the response to an effort to gain both individual identity and a feeling of belonging.

To feel himself a complete human being, the prejudiced person denies the humanity of others and consequently manifests in himself inhumanity. His effort to overcome his own aloneness and to express his human potential is vitiated by his own 'solution'. His powerlessness is compounded rather than eliminated, since his unity with others derives from the out-group. His own power of ordering the world has left him powerless. He becomes dependent on the out-group to know who he is and to feel in unison with others. He has thus created an out-group which is powerful, a self which is dependent.

Moreover the unity thus created is a false unity, it depends for its existence on the existence of an external agent—'out-group'. The relations within the in-group are, consequently, those of a series. Instead of a firm sense of belonging, the prejudiced person is therefore condemned to the vicissitudes of estrangement, separateness, uniformity and solitude—the very effort that is made to affirm a unique identity and give it meaning turns on itself and leaves the individual utterly alone.

REFERENCES

1 Fromm, E. *The Fear of Freedom*, Routledge & Kegan Paul, London, 1960.

2 Dollard, J. Hostility and Fear in Social Life, *Social Forces*, 17, 1938, 15-26.

3 Lippman, W. *Public Opinion*, Allen & Unwin, London, 1932.

4 Bogardus, E. S. *Immigration and Race Attitudes*, D. C. Heath, Boston, 1928; Changes in Racial Distance, *International Journal of Opinion and Attitude Research* I (4), 1947, 55-62. *Social Distance*, Los Angeles, 1959. (Published privately.)

5 Park, R. E. and Burgess, E. W. *Introduction to the Science of Sociology*, University of Chicago Press, Chicago, 1921. Park, R. E., *Race and Culture*, Free Press, Glencoe, 1950.

6 Bettelheim, B. The Dynamism of Anti-Semitism in Gentile and Jew, *Journal of Abnormal Psychology* 32, 1947, 153-68.

7 Adorno, T. W., Frenkel-Brunswick, Else, Levinson, Daniel, J. and Sanford, R. Nevitt. *The Authoritarian Personality*, Harper, New York, 1950.

8 Fromm, E., *op. cit.*

9 Sartre, Jean-Paul. *Critique de la Raison Dialectique*, Librairie Gallimard, Paris, 1960; *Portrait of the Anti-Semite*, Secker & Warburg with Lindsay Drummond, London, 1948.

10 CARMICHAEL, S. Black Power in COOPER, D. (ed.), *Dialectics of Liberation*, Penguin, p. 154.

11 FROMM, E., *op. cit.*, p. 37.

12 FROMM, E., *ibid*, p. 43.

13 *Ibid*, pp. 121-122.

14 *Ibid*, p. 154.

15 *Ibid*, p. 160.

16 MERTON, R. K., quoted in JAHODA, M.: *Race Relations and Mental Health*, UNESCO, Paris, 1960, p. 13.

17 BETTELHEIM, B., *op. cit.*

18 For a discussion of the concept 'seriality' in English, see LAING, R. D. and COOPER, D. G.: *Reason and Violence. A Decade of Sartre's Philosophy, 1950-1960*, Tavistock, London, 1964, pp. 120-128.

19 LAING, R. D. and COOPER, D. G., *ibid*, p. 124.

2

PSYCHOLOGY OF RACE PREJUDICE

M. C. Frame

Introduction

A complexity of factors, intrapsychic, social and cultural, each of different intensity at different times and in different individuals and communities, has relevance in the psychology of racial prejudice. No simplistic formulation is possible to explain the phenomenon. However, it is possible to isolate, in general terms, a number of factors which have significance in any specific situation.

It has become fashionable to label anyone who exhibits racial prejudice as 'neurotic', but this is patently inaccurate. In some, usually those in whom strong personal motivation may be indicted, racism can be clearly seen as an expression of underlying neurosis. In others, where strong cultural influences are operative, the appellation as 'sick' would strictly have much less relevance.

In the natural history of man, both individual and collective, a deep antipathy, secondary to a perception of threat of anything different or differing from the subject, is strongly evident in early years. In adult life, due largely to advances in technology, particularly in the field of communication, and with the increasing maturity and sophistication of man, absolute rejection on the basis of difference is a less prominent automatic feature of life today. However, dyssocial family and community atmosphere at critical periods of life may result in fixation at more primitive behaviour pattern levels, just as may personal intolerable stress in later life, result in regression to these levels.

Although no such dichotomy is actually applicable, it is convenient to study racism from the point of view of the individual in the first place, and secondly of that of the community. In reality both have equal relevance, the one often reinforcing and perpetuating the other.

Individual Sources of Prejudice

In the individual, the basis of racism lies deeply rooted in psycho-social development. Prenatally, the organism develops in a quiet, protected environment. At birth, the infant is projected into a milieu in which it is beset and bombarded by a wide variety of stimuli from which it has comparative minimal protection. This is, and must be, a state of relatively high anxiety and from which evolves man's first and most persistent drive, namely, the motivation to rid himself, somehow, of untoward feelings of anxiety, particularly those for which the reason is not consciously perceived. The habit of externalization is developed at a very early age and becomes an integral feature of personality. Later utilization is important in a manifestation of racial prejudice.

24

In order to maintain some sort of homeostastis or equilibrium in the inner life, various mental mechanisms are utilized by man to defend against unconscious bad or primitive impulses reaching awareness.

Sexual and aggressive tendencies are two such impulses frequently repressed. Anxiety concerning these is alleviated by projecting them on to some convenient 'other', who now is seen to possess them and is regarded as an inferior for this reason. Bettelheim and Janowitz in their book 'Social Change and Prejudice' consider that such people have low conscious anxiety—they write:—

> 'The greater underlying anxiety of a person, the more prejudiced he is because the pressure of his anxiety weakens his personal control. Thus weakened, he seeks relief through prejudice which serves to reduce anxiety because prejudice facilitates the discharge of hostility and if hostility is discharged, anxiety is reduced. Prejudice reduces anxiety because it suggests to the person that he is better than others, hence, does not need to feel so anxious.'[1]

At birth, the infant is completely unaware of any existence beyond his own. His world comprises his own needs and their magical fulfilment. In normal development, this absolute narcissism is superseded by an awareness of objects beyond himself, and a progressive need to relate to these objects becomes evident as the individual matures. With the personality development, the object relationships become more complex and essential to the expression of basic needs. There is a vital necessity to identify with a number of these external objects. In order to ensure continued acceptance and love from these objects, there is in the individual the highly charged need to rid himself of any desire, instinct or trait which might encourage rejection of himself by these important 'others'. So that he may achieve these objectives, a dangerous and archaic externalization mechanism called 'projection' is frequently employed, by people of all classes, colours, cultures and levels of intelligence. This process, which has been previously briefly mentioned, may be described as the unwitting attribution of ones own traits, attitudes, or subjective processes to others and is central to the psychology of racism.

Another important aspect in the genesis of prejudice in this neurotic group is the use of a mechanism called 'displacement'. This differs from projection, in that it is the attachment or affect or feeling to something other than its proper object. Hostility may be felt towards an object or person to whom it would be dangerous for the subject to express such feelings. These hostile feelings are then transferred to another object which apparently has not the ability or power to retaliate. The uncomfortable emotion is thus discharged and some sort of inner equilibrium is re-established. This process is once again, of course, quite unconscious.

In the personal life of the individual, innumerable and variably engendered highly complex conflictual situations occur, arising from intrapsychic and environmental sources. How well the individual is equipped to deal with such conflicts would depend on a multitude of inter-related factors, constitutional, environmental and historical. Should the problem seem insoluble, there develop feelings of threat to the security of the person, accompanied by overpowering feelings of anxiety. The fundamental need to dissipate unbearable anxiety feelings may result in the use of these unconscious mechanisms just described, and in the conditioned person, the object of such externalization displacement could be a 'scrapegoated'² group or individual. The effect on the mental health of people who manifest such behaviour, must of necessity, be deleterious. Motivation to come to grips with absolute basic conflictual matters is dissipated as the anxiety is relieved by these vicarious methods, thus negating the need to manage them realistically. Lack of resolution of conflict would mean that the danger of constant repetition of the uncomfortable feelings is inevitable, and perception of realities would be distorted, with resultant comparatively poor life performances in a number of spheres. The opportunity of countering feelings of lack of personal worth by so simple, albeit neurotic, means is too valuable to be easily relinquished, and subsequent irrational bigotry becomes almost a permanent feature of personal life. The intensity and frequency of the show of prejudice in these people would necessarily be directly referrable to totally unrelated events, and would be unpredictable and inconstant. In these communities, where racial bigotry may be considered endemic, the result of displacement or projection of the untoward emotion on to the socially designated victim, or victim group, would be considered rational by the rest of the community, and subsequently not be recognized as formal neurotic behaviour requiring energetic and consistent management in the interests of the individual and community. On the other hand, because of its efficiency as an immediate tension reducing mechanism, this behaviour becomes increasingly necessary for the subject or patient, and he steadfastly maintains his belief.

Community Sources of Prejudice

The racist community has a need to condone and encourage the behaviour manifestations described above, as reinforcement of its own ingrained bigotry and irrational beliefs. A system of transaction, not open to critical examinations, rationalized and stylized, develops to perpetuate and propogate the myth of racial superiority. The automatic feeling of superiority achieved without the effort usually necessary to attain this status, merely by the creation of an artificially designated inferior-perceived group, is an emotionally expensive device not easily relinquished by a community able to perpetrate self-deception with such remarkable ease.

Besides being a straight-forward manifestation of individual maladjustment, a number of other processes can be recognized as contributory to the psychology of prejudice. One such would be the learning process, and in racialistic communities, there is evidence that the prejudice set is learnt in the very early years of the child's life. A careful study in a community of this type evinced clear evidence of racial prejudice in a majority of children in the pre-school age group 3-5 years. In otherwise apparently normally adjusting children, prejudice-loaded response to colour-laden questions almost universally favouring the black inferiority fallacy was present in the majority. The beginning of such learning experience is easily traceable to transactions which occur in the family group. The family transmits, almost by a process of psychological contagion, values which it accepts or needs to accept either to maintain its own cohesiveness or to ensure its place as an integral part of its community. The probable value of the majority of such attitudes is not questioned, but the fact that certain obviously destructive attitudes are not critically examined is poor commentary on the adequacy and maturity of such families. One of the more pernicious doctrines deeply rooted and inexplicably culture-bound in some areas, is the idea of the superiority of a particular race, a belief which has almost a delusionary quality. This manifestation has been termed 'ethno-centrism', which, in fact, encourages unmerited overvalue of the individual based merely on his accidental ethnic origin to the detriment of other ethnic groups. Together with other related false beliefs, this leads to the ultimate development of a non-justified privileged elite. As an example of this, one may look at 'the members of a club' in the deep south of the United States. These will be perceived as adult, white, protestant males. In general, it will be fair to say that the value judgments learnt in the family constellation will be largely those of the community of which it is a part. Actually, then, these learned, racist notions would be reinforced in school, college, work, social and cultural situations, and there is sufficient evidence to prove this to be the case.

Based on his unwillingness to accept the fact of his own imperman-ence, insecurities are easily aroused in man.[3] Exploitation of this psychological truism for political, economic, legalistic or social advantages is a common feature of contemporary life. For whatever reason, the perpetrators whip up feelings of insecurity by a variety of techniques, and then produce a cathartic experience by skilfully directing the anxiety and hostility at some handy victim. Hitlerian scapegoatism of the Jews is a good example of this, as is the negrophobia of white southern Africa.

When the integrity of the organism is threatened in any way, defence mechanisms, designed to lessen the immediate feeling of discom-fort, are brought to bear with varying degrees of success. It is obviously far more simple to combat an externally received threatening object than vague, ill-defined and poorly conceptualized intrapsychic, conflictual situations. Early in his life, man learned to externalize his bad feelings onto some outside object and deal with this. Biblical reference is made to this technique when, amongst the ancient Israelites, a pure white goat, on which the priests ceremonially heaped all the sins of the people, was subse-quently driven into the wilderness to die. Folklore is replete with tales of symbolic endowment of animals with the unwanted traits and feelings of the people, followed by the sacrificial slaughter of the animal, together with ritual cleaning ceremonies which subjectively relieved early man of intolerably uncomfortable feelings based on guilt, malevolence or sub-conscious knowledge of his own vulnerability and impermanence. From these practices the term 'scapegoat' evolved. The historical advance of the sacrifice surrogate or scapegoat to witches, incubi and finally to men of other tribes, nations, religions, creeds or colour, is obvious and needs no elaboration. History is studded with examples of the techniques of 'scape-goatism' used to relieve the anxiety of both the individual and ethnic collective subconscious.

Effects of Racial Prejudices

When examined from any point of view, in particular, psycho-social, the effects of racial prejudice are disastrous. A mythology has sprung up in which a number of stereotypes are prominent, all disparaging, and whose source and derivation cannot be traced. Examples of these un-warranted beliefs unduly held and expressed, are that the English are rigid and unbending, all Scots are misers, Frenchmen are lecherous.

Perhaps the most pernicious is the belief and expectation held by many
white of coloured people. The noncritical disparaging assessment by these
bigots automatically places coloured members of the community in an out-
group, seriously and unwarrantedly disadvantaged. Members of the victim
group are frequently perceived as destructive, barbaric, prone to unprovoked violence, envious, sexually uncontrolled, possessing lower
intelligence, fit only for menial work, dirty, devoid of sensitivity and
unappreciative of the kind efforts of the dominating group regarding
their welfare. From such attributes develop social, economic, vocational
and political actual positions of disadvantage, dictated by custom, or in
some cases, legalistic pressures. Subsequently, in certain communities or
countries, the coloured person is forced to accept all the agonies of
second class citizenship. He usually has no say in the structure or content
of the political or parliamentary institution of his town or state. His
housing is inferior and usually expensive. His earning power compares
poorly with labour peers of the dominant group. Educational opportunities
are fewer and inferior. Recreational facilities are poor and services of
all kinds are usually inferior. The inevitable result of this is greater
morbidity and mortality in the disadvantaged group, more social dis-
organization, less family cohesion and far less sensory stimulation, with
the resultant motivational deprivation and an ever present hostility and
frustration. All the elements of a self-fulfilling prophesy are extant and
in such an environment many of the predictions of the dominant group
are inevitably realized, no matter what the composition of the victim
group. The combined effect of persistent propaganda, coupled with the
very real disadvantaged style of life which the victim group has to accept,
frequently seriously distorts the self-perception of members of this group.
The resultant poor ego strength, and rejection of other members of the
family and the total current community, interferes seriously with
individual psychological development. Pathetic attempts at making physical changes so that closer physical resemblance to the in-group are often
made, such as hair straightening and artificial skin lightening amongst the
Negroes, indicates that amongst the defeated majority, white is regarded
as right and being black is in itself something inherently bad. Those
elements of inter-personal experience, vital to the development of an
adequate psyche, are consequently denied to members of the out-group.
A constant protective environment in the maturing individual, adequate
identity figures, opportunities for self-expression, sufficient play opportunities, social acceptance and a host of other essential ingredients to the
normally developing and maturing individual are not available, due merely
to the misfortune of being incidentally born into the particular out-group.

A considerable bibliography concerning racial prejudice is developing.
Particular attention is being paid to the myth of racial or ethnic
superiority,[4] and the destructiveness of such false beliefs when they
become institutionalized. Assumptions based on records of historians which
have never been validated, but which form the basis of many present day
opinions are being examined and reassessed. Historical reports, hitherto
uncritically accepted, are being proved to be unreliable and contradictory.
Generalizations about behaviour manifestation of black people, previously
regarded as attributable to genetic factors, have been shown by research
to be common to any impoverished or socially castigated group.

During the past two decades, evidence of change has been increasingly noticeable. The impotence of the so-called liberals as agents of change has been recognized, and a backlash of some vehemence and strength is being mounted by grass-roots members of disadvantaged groups. Ominous signs are appearing, and unless the great, uncommitted masses of advantaged people begin to look seriously at the destructiveness of accepting without examination, the great White Myth, there is a very real danger that the entire society as now structured, will undergo violent and not evolutionary change. A place in the sun for disadvantaged groups must always be the true indication of the degree of civilization which any community has achieved.

REFERENCES

1 BETTELHEIM, B. and JANOWITZ, M. *Social Change and Prejudice,* London. The Free Press of Glencoe, 1964.

2 PRUDHOMME, C. Editorial, *American Journal of Psychiatry,* 127:6, Dec. 1970.

3 *Ibid.*

4 G.A.P. Report No. 37, G.A.P. Publications Office, New York, May, 1957.

3

THE NATURE OF RACE PREJUDICE IN AUSTRALIA

S. Encel

Racialism is deeply embedded in the structure of Australian society. Although it takes a variety of forms, they may be regarded as related aspects of one central phenomenon. There are four aspects of racialism which have been particularly important in Australian social development:—

   (i) Fear of the 'Asian hordes' or the 'yellow peril'.

   (ii) Discrimination against, and repressive treatment of Aborigines.

These two aspects have a long history. More recently, two others have become important.

   (iii) Suspicion of separate ethno-cultural identity among immigrant groups.

   (iv) Solidarity with the white racialist regimes of Southern Africa.

Calvin Hernton, in a searching examination of black-white relations in America, attempts to define racism on a comprehensive basis by describing it as —

> 'the learned behaviour and learned emotions on the part of a group of people towards another group whose physical characteristics are dissimilar to the former group; behaviour and emotions that compel one group to conceive of and to treat the other on the basis of its physical characteristics alone ... When people live in a society where such things are formally and informally taught and learned and are practised, it is inescapable that the ideology of racism becomes a functional institution, originally interwoven with every other ideology and institution of that society'.[1]

Like most other definitions, this is incomplete. By concentrating on the problem of colour, Hernton has confused it with a more general issue. The emphasis on physical differences ignores the enormous amount of racial hostility directed against people who are socially rather than physically distinct, of which the prime example is anti-Semitism. The emphasis on learned behaviour implies that some other kind of behaviour can be learned, which understates the pervasiveness of racial hostility and the way it can flare up in situations where it has apparently never existed—a good example being hostility towards immigrant workers in western Europe in recent years.

A more elaborate approach is to be found in the work of Michael Banton, who distinguishes three distinct models of racial hostility.[2] The first is the 'ideological' model which postulates a racial struggle rather like the class struggle. This may be a real struggle, as depicted by theorists of racial superiority and inferiority from Gobineau down to the late Dr. Verwoerd. (The latter, it may be noted, was not concerned only with colour; he first achieved prominence in 1936 as an opponent of Jewish migration into South Africa from Nazi Germany.) In the Marxist version it is an example of 'false consciousness' or deliberate deception to cloak economic exploitation. The most systematic Marxist writer on the subject is a black American scholar, Oliver Cox, who argues that racism is 'propagated among the public by an exploiting class for the purpose of stigmatizing some group as inferior, so that the exploitation of either the group itself or its resources or both may be justified'.[3] Cox's view echoes the writings of J. A. Hobson, the author of *Imperialism,* who declared that the ideology of the white man's burden was a thin camouflage for the economic motives of imperialism: 'a convenient theory of a race struggle for the subjugation of the inferior peoples'. Lenin, taking up Hobson's thesis at the height of the first world war, reiterated this view and maintained that imperialist policies had been successful in dividing the international socialist movement by offering the workers some of the fruits of colonial exploitation.

Banton suggests that the ideology of racial inferiority is appropriately called *racism,* while the term *racialism* should be reserved for the practice of discrimination and repression against particular racial groups. There is some value in this distinction, but not perhaps in the way that Banton intends. One might say, using his terminology, that racialism is widespread in the U.S.A., but racism is influential only in the South. One might also distinguish Australia from South Africa in that the latter is clearly racist in theory as well as racialist in practice; in Australia, racialism is practised against Aborigines but with little in the way of racist ideology, whereas racism is clearly influential in relation to immigration policy but racialism, in consequence, has few opportunities to manifest itself. In general, however, the distinction between racism and racialism is of little operational value because it is hard to conceive of one without the other. In addition, as Banton himself points out, racial hostility can be attributed to at least two other modes of social inter-action, i.e. the *prejudice* model and the *discrimination* model. These three models are complementary, and in most real-life situations all three can be shown to be operating.

The prejudice model is derived from individual psychology, and its development has been profoundly influenced by psychoanalytic thought. This is the case with Sartre's brilliantly perceptive *Portrait of the Anti-Semite,* as it is with the work of psychiatrists like Money-Kyrle and Dicks in England, or the team which produced *The Authoritarian Personality* in the U.S.A. The latter book is particularly important because it links the prejudiced personality with the concept of *ethnocentrism,* first coined by W. G. Sumner almost fifty years earlier. In this case, racialism becomes a manifestation of individual traits which are widely distributed and gain in importance if the social situation encourages their manifestation. The discrimination model, on the other hand, is essentially a social-psychological construct, which emphasizes group membership as the source of individual behaviour. Its theoretical origins owe something to the German sociological theorist Georg Simmel, who described the 'web of group affiliations' which an individual forms in the course of his personal development; it also owes much to research in the United States, including the pioneering work of Bogardus on 'social distance', a technique used in Gunnar Myrdal's monumental study *An American Dilemma* (1941) and most recently in the work of Melvin Tumin, an American sociologist who studied mutual acceptability as it applied to Englishmen, Americans, Germans, Jews and West Indians.[4]

All three models are relevant to the social impact of racialism in Australia. The most popular orthodoxy is that which explains the effect of racialism on immigration policy—the 'White Australia' policy—by attributing it to a concern with living standards that might be undermined by an influx of cheap Asian labour. This ideological explanation has recently been given a severe drubbing in the work of the historian Humphrey McQueen, whose book *A New Britannia* contains the uncomprising assertion that 'racism is the most important single component of Australian nationalism'.[5] He rebukes a number of other historians, especially those with radical sympathies, for their neglect or wilful distortion of the strongly racialist character of the Australian Labour movement. 'Instead of combating racism as a tool of oppression, Labour leaders have almost invariably articulated and reinforced it ... (the Labour movement) was racist before it was socialist.'[6]

The demand for a white Australia in the last two decades of the nineteenth century was a principal factor in the federation of the Australian colonies, and one of the first legislative acts of the new Federal Parliament was the Immigration Restriction Act of 1901. *The Bulletin,* mouthpiece of the radical nationalism of the period, carried on its masthead the motto 'Australia for the White Man', which it discarded only in 1961 after a change of ownership. The Brisbane *Worker* hailed the legislation as saving Australia from 'the coloured curse', and, in 1905, the federal conference of the Australian Labour Party declared that its policy was 'the cultivation of an Australian sentiment based upon the maintenance of racial purity'. Officially, the Labour movement was in favour of White Australia because an influx of Asian labour was a threat to the living standards of Australian workers; unofficially, the economic motive and the racialist motive were inextricably interwoven. In the words of Manning Clark, 'the believers in the brotherhood of man and equality of all in the sight of God were silent. So the men who believed that the unity of labour was the hope of the world united with the apostles of Christian civilization to preserve Australia for the white man'.[7]

As Yarwood has pointed out in a careful study of the period, a mixture of racialist and utilitarian attitudes was common to members of all parties, and was fully exposed during the debates on the 1901 Act.[8] The Prime Minister, Edmund Barton, quoted at length from *National Life and Character,* written by C. H. Pearson, a former Minister for Education in Victoria who had warned Australians about the dangers of being swamped by an inferior race. Isaac Isaacs, later to be Chief Justice and Governor-General, warned against the 'contaminations and the degrading influence of inferior races'. (Did Isaacs, one may wonder, ever reflect during the 1930s and 1940s—he died in 1950—on his choice of words when the Nazis destroyed millions of Jews in the name of this doctrine?) The Labour leader, J. C. Watson, declared that his objection to coloured immigration, although influenced by 'considerations of an industrial nature', was mainly due to the 'possibility and probability of racial contamination'. The statistician and economic historian, T. A. Coghlan, wrote in the London *Times* in 1908 that the 'ethnical' objection to the coloured races was the most important, and that 'the economic objections might perhaps be waived were the other non-existent'. The Brisbane *Worker* called for a state composed of a 'multitude of perfect human units' (the drawbacks to perfection being obvious), and *The Bulletin* played on race prejudice constantly by its use of words such as 'mongrelisation' and its cartoons, which depicted the coloured man as a grinning caricature of humanity. In the context of this discussion, perhaps the most revealing sentence was uttered by Barton in a speech in parliament in September 1901, after the Immigration Restriction Act had become law: 'I do not think that the doctrine of the equality of man was really ever intended to include racial equality'.

The development of the prejudice and discrimination models reflects a belated recognition of the importance of sexual fears and frustrations in racial hostility. Hernton's book, already quoted, is full of poignant examples of the 'sexualization of racism' or the 'racism of sex' which help to reinforce and perpetuate the unequal social relations that exist between black and white in the U.S.A. An earlier study by the distinguished psychologist Gordon Allport[9] contains numerous examples of the sexual element in race prejudice; in particular, Allport demonstrates how blackness has been linked with masculinity to an extent where black women normally become dominant partners in lesbian relationships, while white lesbians have found it possible to form lasting heterosexual relationships with black men. The connection between racialism and repressed homosexual traits has been the subject of frequent comment in the case of Nazi racialism, where it was manifested in a variety of ways within the Nazi movement itself (such as the enormous stress on masculinity and male 'purity'), in the use of sexual perversion and terrorism within the concentration camps, and in the lurid sexual imagery of Streicher's anti-Semitic weekly *Der Sturmer*. The observation is of special relevance in Australia where the tradition of 'mateship' is under critical examination from various points of view, including the suggestion that it reflects strong tendencies towards homosexuality, which are repressed and redirected because of strong social hostility towards it. Mateship, as a number of people have now pointed out, involves the exclusion of women from the circle of mates, and in the pastoral occupations where the tradition is strongest it also applies to Aborigines. Sexual hostility to coloured people was a constant feature of racialist sentiments during the peak period of 'White Australia' agitation during the generation before 1914. When a Japanese naval squadron visited Australia in 1906, *The Bulletin* printed stories accusing the sailors of distributing pornographic postcards, and alleged that the ships were full of naked prostitutes.[10] William Lane, one of the apostles of mateship and of socialism, wrote in a union paper that he would rather see his daughter dead than kissing a black man or 'nursing a little coffee-coloured brat that she was mother to.'[11] His novel *The Working Man's Paradise* (1889) is saturated in anti-Chinese prejudice which takes a similarly explicit sexual form. Another apostle of mateship and socialism, Henry Lawson, spent the last twenty years of his life writing racialist verse where the sexual implications of a future 'race war' are visible from time to time.[12]

So far, we have described racial exclusionism in terms of the ideological and prejudice models, but discrimination is at least as important. In the Australian setting, racial discrimination may be seen as an essential component of a mixture of attitudes and policies reflecting the insecurity of a group of white settlers in a remote British colony. As McQueen remarks, Australia could become a nation only through the reconciliation of democracy with nationalism, racialism, imperialism, and militarism, symbolized by the mass sacrifice of Gallipoli.[13]

Australian attitudes towards the outside world have been dominated by three considerations. The first is the obvious physical fact that the Australian continent, with its long and exposed coastline, cannot be defended by its own population. Second, there is the cultural and psychological tie to the British Isles, which remains the outstanding component of the Australian identity. This consciousness of British identity has frequently been at odds with the third factor, i.e. the problem of our relations with Asia, which, for over a century, has been the source of real or imagined threats to Australian security and the maintenance of European culture on a faraway island. The history of Australia's external relations is one of reaction to some kind of threat—usually imaginary—and this reaction has been a powerful influence on social norms within Australia itself. The source of the menace has varied, including French, Russian, German, Chinese, Japanese, and Indonesian imperialism at various times, but it has been particularly strong when accompanied by colour prejudice. Fear of Japan, in particular, was responsible for the success of the movement for universal military training, which was introduced by a Labour government in 1910. W. M. Hughes, later Prime Minister, was the strongest advocate of compulsory training; he reminded his fellow MPs that they lived 'only a few days' steaming distance from countries inhabited by nearly 1000 million of coloured people'.[14] His colleague George Pearce, later to be Minister for Defence for a total period of thirteen years, told the Senate that 'our White Australia legislation is so much waste paper unless we have rifles to back it up' and that Australia needed 'twenty million standing behind guns'.[15] In July, 1916, Hughes declared in a florid speech that 'we have nailed the flag of White Australia to the topmost minarets of our national edifice'.[16]

These attitudes continue to be influential to the present day, and a suitable conjunction of circumstances can bring them to the surface. This occurred during the debate in the Federal Parliament in 1957 on the ratification of a trade treaty with Japan, when the discussion turned, not on the content of the treaty, but on the dangers to Australia of allowing itself to become involved with Japanese. An analysis of attitudes towards migrants from different countries based on a number of opinion polls and surveys, was made a few years ago by Huck.[17] Although attitudes towards European migrants have changed substantially as a result of post-war immigration policy, resistance towards non-European migration and towards intermarriage have remained fairly constant, with fluctuations affecting the relative unpopularity of different Asian nationalities.

The treatment of Aborigines in Australia is linked with the other aspects of racialism through the operation of the three models of racial antagonism already described. The ideological origins of black-white relations are suggested by the American historian Louis Hartz, who identifies a common pattern of racialism in the countries colonized by European settlers following the Protestant Reformation. This applies to Australia as it does to the Americas and to southern Africa. Calvinist Protestantism, according to Hartz, made it possible to regard coloured people with pagan cultures as morally and also biologically inferior. Slavery, forcible conversion, suppression and even extermination thus become morally justifiable at the same time that egalitarianism among white man becomes firmly established.[18] One does not have to agree entirely with Hartz's emphasis on evangelical Christianity to accept the general conclusion that societies based on European colonization all show the same paradoxes of equality among white man and suppression of the coloured man; a philosophy of individualism governing relations between white man, but a definition of the coloured man in terms of collective characteristics. Gunnor Myrdal, in his monumental study *An American Dilemma*, noted that American individualism, and especially the ethic of individual success, make things harder for the negro because he has to prove his individual worth by succeeding in a competitive environment where he competes from behind scratch. Similar rationalizations about the natural inferiority of Aborigines help to justify suppression and discrimination, even if they are dressed up in an air of tolerance and humanity. A leading article in a Melbourne daily newspaper in 1938 asserted the 'self-evident truth' that Aborigines were a backward and low race, who could not be treated as civilized people, but should be looked upon with the 'broadest tolerance and humanity' merited by the dying relic of a dead past.[19] Similar sentiments had been voiced ever since the early years of black-white contact, although often with less charity. The pastoralist Alfred Giles, writing in 1899, denied that the blackfellow should be regarded as a noble savage and described his songs, rites and ceremonies as 'utterly revolting and fiendish'. He added a familiar note of sexual doublethink by describing the possibility of chastity among black women as 'preposterous'; black women could only be outraged, he asserted, by stopping their supply of tobacco.[20]

The result of these racialist attitudes was the establishment of a system of segration and repression which has many parallels with the *apartheid* laws of South Africa. It has received less attention because, unlike South Africa, the system operates in rural areas and small towns away from the metropolitan cities, and affects only a minority of the population. In Queensland, law and practice find their statutory basis in the Aboriginals Protection and Restriction of the Sale of Opium Act of 1897. Subsequent legislation and regulations retain the segregationist philosophy of this Act. The legislation established reserves where the resident Aborigines were under the virtually complete control of the superintendent and the local police, with no access to the legal system which governs white society.[21] The Queensland laws give the authorities wide powers of definition as to who is or is not an Aborigine, and set up a system of accounts which prevents Aborigines from handling their own wages. Persons defined as Aboriginal wards of the State are not even allowed to marry without permission. The Queensland legislation is not unique. It was followed closely by the Aborigines Act passed by the West Australian state parliament in 1905, and the administration of Aboriginal affairs in the Northern Territory by the Federal government runs along similar lines.

C. D. Rowley[22] has recently argued at length that the treatment of Aborigines cannot be separated from race relations in general. The assumption that Australia must be kept free from interracial tensions through a restrictive immigration policy is ironic in its neglect of relations with Aborigines. Historians have tended to play down the effects of white settlement on Aboriginal life and treated the moral and political issues as past history. (It may be added that this neglect cuts across political sympathies. Radical historians have been concerned to paint a more favourable picture of the Labour movement by ignoring the racialism evident among trade unions, notably the Australian Workers' Union, which, for many years, refused to admit Aborigines to membership. In 1924, when applying to the Arbitration Court for an award to cover the pastoral industry, the A.W.U. specifically asked the Court to restrict the employment of Aborigines. The ban on membership was not lifted until 1969. The new rules of the A.W.U., adopted in that year, contain a long and detailed list of those racial groups which are eligible for membership. Similarly, it was not until the 1960s that the North Australian Workers' Union took advantage of the arbitration system to press for equal pay for Aborigines in the pastoral industry, despite the fact that this case could have been presented at any time in the preceding forty years, and that Aboriginal stockmen had contributed greatly to cattle raising throughout this period.)

Rowley goes on to suggest that refusal to admit Aborigines as equals is the deep-lying reason for the repeated deferment of policies designed to provide equality in practice. (In April 1971, Mr. Justice Blackburn of the Northern Territory Supreme Court refused an application by the Aborigines of the Gove peninsula for a legal title to the area, which is being mined for bauxite. In his judgment, he provided striking evidence in favour of Louis Hartz's thesis. The 'philosophical justification', the learned judge declared, which supports the colonization of the territory of 'less civilized peoples' was that the earth was open to the industry and enterprise of the 'more advanced peoples' who were therefore entitled to dispossess, if necessary, the less advanced.[23]) Rowley notes also that official accounts, including school textbooks, 'bowdlerize' the facts of repression, so that few people ever learn about the extreme violence shown towards Aborigines through murder, rape, cruelty, cultural deprivation and economic dispossession. There are still persons living who could kill an Aborigine with impunity, if not legality, when they were young, but the general public regards this as an incident of a remote past. Sir Paul Hasluck, Governor-General of Australia, who was an early student of race relations, found it necessary to apologize to his readers for the 'sensational' character of the incidents recounted in his book *Black Australians*, published in 1939.[24]

Racialism in Postwar Australia

The maintenance of a white Australia and the repression of Aboriginal Australians are the two traditional manifestations of racialism in this country. Since 1945, they have been joined by two additional phenomena which reflect some of the important social changes of the postwar period —in particular, the impact of a large-scale immigration programme and the internationalization of racial conflict. Before 1945, 90 per cent of immigrants to Australia came from the British Isles, but since then the proportion has been only about 40 per cent. Non-British settlers, together with their children born in Australia, now make up nearly one-fifth of the total population. Between 1947 and 1969, Australia had received 278,000 migrants from Italy, 165,000 from Greece, 111,000 from Holland, 100,000 from Yugoslavia, 83,000 from Germany, 83,000 from Poland, and 60,000 from Malta.[25] (The figures are net in each case.) Moreover, some of these groups have shown a strong tendency to concentrate in districts within the big cities, especially Melbourne, Sydney and Adelaide. This has created 'problems' of assimilation, in that such ethnic concentrations naturally stimulate the growth of ethnic consciousness and a distinctive sub-culture. The situation is problematic only in the sense that it disturbs traditional racialist assumptions about homogeneity, i.e. the picture of Australia as a white Anglo-Saxon Protestant (WASP) community. Assimilation is an ideological corner-stone of the postwar immigration policy, and makes it possible for a wide variety of nationalist and patriotic groups, of differing political complexions, to accept immigration as compatible with the preservation of the Australian way of life. The prospect of ethnic pluralism disturbs this 'melting-pot' theory and provokes injunctions to migrants to become 'good Australians' as quickly as possible. The annual Citizenship Convention organized by the Immigration Department provides an official platform from which the message of assimilation can be sounded loud and clear. In April, 1971, an official pamphlet published by the Immigration Department referred to the generally accepted aim of a 'socially homogeneous and cohesive population' unmarred by 'self-perpetuating enclaves and undigested minorities'.

Discrimination on ethno-cultural grounds, though greatly stimulated by postwar immigration, is not a new phenomenon. Italian settlers have suffered from it for years. Starting in the 1890s, Italian immigrants took up jobs on the sugar-cane fields of North Queensland; later Italians also settled in the Murrumbidgee Irrigation Area. A British Preference League, set up during the depressed 1930s, was successful in enforcing a quota of 25 per cent for non-British cane cutters, and somewhat similar examples of discrimination occurred in the M.I.A. The Returned Services League tried to persuade the Federal and State governments during the 1939-1945 war that all foreigners should be ousted from the canefields after the war in favour of ex-servicemen. To union officials, the attempts of European workers to earn more by working harder in order to buy their own land and achieve security are often seen merely as 'scabbing' on their fellow-workers. As the secretary of the A.W.U. in Queensland declared in 1958, the migrant workers 'wanted to work as long as they could, break down every union rule, and yet get every penny they could by using the award . . . . It is time they learnt our ways'.[26]

Anti-Semitism, the classic manifestation of racial discrimination in the Christian world, has also played its part in moulding racialist attitudes in Australia. Anti-capitalism, support for white Australia, opposition to British imperialism and anti-Semitism provided a rich mixture of radical attitudes before 1914. *The Bulletin* invented a composite character titled John Bull-Cohen, or British imperialism acting at the will of Jewish financiers. A radical journalist, H. I. Jensen, wrote in *The Rising Tide* (1909) that Australia and New Zealand were allowing themselves to be fleeced wholesale by 'hooknosed moneylenders' in the shape of British capitalism. During the 1914-18 war, a left-wing MP, Frank Anstey, made the same equation of British imperialism and Jewish finance in a pamphlet called *The Kingdom of Shylock*. Even as late as 1947, a trade union newspaper welcomed the proposed nationalization of the banks by the Chifley Labour government on the grounds that it would discomfit the Jewish bankers.

Within the last year or so, the normally latent character of anti-Semitic prejudice has been activated by disputes over the black-balling of

Jews from exclusive clubs. The centre of the argument was the Melbourne Club, one of the oldest institutions of its kind in Australia. The only Jew ever admitted to it was Sir Isaac Isaacs, who refused to use the club because of its discriminatory policies. Although these policies have been known for many years, their operation rarely becomes public because the objects of discrimination are unwilling to endure the quasi-martyrdom involved in breaking the taboo of silence. The situation has changed because racialism in any form is now a topic for front page news, and the black-balling of a prominent Melbourne businessman, Mr. K. B. Myer, in 1970, brought the Melbourne Club into this unwanted position of public exposure.

Throughout the world, race relations have become international relations, and Australia, fondly protected from interracial tensions for so many years by the simple device of exclusion, has found that the device is not good enough. Two remarkable editorials published in the Sydney *Daily Telegraph* on July 27th and 28th, 1967, underlined the connections between colour prejudice and international alignments. Following disturbances in Detroit and other American cities, the *Telegraph* wrote that 'if every time Negro revolutionaries decided to burn and kill, those maintaining the law killed 500 Negroes, the Negroes might decide to stop burning and looting. Surely the time has come for the American nation to take the kid gloves off and deal drastically with this lawless minority'. Apparently public reaction to this editorial was stronger than the *Telegraph* management had expected, for it was followed the next day by a further statement to the effect that the shooting of Negroes was meant to refer only to actual rioters caught in the act, but that 'a country which is involved in a long and arduous war against Communism in Vietnam simply cannot afford to permit little civil wars to break out in the home front'.

This line-up with the forces of 'law and order' is matched, in the *Daily Telegraph* and elsewhere, by direct or implied support for white supremacist regimes in southern Africa. Mr. E. H. St. John, whose brief career in the Federal Parliament (1966-69) was punctuated by a number of spectacular incidents, was opposed in the blue-ribbon Liberal seat of Warringah by an 'independent Liberal' candidate who attacked St. John because of his involvement in the affairs of the South African Defence and Aid Fund. He succeeded in attracting a significant number of Liberal votes to his support. In Federal Parliament, there is a sizeable group of Liberal members who have pressed the government to establish closer relations with South Africa and Rhodesia. In September 1968, for instance, a group of Liberal back-benchers strongly opposed government policy of supporting United Nations sanctions policy against Rhodesia. Some urged the government to withdraw from the U.N. Others attacked the 'black takeover' of the U.N., and its 'double standard' towards South Africa and Rhodesia.

This rising tempo of argument about racialism and its place in Australian politics helps to account for the heat generated by the issue of *apartheid* in sport. The posture of a country towards racialism on the international plane is likely to be directly related to the part played by racialism in its internal affairs. The United States, though racialist in practice, would like to show that it is not racist in theory, and its international stand against *apartheid* has been correspondingly firm. Countries like Britain, Australia, and New Zealand, which have not yet admitted to themselves that racialism is part of their social fabric, are correspondingly equivocal and hypocritical in their public reactions to the challenges with which they are now increasingly confronted. In the meantime, they are being gradually drawn into a web of economic, cultural and sporting relationships with the South African government, which is exploiting their equivocations in an attempt to build up an international body of support— even to the extent of discouraging its own automobile industry in favour of Australian imports, so that the prosperity of the Australian industry will depend more and more on friendly relations with South Africa.

Incidents involving racialism and racial discrimination occur so rapidly these days that they seem to join up like the frames on a moving picture. Unlike the movie, this impression of continuity is not an illusion. Race relations have become a continuous theme of everyday life in Australia. As a result, phenomena which once seemed to be disconnected now run together much more obviously. For many years, it was possible to imagine that policy towards the Aborigines was a separate issue from the assimilation of non-British migrants or the exclusion of Asians. It is much easier now to see these as connected aspects of the one central question of racialism—an issue which, in Australia as elsewhere, is assuming the same kind of basic political character that the class struggle used to have for an earlier generation. Demonstrations against *apartheid* in sport, court cases over Aboriginal land rights, reports of anti-Semitism in clubs, expulsion of Asian students, speeches by the former Prime Minister on multi-racialism, public disputes among Labour politicians over immigration policy—this succession of almost daily occurrences underlines the continuity and intensity of general concern with racialism.

Among recent statements on the subject, few have been so illuminating as that by Mr. Arthur Calwell, former leader of the federal parliamentary A.L.P., who inaugurated the massive postwar migration policy as first Minister for Immigration. Mr. Calwell's prejudice against coloured migrants is well known, and was manifested by several decisions made during his term as minister. Perhaps his most famous utterance on the subject was the remark that 'two Wongs don't make a white', in justifying his opposition to allowing the Asian spouses of Australian nationals to settle in Australia. In April, 1971, Mr. Calwell intervened in a dispute between his successor as Labour leader, Mr. E. G. Whitlam, and Labour's 'shadow' Minister for Immigration, Mr. F. M. Daly. 'Racialism and nationalism', he declared, 'are, in my thinking, synonymous words.' Mr. Calwell (doubtless unconsciously) thereby provided a direct confirmation of Humphrey McQueen's conclusion that 'racism is the most important single component of Australian nationalism'.

This is, indeed, the crux of the matter. Australians have, throughout their history, felt threatened because of their exposed position as an isolated European outpost in the South Pacific, and their racialism is, in part, a reaction to this fundamental insecurity. Colonial dependence on Britain was, for a long time, the answer to this problem, and Australian racialism springs also from the desire to maintain the British identity. We can no longer depend on Britain, and the United States will not provide an effective substitute. The task of maintaining some kind of national identity, without colonial dependence, without racialism, and far away from Europe, is a task of appalling difficulty which must nevertheless be faced.

REFERENCES

1 HERNTON, CALVIN C., *Sex and Racism*, London, Deutsch, 1969, pp. 149-50.

2 BANTON, MICHAEL, *Race Relations*, London, Tavistock, 1967, pp. 7-10.

3 COX, OLIVER C., *Caste, Class and Race*, New York, Monthly Review Press, 1959, p. 393.

4 BANTON, pp. 389-90.

5 McQUEEN, HUMPHREY, *A New Britannia*, Melbourne, Penguin, 1970, p. 42.

6 *Ibid*, pp. 50-53.

7 CLARK, C. M. H., *A Short History of Australia*, London, Mentor, 1964, p. 193.

8 YARWOOD, A. T., *Asia Migration to Australia*, Melbourne, M.U.P., 1964, pp. 22-35, *passim*.

9 ALLPORT, G. W., *The Nature of Prejudice*, New York, Addison-Wesley, 1954.

10 McQUEEN, p. 70.

11 *Ibid*, p. 48.

12 *Ibid*, esp. pp. 111-116.

13 *Ibid*, p. 89.

14 Commonwealth Parliamentary Debates, Vol. 37, p. 1289.

15 *Ibid*, Vol. 41, p. 5679.

16 SISSONS, D. C. S., 'Attitudes to Japan and Defence, 1890-1923.' M.A. thesis, University of Melbourne, 1956, p. 79.

17 HUCK, ARTHUR, *The Chinese in Australia*, Melbourne, Longmans, 1968, ch. 7.

18 HARTZ, LOUIS (ed.), *The Founding of New Societies*, New York, Harcourt Brace, 1964, ch. 1.

19 *The Argus*, 17.1.38. I am grateful to Mr. F. S. Stevens for drawing my attention to this quotation.

20 Giles' report was quoted in the Queensland parliament in April, 1965.

21 For an analysis of the working of 'settlement courts' where superintendents exercise judicial powers, see C. M. TATZ, 'Queensland's Aborigines', *Australian Quarterly*, Vol. 35, No. 3, 1963.

22 ROWLEY, C. D., *The Destruction of Aboriginal Society*, Canberra, A.N.U. Press, 1970, chs. 1-7, *passim*.

23 *The Australian*, 28.4.71.

24 ROWLEY, *op. cit.*, p. 7.

25 PRICE, C.A., 'Immigrants', in A. F. DAVIES and S. ENCEL (eds.), *Australian Society*, Melbourne, Cheshire, 1970.

26 *Courier-Mail* (Brisbane), 23.1.58. Quoted by J. A. HEMPEL, *Italians in Queensland*, A.N.U. Department of Demography (duplicated), 1959.

PREJUDICE AND NEW ARRIVALS

4

MINORITY GROUPS AND PROBLEMS OF ADJUSTMENT

A. G. Doczy

At a recent conference on the welfare of Australian ethnic minorities, my lunchtime neighbour, a native of Papua, said to me that he could not understand the inclusion of European immigrants in the 'ethnic minority' category. 'What is so special about white immigrants' problems?' he asked. 'They have the same colour as white Australians, live a similar life, get the same wages, and so on ... . They don't know what discrimination is.' He went on for a while in the same vein before it was my turn to answer. This chapter presents a somewhat expanded version of my reaction to my Papuan colleague's remarks.

Admittedly, it would be foolish to maintain that the colour of the immigrant's skin is not noticed by members of the host population or that Caucasian newcomers and, especially, their descendants, have no better chance of being on equal footing with 'white' Australians than have members of the non-white races. However, European immigrants (and, it may be added, their offspring), *as a group*,[1] are more or less seriously handicapped as a result of their immigrant status. 'Problems' are related to such things as feeling discriminated against by Australians, communication difficulties, economic stress, etc. A considerable volume of research has been devoted to the problems of immigrants in this country. Authors of important publications in the area include W. D. Borrie and C. A. Price (historical and demographic aspects), J. Zubrzycki (sociological and demographic), R. Appleyard (economic and demographic), J. Krupinski and A. Stoller (psychiatric and psychological), A. Richardson, R. Taft and their Western Australian co-workers (psychological aspects). Being an ex-member of the last-mentioned team, I propose to present a sample of Australian studies of immigrant adjustment under the following four headings:—

    (i) Acculturation.
    (ii) Social Interaction.
    (iii) Identification.
    (iv) Satisfaction.

The connection referred to in the last sentence is that the proposed break-down is based on the combination of two Western Australian approaches to research on immigrant adjustment. One is Taft's assimilation model[2] and the other Richardson's scalogram analysis of the stage-sequence of the adjustment process.[3]

Studies of adults and children will be treated separately, for various reasons. The chief reason is that, as research in the field of child and adolescent psychology has shown, children and adolescents are not 'miniature adults'. Immigrant-adjustment studies, too, support the notion that it is not permissible to generalize from findings on grown-up immigrants to the adjustment of immigrant's children or *vice versa*.

Whenever possible, the findings on immigrants will be compared with those on matched[4] Australian control groups.

Acculturation

The term 'acculturation' refers here to the immigrant's acquisition of cultural knowledge and skills, i.e., knowledge of the customs, folkways, mores and skills characteristic of the life of the host population—in our case, of 'the Australian way of life'. Perhaps the most relevant and most often discussed skill in our context is mastery of the host language. While this variable is not a necessary condition of satisfactory immigrant adjustment,[5] communication skills usually greatly facilitate mixing with the hosts, which, in turn, usually facilitates adjustment in the new country. Indeed, language has been referred to (indirectly) as 'the most visible of the symptoms of assimilation'.[6]

The probably not surprising main finding in the area of mastery of spoken English is that, while Dutch immigrants and their children speak English well and converse in it in their homes, the opposite trend has been observed in the case of adult immigrants from central and southern Europe.[7] It is mainly the latter group to which these words seem to refer:—

> 'Immigrants over the age of 35 years, especially if of poor educational background, find the acquisition of new language skills extremely difficult, and this may constitute a distinct problem of adaptation.'[8]

Mastery of spoken English is only one of the cultural skills studied in its relation to the immigrant-adjustment process. Other acculturation variables include knowledge of the 'heroes' of the hosts (for instance, famous Australian sportsmen) and knowledge of Australian slang expressions (such as 'offsider' or 'Buckley's chance'). The latter has turned out not only to be a sharper measure of assimilation and adjustment than knowledge of 'straight' English but also to be one of the best predictors of those processes. Richardson's 20-item slang test[9] and its variations have been used in a number of studies. It has been found, among other things, that, after having been in Australia for five to seven years, the Dutch adults scored only about half of the Australian adult average and even the British (skilled manual workers and their wives) scored only approximately three-quarters.[10]

Concerning the linguistic adjustment of immigrants' children, there seems to be no doubt that they tend to fare much better than their parents. The quotation below presents an extreme case of a relatively wide range of findings:—

> 'It is doubtful whether an average adult Italian migrant can be linguistically assimilated. With children it is different and their assimilation, both of those born in Australia and those born in Italy, is rapid, once they enter Australian schools. They converse in English from preference both during and after school hours. They retain a knowledge of the original dialect only as far as it is necessary to converse with their parents or . . . grandparents.'[11]

Even if one accepts this bright picture as a summary of the Australian

findings on knowledge of 'straight' English, other measures of acculturation suggest a different state of affairs. Let us look at a typical set of
slang-test results. Table 1 presents a highly condensed version of the results
on a modified 20-item Richardson slang-test, given to British, German,
Greek, Italian and Yugoslav immigrant boys and to an Australian control
group in Sydney.[12]

TABLE 1

Knowledge of Australian slang words
(Sydney boys)

	Non-British		British		Australian		
	f	%	f	%	f	%	Total
High (12+)	41	17	41	47	336	69	418
Low (11−)	194	83	46	53	154	31	394
Total	235	100	87	100	490	100	812

Even a cursory glance at the table reveals marked differences, the
Australians scoring significantly higher than either immigrant group and
the British scoring significantly higher than the non-British.[13]

All other measures of cultural knowledge and skills show a similar
trend, though the differences are not as 'dramatic' as in the case of knowledge of Australian slang words.

As mentioned earlier, while we are concerned here mainly with
ethnic-group differences, we should not forget about individual differences
within the groups. Table 1 is only one of countless tables[14] which may
serve as reminders. For instance, in spite of the strong general trend shown
in Table 1, 17 per cent of the non-British immigrants scored higher than
31 per cent of their Australian peers.

Social Interaction

In our context the term 'social interaction' stands for the frequency
and quality (depth) of immigrants' mixing with Australians. How often
is x immigrant in the company of Australians? How long does he stay
with them? What kinds of activities do they share? Are they together by
choice or by chance? Are they working companions, schoolmates, acquain-
tances or friends? These and similar questions are asked when the variable
'social interaction' is being studied. The variable may be divided into two
components:—

    (i) The 'overt' behavioural component; the immigrant's actual, vis-
        ible participation in the activities of Australians (e.g. visiting
        Australian friends).

    (ii) The 'attitudinal' component; this refers to the degree of mutual
        acceptance of hosts and immigrants.

The two components are, of course, intimately related. 'Social-
distance attitudes', as the attitudes involved are often called, determine,
or, at least, influence, the frequency and depth of mixing. At the same
time, mixing is bound to lead to the development or modification of

social-distance attitudes. Since these deep-seated springs of human behaviour represent the single most important aspect of racism, as well as of other manifestations of group relationships, I shall spend a little more time on them than on the overt aspect. Concerning the latter, let us suffice to refer back to the language factor and to state that the immigrants' mixing with Australians follows a similar pattern. To be a little more specific, adult European immigrants, with the exception of the British and the Dutch, are likely to be found to mix more with their original ethnic group than with the hosts, even if some of them have contacts of various degrees of intimacy with Australians. In general, the higher the immigrant's education the more likely his social intercourse with Australians. A notable exception to this 'rule' is the elderly 'intellectual' who received all his education in his country of origin and who is, or thinks he is, too old to speak satisfactory English.[15] This, by the way, seems to be a specific case of age affecting social interaction, the relationship being an inverse one (i.e., the younger mixing more). For obvious reasons, children of immigrants, especially school-age children mix more often and more easily with their Australian counterparts than do adult newcomers, although investigators report different findings concerning the extent and depth of mixing. For instance, Hempel writes:—

> 'Children adopt fully the behaviour of other school children and are indistinguishable from their school mates. This occurs independently of whether the children live in areas of great density of Italian population or not.'[16]

On the other hand, while my Perth[17] findings in this area do not contradict this statement, my findings on the daily mixing of Australian and Italian boys, in areas of great density of Italian population, do. Forty-four per cent of the Australian control group and only seven per cent of the Italians mixed exclusively with Australians.[18]

Let us turn to social-distance attitudes. Table 2 sums up the results of a Western Australian quota sample study.[19] Two hundred and thirty Australian-born respondents were asked to indicate whether or not they were willing to admit members of each national group listed in Table 2 to

TABLE 2

Social distance attitudes of 230 residents of Perth (1960)

Immigrant Group	Allow to live in Perth	Willing to meet socially	Would accept as a working companion	Would admit to close friendship	Positively favour their further immigration to Australia
English	98	97	96	96	90
German	93	82	86	71 (93)	65
Dutch	92	82	88	70	79
Polish	92	80	82	64	57
Italian	90	79	82	63 (92)	45
Jewish	91	71	77	61	50
Malayan	83	67	71	55 (77)	28

various relationships ranging from 'allow to live in Perth' to 'positively favour their further immigration to Australia'.

The data reported, especially those contained in the last two columns, would seem to suggest some degree of xenophobia and anti-Semitism on the part of many Australians. However, Taft reports that there was a substantial change to favourable attitudes of Australians to foreigners after 1960. The figures in brackets in Table 2 are examples of the 1965 findings.[20] Taft concludes:—

> 'Thus, barring any circumstances that might bring about a marked change in the present position the attitudes of adult residents of Perth towards persons of European origin should no longer be an important consideration in the adjustment of immigrants.'[21]

I do not know how much this applies to other parts of Australia. All I can do is to make a brief digression from the presentation of dispassionate research and to imply a value judgment in saying that I hope we would find similar changes elsewhere, too.

With regard to the *'vice versa'* aspect, i.e., the adult immigrants' social-distance attitudes to Australians, studies in this country seem to suggest that those attitudes are 'relative to the reciprocal attitudes and behaviour of the latter (Australians)'.[22] This may be illustrated by a response to an open-ended question given by a 55-year-old immigrant (non-British) factory worker, former army officer and a university graduate:—

> 'Australia is a country without a soul . . . high standard of living, as far as the stomach is concerned . . . indifferent, selfish life in the family . . . the ultimate aim is money . . . minimum interest in study and art; no interest in these aspects in the lower classes.'[23]

I leave it to the reader to guess this immigrant's specific responses to social distance scales as well as the degree of his assimilation and adjustment.

To illustrate the social distance attitudes of children in Australia, let us have another look at my Sydney sample of young adolescent boys.[24] They were asked to state their preferences for one of the following three groups: (1) Australian boys, (2) British immigrant boys and (3) European non-British immigrant boys. Table 3 reports the results.

The table clearly shows that the majority of the immigrant boys (74 per cent of the non-British and 64 per cent of the British) tend to prefer immigrant boys of their own 'brand' to members of the other immigrant group and to Australian boys. On the other hand, 95 per cent of the Australian sample showed preference for Australians. In order to obtain some indication of the degree of social distance, the boys were encouraged to expand on their responses by reacting to the following sentence, 'If you would like to write a few words about this (preference for one of the groups), please do so.' About one-third of the subjects in each group volunteered. While a small percentage of the responses indicated a tolerant attitude to the out-groups (for instance, 'they are not really different'; 'they are the same to me'; 'it depends on what they are like'), more than 80 per cent of the responses were abusive. The 'typical' Australian response may be summed up by the following statement, give or take a couple of words, 'I hate greasy garlick-sucking wogs'. The immigrant boys' main complaints are somewhat reminiscent of the adult response quoted above. The boys thought that Australian boys of

TABLE 3

Social distance attitudes of Sydney boys

X	Non-British f	Non-British %	British f	British %	Australian f	Australian %	Total
2	54	23	28	32	464	95	546
1	6	3	3	3	11	2	20
0	175	74	56	64	15	3	246
Total	235	100	87	100	490	100	812

LEGEND

(a) Non-British responses
  2 = prefers Australians
  1 = prefers British immigrants
  0 = prefers Non-British immigrants

(b) Australian and British responses
  2 = prefers Australians
  1 = prefers Non-British immigrants
  0 = prefers British immigrants

their age were 'soulless', 'rough', 'insensitive', 'not interested in the finer things' and so on. Those few immigrants who made favourable remarks reported their appreciation of fairness, sportsmanship and lack of racial discrimination, on the part of Australians.

It is interesting to note that in an earlier study in Perth[25] not only were found much less 'dramatic' manifestations of discrimination, but also the differences between the choices of immigrants and Australians were insignificant, statistically speaking. In that study, however, the respondents had to record their attitudes to each of their classmates, instead of reacting to groups. I have no space here for the analysis of the differences between the two sets of results because of the large number of complicating factors to be taken into consideration (for instance, socially desirable responses, politeness, and so on, on the part of the favourably disposed boys). Whatever the interpretation of the different findings, it is possible that, while children (at any rate children like those constituting my sample) prefer to mix with members of their own group, they are also reasonably tolerant of members of the other group. This category would not include, of course, the respondents who made abusive remarks.

Mutual acceptance by one another of European immigrant children and their Australian classmates has been studied by a number of Western Australian research workers. The studies[26] have all found differential acceptance patterns. The degree of non-acceptance has ranged from what may be called mild disapproval[27] to outright rejection[28] of immigrant children by their Australian peers and, in some cases, *vice versa*.

I would like to end this section by stating that even if the 'wog-haters' outnumbered the 'tolerants' in this country it would not be a phenomenon peculiar to Australia. At the conference mentioned, the audience was reminded of 'the case of pupil Snipe from a London dock-land school'.[29] Snipe stated his social-distance attitude as follows, 'Forriners is stoopid bastuds'. According to the investigator, this response was not an idiosyncratic one, either, 'but a laconic summary of the reaction of the whole class'. The class proceeded to participate in a term's project devoted to show the children some of the good points of different nationalities. Through books and films the pupils were exposed to famous foreigners, including sportsmen, scientists, great men and great deeds of ancient Greece and Rome and so on. After this intensive programme, Snipe produced another 'laconic summary' of the consensus, writing 'forriners is kunnin bastuds'.

Identification

By the term 'identification' ('group identification', 'reference-group identification') I shall mean here 'the process wherein the individual so strongly feels himself a member of a group that he adopts its ideas, beliefs and habits'.[30] In other words, the individual identifies himself as being 'one of them', i.e. as a member of a given group (e.g., 'bikie', Italian, Australian).

According to Taft, 'Identification with Australia appears to be the central aspect' of the immigrant-adjustment process.[31] He reports on the identification of adult immigrants as follows:—

'The degree of identification with Australia varies considerably from one immigrant group to another. In some groups, after less than 10 years in Australia, more than 30 per cent of the immigrants identify themself more with Australia than with their country of origin, and in most of the groups, more than 60 per cent have more Australian than homo-ethnic friends. ... However, the vast majority of immigrants are cautious about adopting Australian nationality.'[32]

With reference to the last point of this quotation, the phenomenon which may be termed 'the naturalization paradox' is noteworthy: some immigrants (not many) usually highly educated ones, become naturalised at the earliest opportunity, because of their belief that an Australian passport is an advantage when one wants to *leave the country*.

There are wide nationality-group-differences regarding degree of identification. The most highly 'identifying' group is the British (both sexes), whereas the lowest scoring group is composed of well educated Baltic immigrants.

For illustrating the ethnic identification of children I propose to look at two indices on which immigrants and Australians differed very significantly. The first was the response to the question, 'Do you consider yourself to be a "dinkum Aussie"?'[33] The response to this question may seem to reveal the obvious and may, therefore, seem trivial. It did not seem obvious, however, to a number of teachers at the time of the pretest and the 'warming-up' stages of the study. The comments of these teachers on their immigrant pupils may be summed up in these words: 'There is absolutely no difference between most immigrants and Australians in my class; they dress alike, speak alike and think alike. Why, I did not even know till now that some of these children were not Australians.'[34] When comparing this kind of view of the teachers with their subsequent rating of immigrant, second-generation and Australian boys,[35] one cannot escape the conclusion that the myth of the 'inevitably rapid assimilation of immigrants' children' is due, at least partly, to lack of conscious observation of their daily behaviour and lack of an attempt at a systematic evaluation of their attitudes.

Table 4 reveals that 25 per cent of the immigrant subjects gave a firm 'yes' answer, which suggests that, whatever the meaning of this answer (i.e., is it an indication of identification or of the desire to identify with Australians?), the process of assimilation and adjustment of these subjects seems to have been under way. This is supported also by the number of the 'in-between' responses (17 or 29 per cent). Forty-six per cent of the immigrant subjects, on the other hand, seem to have considered themselves 'outsiders'. This is a strikingly high percentage if the relatively long time of the immigrant subjects' residence in Australia (six plus years) is taken into account. Parenthetically, even more striking concerning the Australian-born offspring of the immigrants: 41 per cent of the second-generation subjects indicated identification with Australians, another 41 per cent gave 'in-between' responses and 18 per cent seemed to think that they were 'outsiders'.

TABLE 4

Responses to the question, 'Do you consider yourself
to be a "Dinkum Aussie"?' (Perth boys)

Response category	Non-British immigrant		Non-British sec. gener.		Australian		Total
	f	%	f	%	f	%	
Yes	15	25	9	41	75	93	99
In-between*	17	29	9	41	6	7	32
No	27	46	4	18	0	0	31
Total	59	100	22	100	81	100	162

* Response like 'undecided', 'not quite', etc.

The second index I would like to talk about is one of the measures of the immigrant's ethnic identification involving both his old and his new country. The boys were asked for which team they would 'barrack' in case of a sport contest between the Australian national team and the national team of their 'favourite European country'. For their response they used a seven-point scale, the point-values ranging from six ('I would barrack for the Australian team whole-heartedly') to zero ('I would barrack for the European team whole-heartedly'). The subjects had to follow up this response by another, this time predicting their Australian peers' modal response, using the same scale. High identification was inferred, of course, from little or no difference between a respondent's own score and his prediction of the Australian score, etc.

The table reveals that while 73 per cent of the non-British and 63 per cent of the British immigrant boys scored 'low', only 18 per cent of the control-group responses fell into that category.

Table 5 shows the results:—

TABLE 5

Barracking for Australia (subject's perception of the difference between own and Australian peer-group response) (Sydney boys)

Difference	Non-British f	Non-British %	British f	British %	Australian f	Australian %	Total
None	27	11	14	16	249	51	290
Some	37	16	18	21	154	31	209
Considerable	171	73	55	63	87	18	313
Total	235	100	87	100	490	100	812

The results seem to speak for themselves: no further comment in 'identification' seems necessary.

Satisfaction

What 'satisfaction' means here may be best explained by reference to the ways this variable has been measured by students of immigrant adjustment. Techniques used range from asking a simple question like 'Are you happy in the new country?' to complex and thorough clinical investigation. Other techniques included between these two extremes are sets of direct questions tapping various aspects of the respondent's satisfaction (or dissatisfaction) with his life, (e.g., with house, street, district, etc., in which he lives; with the friends he has; with his job; etc.); relatively straight-forward and 'rough' rating scales of emotional adjustment; questionnaires consisting of indirect questions; and sophisticated personality inventories.

Satisfaction, the immigrant's experience of happiness or stress, should be looked upon here as a *correlate* rather than a facet, in the sense of the previously discussed variables (e.g. identification), of his assimilation. According to Taft, satisfaction is 'the foundation on which an immigrant's potential assimilation rests'.[36]

An example of empirical support of the statement just quoted will illustrate the first group of findings on adult immigrants. It has been repeatedly found that a rather high degree of satisfaction tends to be a prerequisite of identification and acculturation.[37]

According to Stoller, immigration is 'a potential trauma for all immigrants'.[38] This seems especially true for adults. The extent of dissatisfaction (for instance, the one having to do with 'materialised' trauma; lasting emotional stress; or periodical feeling of 'unhappiness') appears to vary with a number of factors. These factors are, among other things: (a) nation of origin; (b) degree of being discriminated against by the hosts; (c) other environmental factors; (d) circumstances leading to emigration (especially whether the individual is a refugee or a voluntary immigrant); (e) cultural background; and (f) individual differences. Let us illustrate this by a summary of Western Australian studies of European immigrants:—

'Generally speaking, the most satisfied immigrants were the Dutch and British, and the least, by far, were the Hungarians. The most satisfied groups were not far below the Australian control subjects, if we pool the various indices of satisfaction.

... to explain why Dutch males in Perth are very much more satisfied than Polish women living in country towns, or why Polish refugee intellectuals are very much more satisfied than Hungarians is not an easy matter. Perhaps there are even cultural differences that would account almost entirely for these results.'[39]

An indirect index of the immigrant's level of satisfaction is his response to a question referring to the degree of his desire to stay in Australia. An analysis of the Perth indices of satisfaction level and desire to stay indicated the following:—

In most of the national groups between 80 and 90 per cent of the immigrants are at least fairly satisfied generally with their life in Australia and do not wish to leave.[40]

As far as immigrants' children are concerned, there is no empirical evidence for satisfaction being a prerequisite of their assimilation.[41] One of the possible reasons for this may be that school-age immigrants' acculturation will begin almost inevitably and automatically shortly after they enter an Australian school. For instance, *most* immigrant children learn *some* English soon after their arrival in the country. It may be added that some aspects of the satisfaction of immigrant adults and children may differ to such an extent as to make comparison between the two generations unjustifiable. For instance, is job satisfaction the equivalent of satisfaction with schoolwork, is satisfaction with wages or salary comparable with pocket money, do the cultural differences present the same problems and lead, consequently, to a similar degree of dissatisfaction? These and related questions should be kept in mind when the undermentioned findings are being examined.

TABLE 6

Satisfaction with life (Sydney boys)

Score	Non-British f	%	British f	%	Australian f	%	Total
High	66	28	35	40	321	66	422
Low	169	72	52	60	169	34	390
Total	235	100	87	100	490	100	812

Analysis of the Perth boys' results has revealed a statistically significantly higher degree of satisfaction of Australians than of European immigrants. The same applies when measures of an emotional-adjustment rating scale (raters: Australian teachers) and when the responses to the desire-to-stay-in-Australia questions are evaluated. Two of the corresponding Sydney findings are reported in Tables 6 and 7.

The tendency conveyed by Tables 6 and 7 is similar to that reported in the previous tables: in general, the Australians are 'better off' than either immigrant group, the British, in turn, being 'better off' than the

TABLE 7

Desire to stay in Australia (Sydney boys)

Score	Non-British f	Non-British %	British f	British %	Australian f	Australian %	Total
High	36	15	46	53	317	65	399
Low	199	85	41	47	172	35	412
Total	235	100	87	100	489*	100	811

* One subject did not respond.

non-British. It would be an interesting exercise to compare the Western Australian adult data with the ones reported in Table 6. However, there are some problems concerning the comparability of the results. I might say, for instance, that only 41 per cent of the Sydney immigrant boys were 'at least fairly satisfied generally with their life in Sydney', using as my criterion of being 'fairly satisfied' a score of five or more on the nine-point scale (zero to eight) employed. But even if the scores are comparable, the Australian control group results—i.e., 77 per cent being 'at least fairly satisfied'—seem to complicate the issue. Would it be more correct to say that not 41 but 53 per cent (i.e., 41 per cent of 77) of the immigrants fall into the category? Whatever the case, it may be said that immigrant children are anything but indistinguishable from their Australian peers in Sydney (and I may add, also in Perth and Brisbane). The same seems to apply to the desire-to-stay-in-Australia data. In the Sydney sample only 19 per cent of the non-British and 53 per cent of the British immigrant boys as against 65 per cent of the Australians scored three or four on a five-point (zero to four) scale. The finding that more than one-third of the Australian boys do not seem to agree with the view that Australia is the best country in the world[42] came as quite a surprise to me. This kind of finding suggests strongly, if nothing else, the importance of using control-groups when studying immigrants.

Concluding Notes

There seems to be no point in summarising this chapter which, after all, is no more than a sketchy summary of a small section of research on European immigrants in Australia. All I want to do here is to restate the essence of my answer to my Papuan colleague, whom I mentioned at the beginning of the chapter. Here it is:—

'There *are* many, more or less serious, problems associated with minority-group status, irrespective of the skin colour of the members of such groups. Further, I would not disagree with you if you said that colour presents additional problems. Finally, I would not deny that the problems involved may be so severe as to make white immigrants' adjustment difficulties look insignificant—in Australia as well as in other countries. Your implied hypothesis that physical and cultural similarity is directly related to adjustment to Australian conditions seems, indeed, to be supported by the general finding that the British immigrants are "on top", followed by the Dutch, etc., etc., whereas the southern Europeans are a long way behind.'

REFERENCES

1 There are many exceptions to the 'rule'.

2 See, for instance, TAFT, R., *From Stranger to Citizen*. Nedlands: University of Western Australia Press, 1965, pp. 11-12. (Also, London: Tavistock, 1966).

3 E.g., RICHARDSON, A. 'The Assimilation of British Immigrants in a Western Australian Community—A Psychological Study'. *R.E.M.P. Bulletin*, 1961 (a), 9, 1-75.

4 E.g., in my studies of 13 to 16-year-old immigrant boys, the groups were matched on sex, age, intelligence level and father's occupational status. To 'qualify' as a subject, the boy had to be living with both of his natural parents.

5 An example of satisfactory adjustment without any acculturation would be the Italian housewife living in an Italian 'ghetto' where she can buy everything she needs (including the services of doctors and lawyers, etc.) without speaking a word of English.

6 E.g., ADLER, D. L. and TAFT, R. 'Some Psychological Aspects of Immigrant Assimilation'. In STOLLER, A. (ed.), *New Faces—Immigration and Family Life in Australia*. Melbourne: Cheshire, 1966, p. 83.

7 ADLER and TAFT (1966), *loc. cit.*

8 STOLLER, A. 'Stress in Immigrants'. In THROSSELL, H. (ed.) *Ethnic Minorities in Australia*. Brisbane: Australian Council of Social Service, 1968, p. 169.

9 See, for instance, TAFT (1965), pp. 87-89.

10 ADLER and TAFT (1966), *loc. cit.*

11 ADLER and TAFT (1966), *loc. cit.*

12 See Note 4.

13 These differences and nearly all others reported are statistically significant.

14 Even tables referring to mastery of spoken English contain some non-British immigrants in the top-score category as well as some Australians in the bottom or near-bottom category.

15 TAFT, R. and DOCZY, A. G., 'The Assimilation of Intellectual Refugees in Western Australia'. *R.E.M.P. Bulletin*, 1961-1962, 9-10, 68-69.

16 HEMPEL, J. A., *Italians in Queensland*. Canberra: Australian National University, 1959, p. 120.

17 DOCZY, A. G. *The Social Assimilation of Adolescent Boys of European Parentage in the Metropolitan Area of Western Australia*. Unpublished Ph.D. Thesis, University of Western Australia, 1967.

18 DOCZY, A. G. *British and Non-British Immigrant Boys in Sydney*. Paper read at the Immigration Conference of the Australian Social Science Research Council, August, 1970. I would like to record here my acknowledgment of the grants provided for my Interstate project by the S.S.R.C.

19 TAFT (1965), p. 18. (Based on RICHARDSON, A., 'Attitudes of Perth People to Migration', *Immigration Quarterly*, 1961 (b), 1, 3-4.)

20 See TAFT (1965), pp. 19-20.

21 TAFT (1965), p. 20.

22 TAFT (1965), p. 18.

23 TAFT and DOCZY (1961-1962), p. 76.

24 See Notes 4 and 18.

25 Doczy (1967).

26 BLAIR, MARGARET. *The Sociometric Structure and Frames of Reference for Two Classes Composed of Three National Groups*, unpublished student investigation, University of Western Australia, 1958: BOWNES, A. F., *A Sociometric Study of Two School Classes Containing a Minority Group of Children with Foreign Home Background*, unpublished student investigation, University of Western Australia, 1951; DAW, JAN, *Assimilation Study of Australians, and British and Non-British Immigrants as Members of a Common Group—a School Class*, unpublished student investigation, University of Western Australia, 1959; EWEN, GERTIE, *Report*, unpublished student investigation, University of Western Australia, 1959; TAFT, R. and BOWNES, A. F., 'The Frame of Reference Used by Immigrant and Australian Children in Mutual Judgments'. *Australian Journal of Psychology*, 1953, 5, 105-117.

27 DAW (1959).

28 BLAIR (1958).

29 C.H., 'Master Snipe on Race Relations'. *Times Educational Supplement*, 1957, 5, 4. Reported in greater detail by CAMPBELL, W. J., in THROSSELL (1968), pp. 104-107.

30 ENGLISH, H. B. and ENGLISH, AVA C. *A Comprehensive Dictionary of Psychological and Psychoanalytical Terms*. London: Longmans, 1958, p. 249.

31 TAFT (1965), p. 66.

32 TAFT (1965), p. 67.

33 Doczy (1967) and DOCZY, A. G. 'Some Aspects of the Education of Immigrant Schoolchildren', *The Australian Journal for Social Issues*, 1969, 4, 63-64.

34 See Note 33.

35 Cf., Note 33. 'Second-generation boys' are Australian-born children of European-born immigrants.

36 TAFT (1965), p. 65.

37 RICHARDSON (1961, a).

38 STOLLER (1968), p. 163.

39 TAFT (1965), p. 65.

40 TAFT (1965), p. 65.

41 Doczy (1967 and 1970).

42 The 'dissenting Australian boys' answered the question, 'Except for holidays abroad, where would you like to spend the rest of your life?' by underlining one of the following prepared responses: (a) 'As much in Australia as in another country' (23 per cent); (b) 'more in another country than in Australia' (8 per cent); and (c) 'Not in Australia, but in another country' (5 per cent).

5

RESIDENTIAL AND OCCUPATIONAL ADJUSTMENT OF MIGRANTS

I. H. Burnley

In a time when immigration restriction policies in Australia have come under increasing scrutiny and criticism, as have the targets of immigration policy in general, it is perhaps prudent if the residential and occupational adjustments of European ethnic groups, more especially those in the major cities, are surveyed. Residential and occupational patterns are two areas which contribute to stereotyped perceptions of minority groups by the dominant population, i.e. the host society. Common stereotypes for example are that southern Europeans 'stick together', are in particular occupations 'to make money', and settle in 'ghettos'.[1] By examining patterns of residential and occupational adjustment of the eight major birth-place groups in Sydney and Melbourne, Australian cities with the largest foreign-born populations,[2] some understanding of integration problems and process of culturally dissimilar populations might be gained, and also an estimate made of likely residential and occupational problems if the colour dimension was added to Australia's growing population diversity through a liberalised immigration policy. It will be shown how residential and occupational patterns are related, and how they in turn influence other variables involved in integration.

In 1947, before the major post war migration programme began, overseas-born contributed only 10 per cent of the total population, most being of British Isles origin.[3] But by 1966, the overseas-born constituted over 20 per cent of the total Australian population, and the United Kingdom born proportion had dwindled from 90 per cent to less than 50 per cent of all overseas-born, although the post war United Kingdom born migration was still important. The most important changes were the growth of the southern European communities, notably the Italian and Greek-born populations, but also the influx of over 170,000 east European refugees and a substantial inflow of German and Netherlands born, all of whom tended to settle in the capital cities, in particular Melbourne, Sydney, Adelaide and Perth and in the lesser centres of Wollongong and Geelong along with a number of small specialised industrial centres. The impact of the Post-War immigration on the composition of the population can be seen from Table 1.

Although the overseas born constituent of the total population was highest in Adelaide of all the capital cities, the non-British born components were highest in Melbourne and Sydney. Thus the United Kingdom born component in overseas-born population increase was only 17.3 per cent in Melbourne and 20.1 per cent in Sydney, but was 43.9 per cent in

TABLE 1

Overseas born population as a percentage of total population in major Australian cities, 1947 and 1966.

City	1947	1966	Total population 1966
Sydney	12.8	22.1	2,446,345
Melbourne	10.2	25.7	2,110,025
Brisbane	12.5	15.0	718,822
Adelaide	8.9	27.2	733,954
Perth	18.8	26.5	512,130
Newcastle	9.7	7.7	223,936
Wollongong	13.9	28.9	169,100
Geelong	6.2	23.4	105,059
Canberra	12.2	26.7	92,308
Hobart	5.0	12.1	119,469

Table 1 Source: Census of the Commonwealth of Australia, 30 June, 1947 and 1966.

Adelaide for the period 1947-1966. By comparison, the southern European (Greek, Italian and Maltese-born) component in overseas-born increase in Melbourne was 41.3 per cent, in Sydney 32 per cent but only 23.8 per cent in Adelaide. Melbourne and Sydney then were the more truly cosmopolitan cities by 1966 and had the largest non-British-born populations. Melbourne in particular had the largest Greek and Italian population with 92,000 Italian-born (over 100,000 estimate by 1970) compared with 53,500 in Sydney and 27,000 in Adelaide, while there were over 60,000 Greeks in Melbourne and 42,000 in Sydney. Populations as large as these, while not as great as those in American cities during the great immigration period prior to 1924, were certainly large enough to sustain a true ethnic group life and to change the population character of several districts of the respective metropolitan areas.

Residential Patterns

The pattern and extent of residential concentration involves numerous factors. Ethnic concentration reflects in part the pattern of socio-economic segregation or stratification of the host society.[4] If an ethnic group has concentrated in one socio-economic category, for instance, unskilled manual workers, then it is likely that residential concentrations of the ethnic group will occur in those parts of the urban residential structure where unskilled workers in general may have to reside because income inadequacies and housing cost factors limit residential choice. Similarly, ethnic groups with higher proportions in professional, white collar or skilled occupations may tend to settle in suburbs with higher proportions of white collar workers. Yet social class is only one determinant of the residential patterns of immigrant ethnic groups or race groups. Cultural values of a given group are important and these may be interrelated with social class. Well educated central Europeans may prefer a certain location because of values and life styles, while north-west Euro-

TABLE 2

Per cent distribution of major birthplace groups in Metropolitan Sydney, 1966

Ecological area / Main L.G.A. of settlement	British Isles	Germany	Nether-lands	Poland	Yugo-slavia	Greece	Italy	Malta	Total popula-tion
Inner metropolitan									
Sydney	5.39	7.59	4.02	7.11	15.81	29.71	7.63	18.02	6.51
Older residential inner suburbs									
Leichhardt	2.02	1.97	1.00	1.16	3.96	5.43	9.30	6.12	2.43
Marrickville	2.33	3.24	1.15	2.79	7.06	20.76	7.77	3.69	3.14
Other	6.32	6.78	3.21	8.35	6.78	7.41	12.92	5.33	6.19
Total older residential inner suburbs	10.67	11.99	5.36	12.30	17.80	33.60	29.99	15.04	11.76
Middle distance suburbs									
Waverley	3.12	4.78	2.27	8.57	1.78	1.77	1.64	1.37	2.60
Bankstown	5.72	9.92	1.75	13.58	5.38	2.36	4.30	4.34	6.54
Other	33.14	20.52	23.42	23.77	26.27	26.26	27.09	7.30	32.24
Total middle distance suburbs	41.98	35.22	27.44	45.82	33.33	30.39	33.03	23.01	41.38
Outer suburbs and rural urban fringe									
Fairfield	4.76	10.88	6.27	10.54	10.79	0.68	8.82	9.40	4.00
Holroyd	2.06	2.27	2.52	2.45	1.85	0.80	2.14	17.90	2.69
Other	35.14	32.05	54.39	21.78	21.42	4.82	18.39	16.63	33.66
Total outer suburbs	41.96	45.20	63.18	34.77	33.06	6.30	29.35	43.93	40.35
Total metropolitan	100.00	100.00	100.00	100.00	100.00	100.00	100.00	100.00	100.00

SOURCE: Census of the Commonwealth of Australia, 30 June, 1966

TABLE 3

Per cent distribution of major birthplace groups in Metropolitan Melbourne, 1966

Ecological area	Main L.G.A. of settlement	British Isles	Germany	Nether-lands	Poland	Yugo-slavia	Greece	Italy	Malta	Total popula-tion
Inner metropolitan	Melbourne	2.98	2.61	1.69	3.65	5.14	4.24	8.98	8.52	3.60
	Fitzroy	0.48	0.56	0.36	0.59	7.01	7.01	5.13	2.87	1.29
Total inner metropolitan		3.46	3.17	2.05	4.24	9.90	11.25	14.11	11.39	4.89
Older residential inner suburbs	Collingwood	0.42	0.37	0.25	0.48	2.55	7.78	1.92	1.96	1.07
	Richmond	0.82	1.15	0.44	1.23	3.71	9.50	2.63	1.72	1.54
	Brunswick	1.09	1.09	0.41	1.34	2.69	7.74	10.98	4.97	2.46
	Other	2.07	1.17	0.78	0.21	2.52	7.32	1.33	2.73	2.03
Total older residential inner suburbs		4.31	3.78	1.88	3.26	10.47	32.34	16.86	11.38	7.10
Middle distance suburbs	St. Kilda	4.32	6.85	2.36	14.52	4.04	2.10	1.07	0.56	2.75
	Prahran	2.54	3.54	1.43	3.91	2.73	8.91	0.95	0.39	2.37
	Caulfield	3.56	4.71	1.91	13.69	2.17	1.95	1.14	0.51	3.61
	Northcote	1.55	1.12	0.68	1.48	3.55	6.92	7.24	1.02	2.66
	Other	29.79	25.13	15.95	29.01	32.98	23.39	33.15	18.83	34.99
Total middle distance suburbs		41.76	41.35	22.33	62.61	45.50	43.27	43.55	21.31	46.38
Outer suburbs and rural urban fringe	Keilor	1.57	6.60	3.64	3.92	6.81	1.01	2.02	10.70	1.92
	Sunshine	4.12	7.11	2.56	8.91	5.57	2.29	2.79	20.37	3.27
	Broadmeadow	3.86	4.89	3.24	4.38	3.79	1.49	4.48	10.12	4.12
	Other	40.92	33.10	64.30	12.68	17.96	8.35	16.19	14.73	32.32
Total outer suburbs		50.47	51.70	73.74	29.89	34.13	13.14	25.48	55.92	41.63
Total metropolitan		100.00	100.00	100.00	100.00	100.00	100.00	100.00	100.00	100.00

SOURCE: Census of the Commonwealth of Australia, 30 June, 1966

peans may prefer different areas such as new suburbs where a domestic plot of land can be cultivated. Some groups may prefer suburban locations which are part of the city fabric and close to the hub of city life without being in the poorest areas, while those with less means and with values involving kinship and subsidiary folk-community identifications such as southern Europeans[5] of peasant origin may congregate where homes can be purchased more cheaply, and where ethnic or folk group life can be maintained. Some apparent concentrations are not the result of specifically ethnic group social interaction at all, but simply reflect the socio-economic status of the migrants and relatively similar social outlook and values.

Turning now to the patterns of immigrant settlement in Sydney and Melbourne, it can be seen from Tables 2 and 3 that there were, in 1966, distinctive ecological distributions, of the major birthplace groups. That of the British Isles born was relatively similar in both cities, with some apparent concentrations in some outer industrial and higher status suburbs (Local Government Areas) but with distributions not markedly at variance with the total population. The Dutch were more decentralised than the total population and favoured rural-urban fringe suburbs. Poles favoured middle distance suburbs—both industrial and higher status sectors, while Greeks were strongly centralised and also concentrated in a few areas within the central suburbs and some middle distance suburbs. Italians too were concentrated within inner suburbs, but less so than the Greeks, and were also found in groups within some middle distance suburbs and out industrial suburban localities or certain rural-urban fringe areas.

A striking fact with Maltese settlers was their major concentrations being in outer industrial suburbs with secondary groupings in the inner metropolitan areas. It should be clear from the tables that despite concentration tendencies, none of the immigrant groups was confined to any one quarter or sector of Sydney or Melbourne; in fact recent arrivals, especially Italians[6] but also Greeks to a lesser extent, have often gone direct to areas outside traditional settlement areas, joining relatives who had already dispersed from concentration areas.[7] Despite this tendency, Greeks were still quite concentrated in 1966 as can be seen from Table 4, which lists coefficients of concentration for the major birthplace groups in both Sydney and Melbourne. Using the Index of Dissimilarity, developed by O. D. Duncan, S. Lieberson[8] and others, the indices are ranked on a continuum 0—100 in which zero equals no concentration and 100 maximum concentration or complete segregation. The concentration score is the percentage of a given birthplace group that would have to redistribute itself by Local Government Areas to have the same per cent distribution as the total population.

Greeks and Maltese were the most residentially concentrated, while British and Germans were the least localised. The Italians were, on a metropolitan scale, moderately concentrated, for although major Italian concentrations existed, substantial numbers resided outside concentration areas. The Italian concentration score was higher at the 1954 and 1961 censuses; since 1961, despite a continuing heavy Italian migration to Australia and both metropolitan areas, numbers of Italians have fallen appreciably in the inner suburbs as a whole. However despite the tendency for overall decline of the inner city Italian population with residential relocation and mobility, several inner city concentrations of Italians remained stable—in

TABLE 4

*Residential concentration scores for major immigrant Groups,
Sydney and Melbourne, 1966*

Birthplace	Sydney	Melbourne
British Isles	7	12
Germany	19	17
Netherlands	25	34
Poland	30	36
Yugoslavia	29	33
Greece	53	45
Italy	27	38
Malta	46	52

Carlton North and Fitzroy (Melbourne) and Leichhardt in Sydney. It could be that the Italian population remaining in old concentrations whose history dates from the turn of the century,[9] has remained because the areas are 'ecological traps' with modest priced housing attracting persons of limited means and communal support needs who are happier in old concentrations with Italian associations and institutions, whereas more mobile and potentially more assimilable persons choose to move further out, although often to secondary concentrations such as Brunswick in Melbourne and Drummoyne in Sydney.

The relatively high Greek and Maltese concentration scores recorded in Table 4 reflect, in part, recency of arrival of Greeks, but also that Greek and Maltese settlement has remained grouped with few secondary concentrations and less dispersion from concentration areas. The moderate Netherlands score reflects concentration in higher status outer suburbs, but not true ethnic concentration which has occurred with Greeks, Italians, Maltese and Yugoslavs more especially in older inner suburbs. The major Greek and Italian concentrations are true ethnic neighbourhoods remaining stable, often due to kinship, and village or region of origin folk-group connections.[10] The close proximity of ethnic shops and services and, in the case of the Greeks, the Orthodox Church, are also contributory factors. The sheer size of Greek and Italian immigrant populations in areas of concentration has encouraged the growth of ethnic institutions, especially shops, often in older premises which were previously closed due to the decrease in population, especially the Australian-born, in many inner city areas where Greek and Italian concentrations have formed. The range of institutions means that it has become possible, especially for migrant women, to seek all their household and social needs within the ethnic services, thus inhibiting assimilation in areas of concentration.

Although extensive ethnic neighbourhoods have formed with both Greeks and Italians in particular, these ethnic populations with areas of concentration have not displaced the host society population. Even in the peak areas of concentration in Melbourne, the Greek born percentage of the population at the collectors district scale[11] was little more than 40 per cent, with equally high Italian percentages in a few parts of Fitzroy, while in Sydney the highest single birthplace component in the population was

33 per cent Greeks in four collectors districts in Redfern and Marrickville, while the peak Italian concentration collectors districts averaged not more than 20-25 per cent Italian-born.[12] In the main settlement clusters,

TABLE 5

Occupations of major birthplace groups (males) in Melbourne, 1966

	British Isles	Germany	Nether-lands	Poland	Yugo-slavia	Greece	Italy	Malta	Australia
Professional	10.0	8.7	8.0	7.0	3.3	0.6	1.1	1.3	11.2
Managerial	9.1	8.0	8.9	20.5	2.6	4.5	5.8	1.3	11.6
Clerical	15.7	10.8	10.9	5.4	8.2	2.1	2.4	6.3	19.6
Skilled manual	29.3	42.7	36.4	24.0	36.0	20.8	29.5	24.2	22.8
Semi-skilled manual	19.7	19.1	19.0	24.2	24.3	30.3	26.0	29.1	20.6
Service and un-skilled manual	15.7	10.5	15.1	18.7	30.5	41.5	34.5	37.5	13.5
Graziers	0.0	0.0	0.0	0.0	0.0	0.0	0.0	0.0	0.1
Farmers	0.2	0.1	1.0	0.2	0.0	0.1	0.5	0.1	0.4
Farm workers	0.2	0.2	0.7	0.1	0.2	0.2	0.3	0.2	0.3
Totals	100.0	100.0	100.0	100.0	100.0	100.0	100.0	100.0	100.0

TABLE 6

Occupations of major birthplace groups (males) in Sydney, 1966

	British Isles	Germany	Nether-lands	Poland	Yugo-slavia	Greece	Italy	Malta	Australia
Professional	10.1	8.6	8.6	7.4	2.6	0.7	1.4	1.4	9.9
Managerial	10.0	8.4	10.4	9.8	3.2	10.1	8.3	1.3	10.3
Clerical	15.2	10.5	11.9	3.9	2.5	1.4	2.4	5.4	19.1
Skilled manual	27.8	42.1	35.4	26.1	23.6	17.5	30.1	24.3	23.4
Semi-skilled manual	19.5	17.0	18.6	26.6	25.0	26.6	22.6	28.7	21.5
Service and un-skilled manual	17.1	13.2	14.4	25.9	31.5	43.5	33.7	35.8	15.3
Graziers	0.0	0.0	0.0	0.0	0.0	0.0	0.0	0.0	0.1
Farmers	0.1	0.1	0.4	0.2	1.4	0.1	1.1	2.2	0.2
Farm workers	0.2	0.1	0.3	0.1	0.2	0.1	0.4	0.9	0.2
Totals	100.0	100.0	100.0	100.0	100.0	100.0	100.0	100.0	100.0

Source: Census of the Commonwealth of Australia, 30 June 1966. Occupations classified in terms of Occupational Code developed by Australian National University Department of Sociology.

Australian born were still present. However, because of the age structure characteristics of inner city areas of settlement, with an ageing host society population with few children, migrant family settlement resulted in a disproportionate number of first or second generation migrant children in schools.

Despite the mobility of some groups, including the Italians, ethnic neighbourhoods are likely to survive with Greeks, Italians, Maltese and Yugoslavs for some decades to come. The neighbourhoods are not ghettos or tenements, however, but are areas of privately owned, terrace and semi-detached villas with Greeks in Sydney, and semi-detached and separate, old but not necessarily poor, homes with Italians in Leichhardt and Drummoyne, Sydney. In Melbourne, terraces are common with the Italians in Carlton, with detached homes in Brunswick, while Greeks own and occupy old semi-detached villas and bungalows in Richmond, Collingwood and Prahran.

The incidence of private ownership is higher for southern Europeans than the Australian born population in Sydney. In 1966, for example, whereas 69.9 per cent of Australian-born household heads in Sydney owned or were buying their own homes (those living in private dwellings), 82 per cent of Italians and 73 and 76 per cent of Greeks and Maltese were owners and buyers.[13] In Melbourne, Italian, Greek, and Maltese home ownership was 82.3, 73 and 70 per cent respectively compared with 74.5 per cent of the Australian-born heads of households. North-west Europeans did not appear to favour home ownership as much as southern Europeans. However there is evidence that some migrants, unskilled and consequently on low incomes, may have rashly committed themselves to private ownership of old homes needing repair, and to repaying mortgages at high interest rates, creating financial stress for the families involved. Yet property ownership is a form of mobility for unskilled and under educated migrants lacking other securities in a new country.[14] As Price and Stimson[15] have noted for Sydney and Melbourne, and Glazer and Moynihan in New York,[16] in areas of migrant private ownership, much improvement to run-down residential suburbs has been made by persons with pride in home possession.

Occupational Patterns

The residential patterns described above become more comprehensible when the occupations of migrants, both on arrival and after a period of time in Australia, are considered. In contrast to migrants from north-west Europe, a large proportion of southern Europeans have been unskilled on arrival. Price[17] found, for example, that of a sample of Displaced Persons' shipping lists, 47.7 per cent of the Yugoslavs were unskilled and a further 18.8 per cent semi-skilled. In the years 1967, 1968 (which can be regarded as typical of the post war period), 64.4 per cent of Yugoslav arrivals were unskilled manual workers while 75.9 and 49.7 per cent of the Greeks and Italians were unskilled compared with only 10.6 per cent of the British.

In 1966 in Sydney (see Table 6), 43.5 per cent of Greeks were in unskilled manual work compared with 33.7 per cent of Italians and 35.8 per cent of Maltese. By comparison only 17.1 and 13.2 per cent of British Isles and German-born were unskilled workers, while the comparable figure for Australian-born was only 15.3 per cent. Proportional differences were similar in Melbourne. The proportions of southern Europeans in professional, managerial or clerical employment were very low, while with the exception of clerical work, proportions of north-west Europeans in white collar work were similar to those of the host society (Australian-born). Proportions of north-west Europeans in skilled trades were significantly higher than with the Australian born. The degree of occupational difference of the various birthplace groups from the Australian-born using the Index of Dissimilarity can be seen from Table 7.

TABLE 7

*Occupational dissimilarity of major birthplace groups
in Sydney and Melbourne, 1966*

Birthplace	Sydney	Melbourne
British Isles	6.4	8.9
German	18.7	20.0
Netherlands	12.6	16.2
Poland	18.4	18.9
Yugoslavia	32.3	34.0
Greece	33.3	37.7
Italy	27.8	33.7
Malta	32.3	34.0

Source: Developed from Table 6

As with residential concentration, north-west European groups were the least occupationally dissimilar from the Australian born population, and the east Europeans (Poles) were moderately dissimilar, while the southern Europeans were more markedly dissimilar. With major concentrations in unskilled work, often segregated in particular factories, e.g. the Greeks in the motor assembly industry especially in South Melbourne, the southern Europeans had less economic choice available in place of residence within the urban social system. Hence working class neighbourhoods in older, cheaper housing areas towards the city centres and in some newer industrial outer suburbs, became more and more southern European in character. Although only 7 per cent of the population of Melbourne was born in the three southern European countries of Greece, Italy and Malta, over 24 per cent of all unskilled workers were born in southern Europe.[18]

The equation of ethnicity and occupational status, and hence social class, becoming evident in Sydney and in Melbourne has implications for the question of social equality in Australian society. Because of the real concentration of socio-economic characteristics, including occupational status, within these two large metropolitan areas, certain areas contain a disproportionate number of non-English speaking persons with low skills on low incomes. Schools in such areas have large numbers of children with language problems, and substantial districts may have problems of occupational and social inequality, including inequality of opportunity compounded by ethnicity.

Conclusion

It has been shown how southern European communities are, in general, more residentially and occupationally concentrated in Australia's large cities than those from north-west Europe and thus less assimilated. It can be seen what would, perhaps, be the case if culturally dissimilar non-Europeans were admitted to Australia in large numbers. But if non-Europeans (and Europeans for that matter) were admitted with occupational ranges and proportions similar to those of the host society, less ethnic concentration would be likely to occur. If Australian society becomes more tolerant of culturally different Europeans through its experience of the large post-war immigration, moderate numbers of non-Europeans could be admitted if provision is made by various Governmental agencies to train migrants for the skills required in a modern urban society, or to encourage migrants with diverse skills to emigrate and not just those with manual skills at present in short supply.

REFERENCES

1 See article series in *The Australian* by OWEN THOMSON, July 21-24, 1970.

2 On a proportional basis, Adelaide has a larger immigrant contribution than Sydney.

3 Census of the Commonwealth of Australia, 30 June 1966.

4 JONES, F. LANCASTER, *Dimensions of Urban Social Structure*. The Australian National University, 1969.

5 PRICE, C. A., *Southern Europeans in Australia*, the Australian National University, 1963.

6 LEE, TREVOR R., 'The Role of the Ethnic Community as a Reception Area for Italian Immigrants in Melbourne, Australia'. *International Migration*, Vol. VIII, No. 1/2, 1970, pp. 50-63.

7 PRICE, C. A., 'Immigrants', in DAVIES, A. F. and ENCEL, S., *Australian Society*, Cheshire, 1970, pp. 181-199.

8 LIEBERSON, S., *Ethnic Patterns in American Cities*. Free Press of Glencoe, 1963.

9 JONES, F. LANCASTER, *The Italian Population of Carlton, A Demographic and Sociological Study*, Ph.D. dissertation, Australian National University, 1962.

10 JONES, F. LANCASTER, 'Italians in the Carlton Area: The Growth of an Ethnic Concentration'. *The Australian Journal of Politics and History* 10, 1, 1964, pp. 83-95; JAKUBOWICZ, A., 'Changing Patterns of Community Organisation', Honours Thesis in Government, University of Sydney, 1969.

11 The average size of collectors district populations was approximately 900 persons in 1966.

12 These figures exclude children born to migrants in Australia.

13 Unpublished census cross tabulations, Census of the Commonwealth of Australia, 1966.

14 CRONIN, CONSTANCE, *The Sicilian Family in Sicily and Australia*, Ph.D. Thesis in Anthropology, University of Chicago, 1967. SPIRO, M. E., 'The Acculturation of American Ethnic Groups', *American Anthropologist*, 57, 1955.

15 PRICE, C. A. 'Immigrants' in DAVIES, A. F. and ENCEL, S., *Australian Society*, Cheshire, 1970, pp. 181-199.
STIMSON, R. T., *Distributional Aspects of Immigrant Settlement in Melbourne, 1947-1961, a Quantitative Analysis*, Paper Read to Section P, ANZAAS Congress, Christchurch, New Zealand, 1968.

16 GLAZER, N. and MOYNIHAN, *Beyond the Melting Pot,* Massachusetts Institute of Technology, Massachusetts, 1963.

17 PRICE, C. A. 'International Migration—Australia and New Zealand, 1947-1968', *International Union for the Scientific Study of Population General Conference:* September 1969, pp. 9.1.12.

18 Approximately 50 per cent of all unskilled workers were born overseas compared with 25 per cent of the total population.

6

PREJUDICE IN THE PROFESSIONS

Moira Salter

It is assumed that discussion of the racial prejudice that exists in Australia's immigration policy generally will be found in the chapter entitled 'The White Australia Policy'. It is not intended to explore it any further in relation to the professional groups, except to point out that highly skilled workers are least likely to be affected, provided their qualifications are considered acceptable for entry into the professions in Australia.

It is this condition—the acceptability or otherwise of overseas qualifications—that largely determines the countries from which professional workers can be drawn. The object of this chapter, therefore, is to provide a brief explanation of how entry to the professional labour market is controlled and then to examine the reasons for the restrictive policies that have evolved in order to determine whether prejudice of any kind has played a part.

Commonwealth and State governments have legislated, as have governments in all countries, to exert protective control over certain professions only. In Australia, these are the wide group of occupations concerned with health; the legal, veterinary and architectural professions; and certain forms of accountancy, engineering and surveying.

Legislation aims, *inter alia,* to protect the citizen against the unqualified by ensuring that only the legally qualified may register with registration boards, and to control the entry of those immigrating from overseas. The first aim, the *raison d'etre* for the legislation, is achieved by stipulating minimum standards or educational qualifications, the second, by providing automatic registration for only those immigrants who have qualified in some nominated countries or institutions that meet these standards, with the added condition for some professions that they should be British subjects and/or that certain minimum periods of residence are required before registration will be granted.

Membership of a professional association is not a pre-requisite to employment—not all professional workers are members of professional associations. The evaluation of an immigrant's qualifications is a matter for the prospective employer or for a registration board, yet professional associations wield immense if indirect power in two ways: (i) because of ignorance of the standing of many overseas qualifications, employers are wont to demand acceptance for membership of a professional association as a guarantee of the standard of training; (ii) amendments to legislation controlling the registrable professions have often emanated from suggestions of registration boards that usually include representatives of the professional associations. It is not uncommon, also, for members of State legislatures to demand assurances that professional associations have been consulted when amending bills are being debated.

Thus, automatic entry of immigrants to the professions is restricted, in some professions, to those with qualifications that are defined by legislation, and, in others, to those with qualifications that are known to employers or are acceptable to professional associations. These are, generally speaking, qualifications obtained in the United Kingdom and New Zealand, expanded in many cases by qualifications awarded in some other countries that are, or have been, within the British Commonwealth, and, in some instances, by qualifications obtained from accredited institutions within the United States. However, the inflexibility that is suggested by this generalization need not necessarily exist. For example, the Commonwealth public service is not bound by the qualification provisions in the State legislation controlling the registrable professions. Again, professional associations will assess an immigrant's qualifications for an employer without rejecting those that are not automatically eligible for membership. There are other professions, also, in which measures have been created that permit the entry of those who are not automatically acceptable. Nevertheless, in the majority of cases, the generalization is correct.

The difficulty experienced by certain groups of immigrants in having their qualifications recognized as acceptable for the practice of their professions was a problem that first became serious prior to the second World War, and continued as a major obstacle to the occupational assimilation of Europeans arriving under the refugee immigration programmes of the post-war period. It could not, in the circumstances, have been resolved by the departure of the European professional and by the cessation of further migration at the intervention of the national governments concerned. Three characteristics distinguished these people from other immigrants: they were stateless—either refugees or displaced persons —without the protection of their own governments and without citizenship in the countries to which they emigrated; emigration was a flight from either persecution or unacceptable political systems and not in response to the incentive of economic differentials; and barriers to professional acceptance existed in each of the countries in which the majority of these people settled. Those that arrived in Australia remained. The qualifications of some were accepted, the qualifications of others were never accorded recognition, but, for many, employment in the professions was only achieved after retraining or through gradual changes in the legislative provisions governing entry to the registrable professions.

The charge of protectionism that could otherwise have been levelled against professional associations and State legislatures is weakened by the fact that substantial numbers of new entrants moved into the professions from overseas during these years. As evidence, the following figures of accessions of immigrants to State medical registers are presented for five years during which displaced persons were arriving in Australia.

On the other hand, there has been, unquestionably, discrimination in registration requirements and procedures, but in trying to discover whether prejudice is in any way responsible for the exclusion of certain groups of immigrants, a dilemma must immediately be faced: that of distinguishing policies that discriminate in order to safeguard professional standards

Accessions to State Medical Registers—1948-1952

	1948	1949	1950	1951	1952	Total
Numbers registered with overseas qualifications	4	97	116	166	132[a]	585

a Excluding Queensland.
   Source: H. R. G. Poate, 'The capacity of the medical profession in Australia to absorb new members', *The Medical Journal of Australia*, 1953, vol. 2, p. 620.

from those that do so because of monopolistic protectionism, or because of some preconceived opinion or bias against the suitably qualified immigrant.

In an attempt to overcome this, the evolution of discriminatory practices will now be examined. Unfortunately, the number of professional occupations is sufficiently large to preclude a detailed examination of each in a single chapter. It is necessary, therefore, to select a profession that is numerically large, that has a strong and influential professional association and that has statutory provisions governing acceptable qualifications. The profession that has been chosen is the medical profession, but, because statutory requirements for the admission of those qualifying overseas are not completely uniform throughout Australia, the examination is focused on a single State, Victoria.

Under the various Imperial Acts and Letters Patent that established the legislative bodies of the Australian colonies, the bodies so created were empowered to make laws provided that they were not repugnant to the laws of England.[1]

The Imperial *Colonial Laws Validity Act*, 1865 gave greater freedom to Colonial legislatures by providing that colonial Acts should be invalid only for inconsistency with Imperial legislation applicable in the colonies. The *Statute of Westminster*, 1931 which repealed the *Colonial Laws Validity Act*, 1865 was adopted by the Australian Commonwealth Government in 1942 with retrospective effect to 3rd September 1939. The *Statute of Westminster* has not been applied to Australian State legislatures, which are subject to the general doctrine of the legal supremacy of the Imperial Parliament. However, State Acts have not been disallowed since 1900.

The Imperial *Medical Act*, 1858 brought into existence the General Council of Medical Education and Registration of the United Kingdom. The qualifications acceptable for registration, listed in Schedule A of the Act, were exclusively qualifications awarded by various bodies in the United Kingdom with provision for registration of colonial and foreign trained practitioners already practising in the United Kingdom. Section 31 of the Act provided that every person registered should be entitled to practise in any part of Her Majesty's dominions. Section 6 of the Imperial *Medical Act*, 1886 repealed this blanket mandate by adding the proviso that they should do so subject to any local law. Section 17 of the amending Act introduced a reciprocity clause: Her Majesty might declare by Order in Council that the Act should apply to those countries which 'in the opinion of Her Majesty affords to the registered medical practitioners of the United Kingdom such privileges of practising in the said British or foreign country as to Her Majesty may seem just.' By 1937, Orders in Council had applied the Act to Ceylon, New Zealand, India, Malta, four Canadian provinces, Hong Kong, the Straits Settlement, Burma, South Africa, Italy, Japan, and the three Australian States in which medical schools had been established.[2]

Medical legislation in the Australian States that followed the enactment of the Imperial *Medical Act,* 1858 included as acceptable the registered medical practitioners of the United Kingdom and, where this had been overlooked (as in Queensland *Medical Act* 1861 which broadly defined medical practitioners as 'any physician doctor of medicine bachelor of medicine licentiate in medicine and surgery surgeon general practitioner or apothecary),'[3] Royal assent was given, but amendment was requested to protect persons registered under the Imperial Act.[4]

By 1865, the list of qualifications acceptable in Victoria, Schedule III of the *Medical Practitioners Statute,* 1865 was almost a facsimile of Schedule A of the Imperial *Medical Act,* 1858. The Victorian Act appeared somewhat broader by listing as additionally acceptable those who had passed through a course of study of three years at some British or foreign university, college, or other body, but the acceptability of any qualification was conditional on the medical practitioner being a British subject. The restriction to British subjects was later repealed[5] at the request of the Faculty of Medicine of the University of Melbourne, as its insertion in the legislation had precluded the conclusion of a reciprocity agreement with the General Medical Council of the United Kingdom.

Imperial Orders in Council applied the Imperial *Medical Act,* 1858-1886 to Victoria in 1890.[6] Medical graduates from the University of Melbourne were eligible to register in the United Kingdom. To achieve this, restrictions within the Victorian legislation had been removed, the only remaining condition being that medical practitioners should be adequately trained. Any who met the criteria laid down in the legislation were eligible, but this general acceptance was to last for only a few years before the reciprocity clause that was later to be used as the instrument to exclude refugees and displaced persons, was introduced into the legislation. Its introduction occurred not as a result of the need to protect the Victorian medical profession against a one-way flow of medical practitioners that the liberality of the legislation had encouraged to immigrate, but from the refusal of certain countries to grant reciprocal privileges to the medical profession of the United Kingdom. As a retaliatory measure, a special sub-committee of the Colonial Committee of the British Medical Association in London was established in 1904 to foster the principle of reciprocity throughout the Empire, and to advocate the expediency of registering only those qualifications that were registrable in the United Kingdom. Their representations through the United Kingdom Colonial Secretary to the Governors of the Australian States were sympathetically received[7] and, in 1906, a reciprocity clause was inserted into Victorian legislation. Under the clause, the Medical Board of Victoria was empowered to refuse registration to persons with qualifications obtained other than in the United Kingdom or in British possessions, unless the registered practitioners of Victoria were entitled to practise, without further examination, in the country concerned. Schedule III of the Victorian Act, the list of acceptable qualifications, was left unaltered except for stringent restrictions on homoeopathists trained in the United States.

The minimum training period was increased to five years to bring it into line with the length of training necessary for registration with the General Medical Council and for graduation through the University of Melbourne.[8] The Victorian conditions for registration of immigrant medical practitioners, which were to remain unaltered until the late 1930s, now required five years training plus either qualifications listed in Schedule III of the Act, or qualifications awarded in countries that granted reciprocal privileges to the registered practitioners of Victoria.

Until 1938, the Medical Board registered all practitioners arriving in Victoria who had qualified not only in the United Kingdom, but also in countries to which Imperial Orders in Council had been applied. From 1935 onwards, registration was refused to a small group of refugee medical practitioners who were trickling in from the United Kingdom, where they had been permitted previous entry for further study on condition they re-emigrated. These had obtained the Scottish Triple Conjoint Qualification after twelve months study and had registered with the General Medical Council before leaving England. The decision to refuse registration by invoking the reciprocity clause, i.e., that the five years of medical or surgical study had been undertaken in Germany, a non-reciprocating country, was reversed by the Supreme Court of Victoria in June 1937 and an appeal to the High Court of Australia was dismissed in August 1937.[9] By 1938, the Medical Board of Victoria had received 123 enquiries from European medical practitioners; of these, 43 were deemed eligible for registration.[10]

In July 1938, representatives of thirty-one nations, including Australia and the United Kingdom, assembled at Evian, at the invitation of the United States Government, to consider measures for assisting political refugees. In October, a bill, later proclaimed as the *Medical Act*, 1938, was introduced into the Victorian Legislative Assembly to strengthen the reciprocity clause to exclude the registration of medical practitioners who had not passed through a regular course of medical and surgical study of five or more years either in Victoria or in reciprocating countries. In December, the Commonwealth Government announced that 15,000 refugees would be admitted over a period of three years.[11]

Despite the prompt reaction of the Victorian legislature to what must have appeared as the imminent opening of the floodgates of Europe, the subsequent massive intake of immigrants under the Commonwealth Government's post-war immigration schemes has been accompanied by a gradual reversal of the exclusionist policies of the pre-war era. In 1946, provisions were made for the registration of those practitioners who had worked in country areas under the National Security (Alien Doctors) Regulations,[12] and who had served in the Australian Army Medical Corps;[13] in 1950, arrangements were made for registration of those who had passed through the final three years of the medical course at the University of Melbourne;[14] in 1951, it became possible for the Medical Board to issue temporary certificates of registration for teaching and research for a maximum period of three years;[15] in 1956, the Board was empowered to register those with medical or surgical knowledge of international standing or of special value.[16]

These piecemeal provisions culminated in an overall approach to the problem of the unregistered practitioner with the establishment in 1957 of a Foreign Practitioners Qualification Committee,[17] composed of nominees and Professorial staff of the Faculty of Medicine of the University of Melbourne, to interview, examine and recommend or reject applications for registration. However, the progressive relaxation over a period of about twenty years would not have occurred but for the shortage of medical practitioners that developed, accompanied by an increasing pool of the unregistered, whose numbers were soon large enough to attract not only the attention of Commonwealth and State governments, each of whom was responsible for the provision of medical services in areas where shortages were most acute, but also the sympathy of the press.

Liberalization of the conditions for registration was directed in each case towards those unregistered practitioners who were already resident in Australia. Until 1971, Victorian legislation remained sufficiently restrictive—by stipulating residential requirements which had to be met before immigrants who were not automatically registrable could be examined by the Foreign Practitioners Qualification Committee—to discourage the immigration of medical practitioners from any but reciprocating countries. At the end of 1970, the Bill of a new Medical Act was passed through the Victorian legislature. This provides for the automatic registration of those medical practitioners who (a) have passed through a course of medical and surgical study of at least five years at an educational institution recognized by the Board in Australia, Great Britain, Ireland, or New Zealand; or (b) hold the Foreign Practitioners Qualification Committee's certificate. Residential periods are no longer to be fulfilled by the latter group, but the Committee is required to consider every application upon its merits and is empowered to interview and examine. The new Act is yet to be proclaimed and it is not yet known whether the Committee will require personal attendance by each applicant.

The reader will note that any qualification obtained in the United States of America is to be subjected to individual examination. This may be some small reprisal for the excessively protective attitude of the American medical profession.

The output of graduates from State Universities has always been inadequate to meet the needs for medical practitioners in Australia. The *Australasian Medical Gazette* reported in 1893 that only 12 per cent of the total number of medical practitioners in Australia and New Zealand had graduated from Australian Universities,[18] but statistics of accessions to Australian State medical registers from 1958 to 1962, nearly seventy years later, show that 31 per cent were from overseas.[19]

The protection of the rights of those registered with the General Medical Council to practise in Australia was, in the early nineteenth century, legislatively necessary, but the Imperial *Medical Act*, 1886 following the *Colonial Laws Validity Act*, 1865 freed State legislatures to frame their own requirements governing acceptability of qualifications. Because of historical, political, racial and cultural bonds, the role of 'migratory elite' has continued to be awarded to those from the United Kingdom. This has ensured that immigrants who are most readily assimilable in terms of both training and professional practice are allowed to enter the Australian medical profession.

The conclusion of a reciprocity agreement to acquire a similar privilege for the Australian graduate in the United Kingdom was due almost solely to the vital importance to the Australian medical profession of the right to register with the General Medical Council. Without it,

Australian graduates would have been denied access to facilities for post-graduate education, training and experience that were not available in Australia, a country whose educational resources in medicine have been, and still are, primarily directed towards under-graduate training.[20] The continuing need for access to these facilities and the continuing necessity to comply with conditions for registration in the United Kingdom not only ensured the maintenance of the reciprocity agreement but, also, to some extent, fashioned the form and content of Australian medical under-graduate training.[21]

It was not a condition of the agreement with the General Medical Council that those registered in the United Kingdom should have the exclusive right to enter the Australian medical profession. The insertion of the reciprocity clause within the medical legislation to protect these rights was at the request of the British Medical Association, an Association that was, until 1962, also the professional association for the Australian medical profession. This was inserted at the beginning of the twentieth century and was simply an instance that was typical of the manner in which professions in all countries were beginning to control the international movement of professional labour in order to protect the domestic market—in this case, and at that time, the British Empire.

Reciprocity agreements facilitating the international movement of workers in professional occupations will only be concluded and maintained if they are of mutual advantage to the professions in the countries concerned. Racial prejudice plays no part. In the example cited here, one has only to glance through the list of countries to which Orders in Council had been applied to realize that they covered a large variety of racial groups.

However, there still remains the possibility that prejudice may have crept into the measures that were created to permit the acceptance of those who were not automatically registrable. These measures were fashioned to cope with the special problems associated with the stateless—a group of people who were without the protection of their own governments and who, in addition, had arrived from countries that had never been a source of professionally trained immigrants at a time when the political situation and aftermath of war in Europe rendered it impossible to approach the Universities or medical schools at which they had been trained. The usual channels of establishing standards or of negotiating reciprocity agreements were closed. It became necessary, therefore, to devise procedures that would ensure that both theoretical and practical training and command of the English language were adequate. These were of three kinds: examination, normally by a committee, usually followed by a period of supervision and a certain period in practice; retraining at a University; and, finally, examination by a committee only.

The first type was associated with recruitment for areas where there were shortages of medical practitioners, e.g., country areas, public hospitals, Papua and New Guinea, and Antarctic bases. This avenue is still open in New South Wales (three years service in a region that has inadequate medical services entitles the medical practitioner to registration) and in Western Australia (registration limited to certain regions or auxiliary services may be granted).

The second type, retraining, required that the foreign medical practitioner should pass through the final three years of the medical course at an Australian University. Registration followed automatically and supervision was unnecessary. This method was used in South Australia, New South Wales and Victoria, and remnants of it remain in Tasmania (a one year training course, followed by an examination and three years service as a general medical officer provides registration).

The numbers of foreign medical practitioners that could benefit by either of these methods were limited but, in so far as restrictions were placed on the number that could enter the Universities, quotas were already being applied to Australians who wished to train as medical practitioners.

The final type was the Committee that was empowered to examine and recommend registration, and to whom any foreign practitioner might apply. This was introduced in New South Wales (an Examining Medical Committee), in Victoria (a Foreign Practitioners Qualification Committee), in South Australia (a Foreign Practitioners Assessment Committee) and in Queensland (oral and clinical examinations conducted by the University). Although the reports of these committees were not published, there is evidence in Parliamentary debates that they functioned without prejudice. For example, it was reported to the Victorian legislature in 1965 that the Foreign Practitioners Qualification Committee had recommended for registration people of Albanian, Austrian, Dutch, Egyptian, Estonian, German, Hungarian, Italian, Latvian, Lithuanian, Polish, Roumanian, Russian and Ukrainian nationality.[22]

A further stage of liberalization was reached in New South Wales in 1963. The reciprocity clause and the restriction of automatically acceptable qualifications to those awarded in the British Empire were removed from the legislation. Additions to the schedules of automatically acceptable qualifications are now proclaimed by the Governor of New South Wales on the recommendation of the Minister of Health.

It is, in fact, difficult to discover evidence that indicates that prejudice is responsible for the distinctions that are made in medical registration procedures. On the contrary, as a consequence of the immigration programme, a degree of flexibility has been introduced that has resulted in different kinds of registration procedures for those who are suitably trained, analogous, perhaps, to a double column customs tariff applied to commodity imports. In this case, the commodity is a medical service of a certain standard that is produced by a qualification obtained after a prescribed number of years at an appropriate training institution. Medical services that do not meet these standards are prohibited imports. The supplier of the commodity, the medical practitioner, is expected to absorb the duty, if any, under the tariff that each State levies through the medical legislation that is administered by the Registration Board. The tariff encourages the import of the commodity that has been produced in nominated countries or educational institutions by permitting duty free entry under column one. A commodity that has been produced in some other country or educational institution may enter under column two, but the duty to be paid by the supplier is an individual scrutiny of qualifications and the possibility that certain other conditions may be imposed.

ACKNOWLEDGEMENTS

The bulk of the material for this chapter was collected as part of the writer's work as a Research Fellow of the Social Science Research Council of Australia, who appointed her to conduct a survey of Professional Immigrant Manpower. The writer is indebted to Professor H. W. Arndt, Mr. D. M. B.-Butt and Dr. P. Luey for discussions and comments that resulted in considerable improvements to the first draft of this chapter, and to Mrs. M. Noakes of the National Library of Australia for assistance in tracing the sources that are quoted in the references.

REFERENCES

1 *An Act for the better government of Her Majesty's Australian Colonies*, 1850 (Australian Colonies Government Act).
Letters Patent erecting Moreton Bay into a Colony with the name of Queensland 1859. *New South Wales Judicature Act*, 1823.

2 Order dated 29th Dec. 1887; S.R. & O. 1913, No. 324; Order dated 9th May 1892; S.R. & O. 1901, No. 797; S.R. & O. 1916, No. 384; Order dated 21st March 1890; Order dated 25th March 1887; S.R. & O. 1913, No. 1364; S.R. & O. 1906, No. 383; S.R. & O. 1910, No. 71; S.R. & O. 1942, No. 142; S.I. 1949, No. 2392, S.R. & O. 1921, No. 1025; Order dated 23rd February 1891; S.R. & O. 1916, No. 626; Order dated 21st March 1890; S.R. & O. Rev. 1904. VIII, Medical Profession, p. 1 (1901 No. 204); S.R. & O. 1905, No. 1295.

3 Queensland *Medical Act*, 1861, sec. 9.

4 Queensland *Medical Act (Amendment Act)*, 1862, sec. 1.

5 Victoria *Medical Practitioners Act*, 1889.

6 Order dated 21st March 1890.

7 A. A. LENDON, 'The Desirability of amending the Medical Acts', *The Australasian Medical Gazette*, 1906, Vol. 25, p. 321.
British Medical Journal, 1906, Vol. 1, p. 203.

8 Victoria, *Medical Act*, 1906.

9 (1937) V.L.R. 237, 291.

10 Victoria *Parliamentary Debates*, session 1938, Vol. 205, p. 2297.

11 Commonwealth of Australia, *Parliamentary Debates*, 16th Nov.-8th Dec. 1938, Vol. 158, pp. 2534-6.

12 National Security (Alien Doctors) Regulations, Regulation 10, made under Commonwealth *National Security Act*, 1939-1943.

13 Victoria *Medical Practitioners' Registration Act*, 1946.

14 Victoria *Medical Act*, 1950, sec. 3.

15 Victoria *Medical (Temporary Registration) Act*, 1951.

16 Victoria *Medical (Registration) Act*, 1956.

17 Victoria *Medical (Registration) Act*, 1957.

18 *Australasian Medical Gazette*, May 1893.

19 Commonwealth of Australia, *Report of the Committee on the Future of Tertiary Education in Australia*, Vol. 2, 1964, p. 97.

20 *Ibid*, p. 106.

21 H. SEARBY, 'Medical Board and Alien Doctors', *The Age*, 13th February 1957.

22 Victoria, *Parliamentary Debates*, session 1965-66, Vol. 282, p. 3362.

7

HEALTH PROBLEMS OF IMMIGRANTS AS EVIDENCE OF PREJUDICE

C. B. Kerr

Due to medical screening before migration, most immigrants arrive in Australia with good health. Should the immigrant become ill, he enters a system which differs in many ways from that in his country of origin. Australians have to select their own doctors and make their own arrangements to insure against the cost of illness. People from the United Kingdom and most European countries are accustomed to receiving medical care as part of a compulsory scheme of social security. The United Kingdom and Europe have no counterpart of the Australian general practitioner who can, if he wishes, assume specialist functions including those of the surgeon. By custom and the provisions for voluntary medical insurance, entry into the Australian medical system is largely via a general practitioner. The main alternative is through the emergency department of a general hospital. Direct access to a medical specialist, so prevalent in southern Europe, is possible but not widely exploited, because the patient is debarred from receiving rebates from a medical insurance fund without prior referral by a general practitioner. Apart from conventional medical resources, the immigrant faces a bewildering complexity of health-related services made up of federal, state or local government agencies and private organization. Effective utilization of the entire health/welfare system is yet another facet in the process of adjusting to a new country—a very important facet due to the handicaps of ill health superimposed on problems of settlement and adaptation. Discussing immigrant families in Western Australia, Saint[1] noted that '... perhaps the commonest cause of catastrophe is the chronic illness or disability of the breadwinner'. This economic vulnerability of families without a working head was shown clearly in the Melbourne survey of poverty.[2]

Utilization of health services is related to personal and cultural features of immigrants. Language is all-important, but so are health expectations and the immigrant's role as a sick person. Then there are special health problems of immigrants—an area of particular importance when considering the origins of any prejudices held by the Australian-born. There is the possibility that hostile feelings directed against a specific illness, disability or other health variation generate prejudicial attitudes or, alternatively, become grafted onto an ethnic stereotype. Prejudice may influence patterns of using the health system; any different conditions that were enforced for immigrants would constitute discrimination. The latter situation might lead to social separation for health reasons—where conflict with the Australian system has led to the creation of ethnically autonomous medical care services.

The information that exists on health of immigrants concerns mainly those from the United Kingdom or Europe. Very little is known about the well-being of Asian minorities, although there has been recent interest in some health problems of Asian students at Australian universities. Surprisingly, no one seems to have looked at the health of Jews in Australia.

Health Problems

Australian vital statistics are recorded in a way which prevents any comparison of mortality rates and disease patterns among different nationalities. However there is nothing to suggest any marked distinction between the overall death-rates of immigrants and the Australian-born (allowing for the younger age-structure of the former). A dwindling excess mortality from tuberculosis in immigrants has almost certainly been balanced by their generally reduced susceptibility to fatal degenerative disease of the heart and blood vessels.[3]

Many immigrants have grown up under very different interactions of environmental and genetic influences. This can be reflected in their own health or that of their descendants. For instance, an early poor nutrition can result in imperfect formation of the female pelvis which leads to a complicated delivery and hence greater risks to the infant. Then again, certain racial groups have accumulated harmful genes, the most spectacular example being thalassaemia, a serious and often fatal anaemia. The gene in question is found among people from Mediterranean countries and especially those from Sicily and southern Italy—regions which provide about 75 per cent of all Italian migrants. However, any mortality from this genetic disorder of southern Europeans is matched in Anglo-Saxons and northern Europeans by other serious inherited diseases rare among Mediterranean people—notably cystic fibrosis.

There are a few other isolated incidences of some unusual cause of death afflicting an ethnic group, e.g. the Chinese in Australia have a sixty-fold increased risk of developing nasopharyngeal cancer by comparison with Caucasians.[4] But all in all, there is no reason to assume that immigrants have a higher mortality rate than do established Australians.

The overall picture of diseases and disabilities in immigrants is similarly rather vague. Some idea of the pattern was obtained from an analysis of medical reasons for admission to hospital in Perth.[1] Varieties of illness suffered by immigrants were the same as in the Australian-born except for the occasional legacy of extreme childhood deprivation, some rare genetic disorders and a few exotic infections. What differed were the relative frequencies—the greater incidence of acute infections, tuberculosis and mental illness among Europeans as compared to Australians and by contrast, a much lower frequency of degenerative heart or vessel disease and chronic bronchitis among the Europeans. Two further observations were made from the Perth study which do not seem to have been subsequently examined. The first was that immigrants formed a significant part of the workforce in dangerous occupations. But no data on health consequences related to country of birth has been published by organizations which employ unskilled or semi-skilled labour, and which attract immigrants through offering high rewards for hazardous work. Nowadays, several industries account for immigrant labour in safety programmes by incorporating multi-lingual warning notices and instructors,

but the whole question of occupational trauma and illness in different
ethnic groups awaits evaluation.

The second finding from the Perth study was the high incidence of
infectious disease among immigrants. This was related to overcrowding in
the home, poverty and poor hygiene. Most of those with acute bowel
infections came from dwellings in the 'down town' metropolitan area of
Perth. Presumably the inner urban communities of eastern Australia show
similar associations between poor circumstances and the traditional
diseases of poverty. The association is well established elsewhere, for
instance, with Asian and West Indian communities in the North[5] and
Midlands[6] of England. Further information on immigrants in other
Australian cities cannot be disentangled from the official statistics on
infectious diseases.

It is not known, either in Australia or the United Kingdom, whether
the illnesses of poor living conditions and defective hygiene reinforce
prejudice against racial minorities. The most likely consequence would
be to exaggerate ethnocentric attitudes towards 'dirtiness' of certain
racial groups. Such views are sometimes glimpsed in medical reports—in
the form of comments about inaccurate use of lavatories[5] and so forth.

Combinations of environmental, economic and personal deprivation are
ingredients in the so-called medical ghettos of western societies.
Australia has nothing like the medical ghettos of certain cities in the
United States where overt racism (mainly white versus black) is judged
to be a major factor both in maintaining a high rate of disease and in
obstructing attempts at a solution.[6a] It is extremely unlikely that a similar
situation could arise in Australian inner city communities with large
migrant populations. Full development of a medical ghetto involves
discriminatory action by the majority in withdrawing conventional
health services from the minority. This has happened in the United
States where doctors have moved out of under-privileged areas which
contain entirely inadequate hospital services. Moreover, a low recruitment rate into the medical profession of members from racial minorities
has prevented any useful replacement with ethnically acceptable manpower. Barriers against similar trends in Australia include a relatively well
developed public hospital system, special provision for the medical care
of indigents and no lack of medically qualified representatives of each
ethnic minority (with the exception of Aboriginals).

Tuberculosis ranks foremost among diseases especially prevalent in
Australian immigrants. Since the early 1950s, this serious illness has been
studied with careful attention to the origin of patients. In 1963, immigrants
in Western Australia had twice the infection rate of tuberculosis found
in the Australian-born.[7] This trend continues[8] as the absolute number of
cases has diminished. Reasons for high rates in immigrants can be
listed:—

   (i) A significant contribution from active or potentially active tuber-
       culous lesions in British full-fare-paying immigrants who are the
       only group not required to undergo statutory chest X-ray exam-
       ination in their country of origin before embarkation.[7]

  (ii) Breakdown and reactivation of old tuberculous lesions leading to
       active disease—a process accentuated by poor living conditions
       and heavy work.[9]

 (iii) Migration from areas of high tuberculosis incidence, especially

Asia. In the latest Western Australian figures,[8] the ethnic category 'other (non-European) birthplaces'—presumably almost all Asians—had the second highest incidence of tuberculosis among ten ethnic groups.

For more than two decades, the Australian medical profession and related authorities have been fully aware of the increased susceptibility of immigrants to tuberculosis; special efforts have been made to combat the problem. It is doubtful whether the Australian public has been similarly aware of the situation and, as a result, incorporated the high risk into prejudicial attitudes based on immigrants being consumptive or dangerous because of tuberculosis. The disease was formerly a major scourge—almost an accepted fact of life among the Anglo-Saxon-Irish colonists. Quantitatively, there have always been more cases in the Australian-born population, e.g. for total cases notified in Western Australia between 1961 and 1968, there were 696 non-Australian-born and 957 of Australian origin.[8] But probably the main reason for assuming no prejudice on the basis of tuberculosis is spectacular success with its treatment. Mass X-ray programmes and chest clinics are fully accepted medical institutions and effective therapy has removed the widespread fears of former times when tuberculosis was generally incurable.

Another class of infectious disease which induces strong ethnocentric reactions is venereal disease. Unattached young males are always at special risk especially when there is transition between cultures with different attitudes to sex and marriage. Such is the case with West Indians in the United Kingdom[5, 6] and with southern Europeans in Australia. For instance, most Greek immigrants come from rural areas where there is close observance of female pre-marital chastity combined with socially acceptable utilization of government-regulated prostitutes.[10] In Australia the Greek immigrant is faced with the same courtship and marriage customs within his ethnic group. But prostitution is neither approved nor medically supervised. The risk of contracting venereal disease is high; it has been estimated that half the prostitutes in Sydney have gonorrhoea.[11]

Despite *a priori* indications that immigrants may be at increased risk to venereal disease, there are no objective data on infection rates by ethnic origin. In 1967 an extensive discussion on the rising venereal disease rates by a federal committee of the Australian Medical Association[12] did not include any mention of the involvement of immigrants. However Adams, surveying attendances for venereal disease in general practices of metropolitan Sydney,[13] found that the doctors included the particular problem of lonely single male migrants as a significant contributory factor to the increasing incidence. Obviously public censure on real or assumed high utilization rates of prostitutes and frequent infections with venereal disease could be a powerful factor in creating hostile attitudes, as is well established for anti-black prejudices in the United States.[14] But lacking firm evidence from Australian sources, the question must remain open.

Mental illness in immigrants has been studied quite extensively, especially in Victoria. As in other countries with immigrant minorities, an excess burden of mental illness has been found in some ethnic groups but not in others.[15] For instance, Eastern European immigrants in Victoria were found to have a six to seven times greater incidence of schizophrenia than the local Australian population; depressive states and alcoholism were frequent among the British; and all immigrant adolescents except those from southern Europe had a higher incidence of personality and behaviour disorders.[15]

The genesis of mental illness in migrants is complex, and numerous studies[16, 17, 18, 19] have dissected the stresses of adaptation and areas of conflict in family life. Some causal factors are unrelated to existence in Australia; these include an hereditary predisposition and a self-selective element in the act of immigration whereby the possession of a pre-psychotic personality inhibited stable personal relationships in the country of origin. Ellard[20] pointed out difficulties in defining mental illness which were imposed by cultural disparaties between ethnic groups, '... perhaps the reason why 50 Greeks manifest hysterical conversion for each Australian is that their behaviour means something quite different and the term hysteria is inappropriate.'

It is difficult to assess what part is played by prejudicial attitudes in the precipitation of mental illness. Ellard suspected the prejudices against immigrants may be significant but could find no evidence.[20] The kind of hostile attitude that Jahoda regarded as mentally damaging[14] was associated mainly with aggressive racial antagonism, overt discrimination and ethnic segregation. Stoller, in analysing stressful factors experienced by immigrants and their families,[19] did not appear to regard conflict with Australians as a powerful source of stress.

Despite higher rates of psychiatric breakdown, there is no evidence of any stereotype of immigrants based on poor mental health. However, Adler[17] considered that Australians attributed a high crime rate to immigrants due, it seems, to the newspaper practice of qualifying names of criminals and other deviants with their national origin. In fact, immigrants do not appear to be over-represented in the courts (with the possible exception of adolescents and young adults in Victoria).[19]

Besides specific problems of physical and mental illness, there is another potential area of health-related prejudice—the war-horse of pseudo-scientific racial theory, perverted Darwinism. In the 1920s, racial hygiene movements in other countries were extremely strong; the Immigration Restriction Law of 1921 in the United States was regarded as official sanction against miscegnation with its 'weakening of the stock', 'racial degeneracy' and similar fantasies. The Rassenhygiene movement in Germany was backed enthusiastically by eminent anthropologists and human biologists. Thus it is somewhat surprising that no comparable movement became established at that time in Australia. Although opinion strongly favoured population by Anglo-Saxons, the debate was remarkably free from accusations of inherent defects in non-British races.[21, 22] The matter does not seem to have been an open issue during evolution of the 'White Australia' and current immigration policies.[23] Needless to say there are no scientific grounds for such views. Walsh[24] discussed the effect of immigrant genes on the Australian gene-pool and concluded that such a mixture held no disadvantages.

The Australian Medical System

There is only one discriminatory component in the health statutes of Australia, and that favours immigrants. They have special conditions for entry into the voluntary insurance scheme. On arrival, immigrants are automatically covered without charge by registered medical and hospital funds for a period of two months. The funds assume that migrants have no pre-existing illness and so there is no waiting period nor possibility of non-recognition for insurance purposes of some chronic illnesses established before signing-on. In these respects, immigrants have a distinct advantage over the Australian-born.

Despite initial concessions for voluntary insurance, immigrants form a relatively high proportion of those not covered against illness. In an extensive survey of the utilization of medical care in western Sydney,[25] where nearly 25 per cent of the sample was born outside Australia, it was found that southern European migrants ranked high among the 14 per cent who had no insurance cover. Cumming, a Greek-speaking Australian doctor with extensive experience of practice both in Greece and Australia, recently looked at health problems in the Greek community of Sydney.[10] He found that the main reason why most young Greek males remained uninsured was because many had been compulsorily covered in Greece with automatic deductions from their wages and they did not properly understand the voluntary nature of the Australian system. Although the latter was explained to all migrants before they were granted a visa, many did not grasp that one has to actively approach an Australian fund for health insurance. The funds make efforts to attract immigrants by employing interpreters and mailing instructions for permanent enrolment during the post-arrival period of free coverage. It seems that personal attitudes of southern Europeans are largely responsible for non-insurance and that this vulnerable situation is not due to any prejudice by default through non-provision of information, or interpreters, and so forth.

Utilization of medical services is a complex matter influenced by numerous personal, economic and cultural factors. The western Sydney survey yielded much information on patterns of utilization related to country of origin. For instance, immigrants from the United Kingdom and Northern Europe were more insistent on specialist medical services than the Australian-born; the latter had lower rates of operations performed on them by specialist surgeons than any other group. In answer to a query about whom they would like to undertake a fairly extensive operation on them (removal of gall-bladder), 23 per cent of Australian-born preferred a general practitioner in contrast to 8 per cent of Northern Europeans and 14-18 per cent of other Europeans and British or Irish-born. Public hospitals, as opposed to private institutions, were used by 81-89 per cent of immigrants and 73 per cent of Australian-born. However, occupational, educational and medical insurance status were additional discriminants in the choice of hospital.

One group of immigrants, those from northern Europe, had somewhat lower rates of utilizing all medical services. When asked about what type of care they would seek if faced with certain specific ailments or injuries, these immigrants showed a reluctance to contact doctors or hospitals unless absolutely necessary. This behaviour was in contrast to the southern Europeans, who, of all ethnic groups, had the highest utilization rates of all services. They were also the group to be most extensively threatened by the thought of illness, having a greater rate of preference for hospital services when confronted by even relatively minor maladies like a sore throat.

The general conclusion emerged, that although immigrants had certain characteristic ways of using the Australian health system—the overall utilization pattern was very similar to that of the Australian-born majority. This finding argues against any discrimination against immigrants which might be suspected if there was evidence of under-usage of medical services. Some attitudes on quality of services were obtained. There was a slight bias here, because in a small proportion of western Sydney households (0.02 per cent), lack of English rendered impossible any communication with interviewers. Thus a language-barrier may have caused greater difficulties in doctor-patient relationships than was observed. With regard to the qualities of their general practitioner, immigrants did not appear to differ in their opinions from the Australian-born—although there must remain reservations on the reliability of observations obtained in the course of a general enquiry into utilization of medical services. Like the Australian-born, immigrants appeared to be looking for the qualities of Congalton's ideal doctor.[26] One-third of the entire sample were critical of their general practitioners; most usually because of defects in the doctor's manner (e.g. abruptness or rudeness) and then because of his actions (e.g. failure to examine or explain) or his service arrangements (e.g. excessive waiting periods or unavailability at certain times).

The results suggest that in western Sydney, at least, there is no obvious discrimination against immigrants in the provision and delivering of medical care. Problems within the system—with hospital services as well as general practitioners—appeared to be distributed throughout the area regardless of nationality. Varying patterns of utilization are difficult to interpret for the purpose of identifying any specific area where prejudice may be involved. The relatively lesser utilization by non-Australians of private hospitals might indicate some adverse attitudes aimed at discouraging immigrants from using such facilities. However, the evidence suggests otherwise because economic and insurance status are major determinants in choice of hospitals and these factors in immigrants are weighted towards utilization of public hospitals. Moreover, certain immigrant groups prefer public hospitals due to prior experience in their country of origin (British and northern Europeans) and the availability of out-of-hours services, interpreters and fellow countrymen among the non-medical staff (southern Europeans).

Some stereotypes may be enhanced by the way immigrants use the system. A physical example is so-called 'Mediterranean back' familiar to hospital specialists, especially orthopaedic surgeons[27] and psychiatrists.[20] This term describes the rather histrionic reaction to the back injury by southern Europeans greatly concerned about the consequences to their one wage-earning skill, physical strength. In the western Sydney survey, it was found that 10 per cent of southern Europeans, if afflicted with backache, would go straight to hospital by comparison to only 4 per cent of all other ethnic groups. Thus a relative excess of Mediterranean people with this particular complaint are seen by hospital specialists. The situation tends to create a stereotype of southern Europeans with back injuries which includes the suspicion of misapplied motivation for purposes of gaining compensation.[27] As Minc has noted,[28, 29] this suspicion of conscious or subconscious malingering is probably not so valid as the patient's concept of himself when ill (i.e. he must be the centre of attention), his suspicion of the doctor with reference to compensation and his irrational belief in therapeutic qualities of investigations such as an X-ray.

A major finding of the western Sydney survey[25] was that the people, including a significant proportion of immigrants, had frequent contact with general practitioners and, on the whole, expressed faith and confidence in their work. Accordingly any adverse attitudes by general practitioners towards immigrants could have serious consequences. There are well-known problems in the doctor-patient relationship associated with language and non-verbal communication.[20, 28] Culture-based concepts of the sick role are frequently in conflict, especially the dramatic responses of southern Europeans which contrast so markedly with the stoicism traditionally required of sick Anglo-Saxons.[10] Many Europeans expect careful explanations of all illness, however trivial, accompanied by therapeutic intervention. These expectations are frequently not met under the more pragmatic conditions of Australian practice. Further conflict could arise from non-appreciation by immigrants of the high status enjoyed by Australian general practitioners. Nowhere in Europe or the United Kingdom are general practitioners so highly regarded as in Australia.

Although such ethnic discriminants doubtless influence the delivery and quality of medical care received by some immigrants, there are several counter-forces which tend to neutralise adverse effects. There is no apparent shortage of immigrant practitioners or Australian-born ethnic representatives to service major immigrant enclaves. For instance, the Greek-speaking community in Sydney almost exclusively attend the practices of medical compatriots or Australian-born doctors of Greek extraction, fluent in their language.[10] It may be noted here that doctors born outside Australia or retaining non-Australian identity appear to acquire the high status generally accorded to medical practitioners and are accepted by the profession and public alike. There are many Asian doctors with large practices among the Australian-born; one ethnic group in particular, the Jews, has made a very notable contribution to Australian medicine.

Another factor of importance in provision of medical services is related to the economics of general practice which requires a high turn-over of patients to flourish.[30] It seems likely that any general practitioner working in a community which contains a significant proportion of non-Australians would be at an economic disadvantage if he did not attempt to meet the needs of immigrant groups.

Even though immigrants tend to use ethnically compatible general practitioners and, to a certain extent, specialists, there is no true social separation on medical grounds because the hospitals are not segregated in any way. Immigrants have no alternative but to enter the general hospital system, public or private. There are no objective data on the experience of non-Australians in hospitals. The western Sydney survey[25] canvassed opinions on institutions in the region, but the situation was atypical due to pronounced inadequacies of hospitals related to rapid population growth. Accordingly, the comments of both the Australian-born and immigrants were concerned largely with physical arrangements and organization of services.

In general, it seems that hospital services have responded slowly to the special needs of immigrants. For instance, because of the young age-structure of immigrants, they have a high utilization-rate of maternity beds. All ethnic groups frequently attend antenatal care clinics in hospitals; for southern Europeans the attendance rate is twice that for the Australian-born.[25] Yet it is only quite recently that interpreters and multi-language notices have appeared in obstetric hospitals. This tardy provision cannot be regarded as an indication of discrimination; more likely reasons are non-appreciation of the communication difficulties of immigrants (after all, if it was really necessary somebody could always be found who spoke the patient's language) and the general inertia that seems to retard change in well-established hospital routines.

In the absence of any comparative data on how immigrants fare in hospital it is impossible to assess the consequences of any prejudice. Anyone who has worked in a large obstetric hospital will have noted a certain amount of disapproval over the family congregations and histrionic behaviour that surrounds the delivery of a southern European mother. There is a direct clash with Anglo-Saxon concepts of what is permissible; in addition, suppression of emotions is a well-known mechanism by which doctors and nurses deal with the disturbing incidents encountered in medicine. But the classical ingredient in the generation of prejudice—an inadequate personality—could well react with hostility and thus compromise the immigrant patient's progress in hospital.

A final point concerns provision for unusual diseases encountered among immigrants. In general, such diseases are well covered by special hospital services in major cities. For instance, there are clinics established for the treatment of thalassaemia; one such clinic has produced an excellent tri-lingual booklet to explain the disease to Mediterranean families.[31]

Conclusions

Although the frequency of certain diseases varies in different ethnic groups, there is no real evidence that specific medical problems contribute to prejudicial attitudes. There are a few disease situations which may reinforce ethnocentric views notably by associating immigrants with the diseases of poor living conditions in large cities.

The Australian medical system contains no obvious features which discriminate unfavourably against immigrants. The latter have preferential conditions for entry into the voluntary insurance scheme. Culturally-based differences create some problems in doctor-patient relationships, but there is no firm evidence that this factor significantly affects the delivery of medical care to immigrants. There may be greater opportunities for prejudice to operate within the hospital system but once again, no adverse consequences can be detected.

REFERENCES

1 SAINT, E. G. (1963). 'The Medical Problems of Migrants', *Medical Journal of Australia* 1: 335.

2 HARPER, R. J. A. (1967), 'A Survey of Poverty in Melbourne, 1966', *Australian Journal of Science* 30: 292.

3 STENHOUSE, N. S. and McCALL, M. G. (1970). 'Differential Mortality from Cardiovascular Disease in Migrants from England and Wales, Scotland and Italy and Native-born Australians', *Journal of Chronic Diseases* 23: 423.

4 SCOTT, G. C. and ATKINSON, L. (1967). 'Demographic Features of the Chinese Population in Australia and the Relative Prevalence of Nasopharyngeal Cancer

among Caucasians and Chinese', in *Cancer of the Naso-pharynx*. Munksgaard, Copenhagen, p. 64.

5 DOLTON, W. D. (1968). 'Social Factors and the Health of Immigrants', *Proceedings of the Royal Society of Medicine* 61: 19.

6 GALLOWAY, J. (1965). 'Immigration in the Midlands', *Lancet* 2: 731.

6a PIERCE, C. M. (1969). 'Is Bigotry the Basis of the Medical Problems of the Ghetto', in *Medicine in the Ghetto*. Ed. J. C. NORMAN. Appleton-Century-Crofts, New York, p. 301.

7 EDWARDS, F. G. B. (1963). 'Tuberculosis Incidence in the Non-Australian-born', *Medical Journal of Australia* 1: 501.

8 Report of the Commissioner of Public Health, West Australia (1969), p. 47.

9 LAST, J. M. (1960). 'The Health of Immigrants. Some observations from General Practice', *Medical Journal of Australia* 1: 158.

10 CUMMING, R. W. (1970), 'The Greek Approach to Ill-health', Project report. Department of Preventive and Social Medicine, University of Sydney.

11 WREN, B. G. (1967). 'Gonorrhoea among Prostitutes', *Medical Journal of Australia* 1: 847.

12 Report of the Federal Co-ordinating Committee on the Problem of Venereal Disease in Australia (1967), Supplement. *Medical Journal of Australia* 1, March 4, p. 17.

13 ADAMS, A. (1967). 'Venereal Disease in an Australian Metropolis', *Medical Journal of Australia* 1: 145.

14 JAHODA, M. (1960). 'Race Relations and Mental Health', UNESCO.

15 KRUPINSKI, J. and STOLLER, A. (1965). 'Incidence of Mental Disorders in Victoria, Australia, According to Country of Birth', *Medical Journal of Australia* 2: 265.

16 KRUPINSKI, J. and STOLLER, A. (1966). 'Family Life and Mental Ill-health in Migrants', in *New Faces*. Ed. A. STOLLER, Cheshire, Melbourne, p. 136.

17 ADLER, D. L. (1960) in 'Uprooting and Resettlement', World Federation for Mental Health, London, p. 100.

18 JOHNSTON, R. (1968), 'Culture Conflict and Culture Tension', S.A.A.N.Z. Conference paper.

19 STOLLER, A. (1969). 'Stress in Immigrants', in *Ethnic Minorities in Australia*. Ed. H. THROSSEL. Australian Council of Social Service, Sydney, p. 163.

20 ELLARD, J. (1969). 'The Problems of the Migrant', *Medical Journal of Australia* 2: 1039.

21 PHILLIPS, P. D. and WOOD, G. L. (1928). *The Peopling of Australia*, Mac-Millan, Melbourne.

22 LYNG, J. (1927). *Non-Britishers in Australia*. MacMillan, Melbourne.

23 LONDON, H. I. (1970). *Non-white Immigration and the 'White Australia' Policy*. Sydney University Press, Sydney.

24 WALSH, R. J. (1963). 'Effect of Migration on the Genetic Pool', *Medical Journal of Australia* 1: 700.

25 ADAMS, A. I., KERR, C. and CHANCELLOR, A. (1971). 'Utilization of Medical Care Facilities in Western Sydney', *Medical Journal of Australia* (In press).

26 CONGALTON, A. A. (1969). 'Public Evaluation of Medical Care', *Medical Journal of Australia* 2: 1165.

27 GREAVES, C. (1963). 'Of New Australian Patients, Their Medical Lore and Anxieties' (Corr.), *Medical Journal of Australia* 1: 910.

28 MINC, S. (1963). 'Of New Australian Patients, Their Medical Lore and Major Anxieties', *Medical Journal of Australia* 1: 681.

29 MINC, S. (1963). 'Of New Australian Patients, Their Medical Lore and Major Anxieties' (Corr.), *Medical Journal of Australia* 2: 121.

30 SCOTTON, R. B. and GROUNDS, A. D. (1969). 'Survey of General Practice in Victoria', *Medical Journal of Australia* 1: 1.

31 Institute of Child Health, University of Sydney (1970), *Thalassaemia: A Guide for Parents.*

PROCESS OF ADJUSTMENT

8

JEWS IN AUSTRALIA

P. Y. Medding

Some forty years ago, it was commonly assumed that the Melbourne Jewish community would eventually lose its identity and become absorbed within the general Australian population. The community was small, inter-marriage was widespread—the 1921 census revealed that 26 per cent of Jewish men and 14 per cent of Jewish women in Victoria had non-Jewish spouses—and if this rate continued it was only a matter of time before the community completely disappeared. The community's leaders were gravely perturbed and the *Jewish Herald* warned 'that our world-old religion is threatened with extinction'.[1] Yet the community did not seem either ready or able to take the institutional action needed to halt this inexorable process.

The synagogues were poorly attended. Hebrew—the language of prayer—was known to few, and comprehensible to even fewer, facilities for Jewish education were abysmal, the spiritual leadership was pedestrian, the performance of Jewish rituals was minimal, Jewish cultural life was non-existent, and Zionism was in its earliest infancy. The newcomer who arrived could look forward to some financial assistance, but little attempt was made to integrate him socially into either the Jewish or the general community, and he was apt to feel lonely and neglected, and often embittered as well, at the patronizing and heavy-handed way in which communal charity was administered. The activities of the few existing institutions were not co-ordinated, nobody spoke officially on behalf of Melbourne Jewry and consequently the community as such, played no role in Australian society and had little impact upon public consciousness.[2] The desire for ethnic survival burned strong in a few hearts, but they were in a tiny minority and not in positions of institutional power where they could do something to improve the situation. For Melbourne Jewry in those days, the chances of survival were very dim indeed.

Forty years later, this situation has been radically transformed. Not only is the community much larger in size, it boasts, in addition, a flourishing network of communal institutions and activities previously undreamt of. Intermarriage has markedly declined,[3] Jewish education is amply catered for, synagogues abound (although only a few are well attended), Jewish rituals are more commonly observed, Zionism has become a focal point of communal existence, whilst a plethora of organizations caters for the community's needs in the cultural, sporting, youth and social service spheres. These activities are co-ordinated by a communal roof-body which includes nearly every major group in the community and which represents it outside. The community has learnt to participate as a community in the affairs of Australian society, and to take a public stand on many issues.

The Socio-Economic and Demographic Setting[4]

The population growth of Australian and Victorian Jewry since 1901 is presented in Table 1, which shows in addition, the proportion of Jews in the total Australian population.

TABLE 1

Growth of Australian and Victorian Jewry, 1901-1961

	Total Australian Jewry	Proportion of Australian population %	Total Victorian Jewry
1901	15,239	0.40	5,907
1911	17,287	0.38	6,270
1921	21,615	0.40	7,677
1933	23,553	0.36	9,500
1947	32,019	0.42	14,910
1954	48,436	0.56	24,016
1961	59,343	0.57	29,932

It will be immediately noticed that Victorian Jewry's proportion of the total has markedly increased over the period under review. Thus they constituted 38.1 per cent of Australian Jewry in 1901, 40.4 per cent in 1933, 46.6 per cent in 1947, 49.8 per cent in 1954 and 50.5 per cent 1n 1961. It is not clear, however, how accurate these figures are, as approximately 10 per cent of the overall Australian population do not answer the question on religion in the census, or claim to have no religion, or to be atheists or agnostics. There are three main approaches to this problem. The first claims that many Jews who have been persecuted in Europe would be afraid to put down Jewish as their religion. The second maintains that nearly all Jews would classify themselves as such, and that even if rationalist or anti-religious, ethnic or social expressions of Jewish identification are still retained. It is impossible to ascertain how many Jews completely deny their Jewish origin, or whether the reality of freedom in Australia has removed fears of self-identification as Jews. The third approach therefore, simply adds 10 per cent to the census figures, bringing the total of Australian Jewry to something over 65,000.

As most of this increase has been due to migration, it is to be expected that the proportion of Australian born Jews in the community will have fallen, corresponding with a rise in the European born. The census tables reveal that in 1911, over 80 per cent of Victorian Jews were born in Australia and the United Kingdom, with the former comprising 63.5 per cent of the total. By 1961, only 37.5 per cent were born in Australia, 6.8 per cent in the United Kingdom, and 56.8 per cent in Europe, with the main areas of origin being eastern Europe with 30 per cent, and

Austria and Germany with 10.5 per cent. The proportion of adults of European origin is, of course, far greater than this, having comprised the vast majority of migrants, both before and after the war. Conversely, the vast majority of Jews under twenty-one are Australian born. Unfortunately the census figures do not break down national origins by age within the religious groups, but clear indications of this trend can be found elsewhere. The 1954 census, for example, revealed that among the Polish born (of whom Jews constituted approximately 30 per cent) the ratio of under twenty-one to over twenty-one was 1:11, whereas that of the total Australian population was 2:3. Similarly, our random sample of adults in the Jewish community in 1961 found that only 12 per cent of those over twenty-one were Australian born. The 1961 census showed that there were approximately 10,000 Jews in Victoria under twenty. Adjusting these figures to include those under twenty-one, and then applying the migrant ratio of 1:11, it is found that nearly 85 per cent of those under twenty-one were Australian born. By subtracting these from the total number of Australian born, the proportion of Australian born adults is approximately 14 per cent, which bears out the findings of our random sample.

In most countries of the world in the twentieth century, Jews have been a predominantly urban people, concentrated in clearly definable sections of the metropolis. Victorian Jews follow this universal pattern. Since 1911, when the proportion living in the Melbourne metropolitan area was 86.6 per cent, it has steadily increased. Thus in 1921 it was 90.2 per cent, in 1933 it was 93.7 per cent, in 1947 it was 95.4 per cent, in 1954 it was 97.6 per cent and by 1971 it had reached 98.5 per cent. Table 2 reveals the areas of concentration and the way in which these have changed since 1901.

TABLE 2

Jewish population of Melbourne, 1901-1961[5]

	1901 %	1921 %	1933 %	1947 %	1954 %	1961 %
City of Melbourne	44.4	28.2	31.4	21.1	11.2	5.7
Inner East	19.3	12.5	6.4	2.6	2.4	1.1
Northern	1.7	7.3	8.6	8.0	11.0	7.4
Western	1.9	2.0	1.5	1.4	1.1	0.9
Southern	6.8	5.5	2.8	1.9	1.3	0.9
South-Eastern	23.2	40.7	44.8	57.2	55.6	60.6
Outer South-Eastern	0.1	0.6	0.9	1.3	5.9	8.7
Eastern	2.5	3.0	3.5	6.1	10.5	12.6
Outer-Eastern	0.1	0.2	0.1	0.4	1.0	2.1

Over the period there has been a steady drift away from the City of Melbourne and the inner eastern areas, representing such suburbs as Carlton, East Melbourne and Brunswick, to the higher class south-eastern, outer south-eastern and eastern municipalities, in which over 80 per cent of Melbourne Jews now live. Among these, the most populous Jewish municipalities are St. Kilda and Caulfield (both south-eastern) with 23.4 per cent and 20.1 per cent respectively, followed by Prahran (south-eastern), Moorabbin (southern), Brighton (southern) and Kew (eastern), in this order, each manifesting between 7 per cent and 5 per cent of the total.

Residence in the higher-class suburbs immediately suggests economic well-being and this is borne out by the census statistics. They show clearly that Jews in Victoria, as in the rest of Australia, are predominantly middle class. Statistics of occupational status in 1961 found that among Jewish males in the work force, 31.3 per cent were employers, 17.6 per cent self-employed and 51.1 per cent employees, compared with approximately 8 per cent, 14 per cent and 75 per cent respectively for the total Australian population. These figures for Jewry do not tell the whole story, however, because of the way in which the census questions are formulated. Those who employ others in their own businesses or trades are told to classify themselves as employers, while managers with the power to hire or dismiss staff are classified as employees. Many Jews, in fact, run businesses which are incorporated as private companies. According to strict legal definitions and for census purposes such directors and managers are employees of the company despite the fact that they own and control it. Even if Jews in such positions give their status as employer, census officials, through elaborate checking procedures, reclassify the responses so as to correspond with the strict legal definition.[6] Thus our 1961 random sample which avoided this problem and adopted a 'commonsense' definition, found 51.2 per cent to be employers, 24 per cent to be self-employed and only 18.4 per cent employees.

TABLE 3

Jewish graduates from Melbourne University, 1940-1959

	Total Jewish Graduates	Total Jewish Graduates %	Total University Graduates %	Jewish Graduates in Faculty %
Arts	199	25.8	26.48	4.8
Law	99	12.8	6.11	10.5
Medicine	220	28.6	15.47	9.3
Science	77	10.0	14.76	3.4
Commerce	74	9.6	12.32	3.8
Engineering	45	5.8	9.54	3.03
Dentistry	27	3.5	3.78	4.7
Education	12 ⎫		3.55	2.05
Architecture	5 ⎪	⎫		1.74
Music	5 ⎬	3.9 ⎬	6.95	2.20
Agricultural Science	7 ⎭		2.46	1.57
Total	770	100.0	100.0	

The 1947 census also tabulated religion according to occupational order for Australian Jewry. Among the males, 29.1 per cent were in administrative occupations including proprietors, directors and managers, compared with 5.3 per cent for the general population, 25.2 per cent were in commercial and clerical occupations compared with 16.3 per cent,

16.4 per cent were craftsmen and 13.3 per cent operatives, compared with 19.9 per cent and 23.4 per cent respectively, and 9.1 per cent were professionals compared with 3.2 per cent.

The Commonwealth censuses of 1921 and 1933 enquired into the educational achievements of the population. When these were divided according to religion, Jews were found to manifest a higher proportion at universities than other groups, the figures being 3.74 per cent in 1921, and 4.26 per cent in 1933 compared with 0.71 per cent and 0.73 per cent respectively, for the total population. Since then, unfortunately, this question has been dropped from the Census Schedule. In order to bring these figures up-to-date, a name count was used to analyse the lists of graduates from Melbourne University in the various faculties in the years 1940-59. The problems of employing name counts are readily admitted, and no claim can therefore be made to exactness, although this method of analysis is sufficiently reliable to indicate approximate proportions in each faculty. Only identifiable Jewish names were included and, if anything, the figures underestimate the total numbers of Jews graduating from the University. The results of this procedure are embodied in Table 3.

In the period 1940-59, Jews constituted 5.05 per cent of all graduates. The most popular faculties are Medicine, Law and Arts, with female students accounting for a large proportion of the latter. In general, the figures clearly demonstrate a strong preference for training in the independent professions.

Melbourne Jewry differs substantially from the rest of the population in its ecological, socio-economic and educational structures, and in these respects it closely reproduces a pattern which is universal among Jewry. In order to understand this structure more fully, it is necessary to analyse briefly the reasons given for this world-wide phenomenon. Four basic approaches are used: historical, economic, socio-cultural and psychological.

The historical approach traces the economic structure of Jewry since medieval times, and suggests that their present profile stems from the fact that they were not admitted into the craft guilds or the professions (including the military) and were legally disbarred from owning land. They were therefore forced into minor business activities, such as peddling, moneylending, and various types of middle-man activity. This occupational experience, familiarizing them with finance and industry, stood them in good stead in the competitive capitalist world and gave rise to Jewish social mobility and middle class status. Nathan Glazer, in explaining the economic success of American Jewry, takes this one step further, suggesting that as a result of having, for many generations, been engaged in middle class occupation, the Jews developed these middle class values such as moderation and foresight, which are instrumental in achieving upward social mobility. Thus the Jewish workers who came to the United States from Europe were not:—

> 'Like the other workers who immigrated with them, sons of workers and peasants, with the traditionally limited horizons of those classes. The Jewish workers were the sons—or the grandsons—of merchants and scholars even though the merchants had only their wits for capital . . . This background meant that the Jewish workers could almost immediately turn their minds to ways and means of improving themselves that were quite beyond the imagination of

their fellow-workers. Business and education were, for Jews, not a remote and almost foreign possibility, but a near and familiar one'.[7]

Kuznets adopts an economic approach in attempting to explain the lack of Jewish participation in agriculture, minor participation in transportation and communications, and concentration in trade, finance, the professions, handicrafts and industry, which constitute universally applicable distinctive characteristics.

In general, the economic functions of a minority are determined by its small size, the period of its arrival and its tendency towards cohesion and distinctiveness. To begin with, the small size prevents the minority reproducing the majority economic profile, while the desire for cohesion becomes translated in the economic sphere into select occupations and industries, to prevent dispersion. Concentration will be further determined by the period of its arrival, for newcomers can fit most easily into those areas of the economy which are not fully manned at the time, namely those expanding rapidly, which also serves to prevent conflict and competition with the native population. Choice is also limited by their economic heritage and traditional occupational skills, but at the same time this may enable them to create unperceived opportunities. Once concentrated in certain areas of the economy, for example commerce, a recently arrived minority is hardly likely to move to other spheres, particularly if the former is still expanding rapidly. Furthermore, certain areas may be shunned for fear of discrimination, particularly if they had originally experienced resistance to entry. Their rise in economic status, therefore, is likely to be significantly larger than that of the total population, because they enter into rapidly expanding areas of greater growth potential, usually at the lowest rungs, and not having established roots, can adjust most easily to changing economic opportunities.[8]

The socio-cultural approach traces the religious, cultural and social sources of middle class values among Jews, suggesting that their possession leads to rapid upward social mobility. Four factors are emphasized: the Jewish religious tradition; the business experience of the Jewish people; their urban psychology; and their minority group status. The Jewish religion is thought to inculcate certain values conducive to the establishment of a middle class ethic, similar in nature to the Protestant ethic, namely, recognition of individual worth and responsibility for individual welfare, non-asceticism, rationality, empiricism, emphasis on literacy, education and intellectual pursuits, cleanliness, sobriety and family purity. The business experience of Jews taught them care, foresight, moderation, the ability to make the most of opportunities, the anticipation of alternatives and the cultivation of clients and customers. Urban life stressed the inter-human struggle for gain, fostered intellectuality, calculability and exactness, and loosened the bonds of the community over the individual, making him responsible for his own welfare. Minority group status and its concomitant social cohesion and solidarity as a defence against a hostile outside world, developed a tradition of group support for individual attempts to attain economic independence and gain protection from the buffets of discriminatory pressures. The desire for independence is apparent in all areas of Jewish economic pursuit, and combined with the tremendous stress on education, has produced the concentration of Jews in the independent professions.[9]

The psychological approach stresses the individual's psychological and cultural orientation towards achievement, that is, the need to excel, willingness to enter into the competitive race for social status, and high valuation upon personal achievement and success. Such motivations are instilled early in life by parents setting high standards of excellence, showing approval of competence and self-reliance in children and granting them independence in making decisions. For upward social mobility, incentive to excel on its own is not enough; it requires planning, hard work and sacrifice to enable it to be put into practice. It was shown empirically, that of all ethnic groups, Jews expected the earliest evidence of self-reliance and manifested the highest valuations of achievement, and the highest mean scores of vocational aspiration, all of which persisted when social class was controlled. Such findings demonstrate that these psychological attitudes among Jews are an important factor in their upward social mobility.[10]

The general arguments based upon Jewish cultural and religious values, business experience, minority status and upon the economics of small minorities apply equally to Australian Jews as to those elsewhere. In order to further check Glazer's theory and to ascertain how many Jews came originally from middle class backgrounds, we enquired into the occupations of the fathers and fathers-in-law of the respondents to the survey. It was found that over 90 per cent in each group were engaged in occupations employing middle class skills, with 64 per cent of the fathers and 60 per cent of the fathers-in-law in small business. It should also be noted that Jewish migrants who came to Australia were required to possess a certain amount of landing capital, which in the years immediately preceding the war was quite considerable. Moreover, communal loan societies also made capital available for establishing newcomers in business, and, after the war, for providing housing as well. Once the primary problem of accumulating sufficient capital to start in business had been overcome, the inherited and acquired experience, judgment, skills and values could be utilized to further their economic ends.

This ability of the community to assist its immigrants financially, and the special occupational distribution of Jewish migrants in Europe prior to their arrival here, constitutes another major difference between Jews and other immigrant groups in Australia. The fact that the Jewish community in Melbourne prior to the large-scale migration after 1945 was predominantly middle class, and highly concentrated in independent business activities, made the task of finding capital, jobs and housing for the migrants much easier than among the immigrant groups which were concentrated in working class occupations. This was particularly true for those who had relatives here. Furthermore, the influx of Jewish migrants, relative to the size of the established community, was quite small as compared with other immigrant groups.[11] Whereas other groups tended to be divided on the basis of regional differences (districts of origin), Jewry tended to be far more cohesive, and in this, the strong Jewish traditions of philanthropy, self-help and feelings of inter-dependence played an important role. Finally, most migrants from other countries were from rural areas and did not possess the middle class skills which produced rapid economic mobility and integration for Jewish migrants. This in turn created a chain process; Jewish migrants, arriving with middle class skills, aptitudes and experience, and benefiting from various forms of communal and individual assistance, within a short time became economically established and in a position to assist further newcomers. Other migrants remaining in working class occupations simply did not possess the resources with which to assist later newcomers.

Retrospect and Prospect

The development of Melbourne Jewry since 1920 has witnessed the invigoration of a community in danger of disappearance. The assimilatory pressures upon it were strong and were steadily taking their toll. The 1960s, by way of contrast, find a community in which group identity and activity in all spheres have been considerably strengthened. Of Melbourne Jewry, it can be said without doubt, that in the last forty years the group-strengthening factors have become predominant; the community has undergone behavioural assimilation, adapting and accommodating to Australian society in economic practices, day to day behaviour, dress and language, but has resisted structural assimilation and not undergone a large-scale entry into its social cliques, organizations, institutional activities and general civic life, culminating in intermarriage. Melbourne Jewry has thus achieved a marked degree of adaptation to Australian soceity while creating and maintaining a complete socio-religious structure of its own.

Melbourne Jewry's provision for its socio-religious needs, as we saw, is extensive. It begins in early childhood and continues right through the life cycle, including the kindergarten, the day school, the youth organization, the university student society, the marriage partner, the synagogue, the residential area, the cultural, sporting, social and welfare organizations, the adult friendship group, the old age home, and finally the cemetery. In all of these activities, Melbourne Jews can, if they wish, follow a path which will never take them outside their own group. The existence of such a vast network of socio-religious institutions and activities has important sociological implications. As we pointed out, each of its separate elements acts to both communicate and reinforce group sentiments, attitudes, practices and values. Whether they be rituals which, by their symbolism, strengthen the moral authority of the group, formal educational institutions which inculcate and perpetuate its heritage, or clubs and friendship groups where Jews mix socially—through them and others as well, the socio-religious group becomes strengthened as its norms and values are communicated and reinforced.

The survey demonstrated this point many times over. What was not quite so obvious is that the findings of the survey question the common assumption that the various forms of Jewish identification and expressions of group belonging have a separate existence of their own: that Jews either keep rituals and are religious, or are Zionists, or join Jewish organizations or have exclusively Jewish circles of friends. Our findings point in the opposite direction, to the existence of clusters of interacting and reinforcing attitudes, norms and behaviour patterns. While the theory of separate forms of identification may be true in certain specific cases (such as secular Zionists and Bundists), in general it may be said that these means of identification cling together.

Two basic syndromes exist. The first includes at least moderate adherence to rituals, strong opposition to intermarriage, support for Jewish day schools, and strong sympathies for Israel, usually correlated with less than university education and limited social contact with Gentiles. The second consists of rejection of rituals, weakened opposition to intermarriage, and support for minimal Jewish education, usually correlated with high education and greater social mixing among non-Jews. (Generally speaking, the former pattern is more likely to be found among eastern European Jews and the latter among Germans and Austrians and Australian born, although these correlations are not as strong as those with education and non-Jewish friendships.) The large majority of Melbourne Jews conform to the former syndrome.

There has been, since 1920, a revolution in communal mentality which has manifested itself in many areas—religion, Jewish education, Zionism, communal leadership, integration of migrants and reactions to anti-semitism. In fact a completely new approach to the position and role of the Jew in non-Jewish society has been developed. In 1920 the emphasis was upon the participation of the individual Jew in the general community. It was felt necessary to de-emphasize many elements of Jewish distinctive-ness and group particularism in the belief that the more Jews were like other Australians, the more easily they would become integrated into Australian society. Sociologically, the theory maintained that structural assimilation was desirable—up to a point. Jews should be active in non-Jewish associations, social cliques, institutions and general civic life, but intermarriage was to be avoided. (Whether it was realistic to believe that it could be avoided under these conditions, is a different matter.) In short, a few basic religious differences were to be maintained, but Jews were not to be socially segregated or institutionally isolated. This was the Australian equivalent of what in Great Britain and the United States was termed Anglo-conformity. The chances of group survival without the net-work of independent socio-religious institutions which both guarantee and represent minority living, were negligible indeed. Yet it seems that communal leaders then, despite the desire for structural assimilation, were clearly opposed to the group's complete disappearance, which is the usual objective of Anglo-conformists.

Melbourne Jewry in the 1960s has rejected this approach, and is searching for a new ideology which will define its minority situation. It is slowly moving in the direction of cultural pluralism. Cultural pluralism emphasizes group distinctiveness, enabling the contributions to society as a whole of different groups as groups. It stands in direct contrast to sociological theories of assimilation (Anglo-conformity)—the complete integration of minorities into the larger society, their acceptance of the majority norms, values and attitudes, in other words, their disappearance, and of the melting pot, which is based upon the assumption that all cultures in a society should eventually be synthesized into a new product, again predicated upon the disappearance of minorities. Cultural pluralism depends upon the continuance of separate religions and cultures side by side, each adding its unique contribution to the whole, but being able to do so only if it can freely develop and maintain its own particularistic socio-religious framework. Cultural pluralism is a new synthesis as far as Melbourne Jewry is concerned. It offers the community the opportunity to participate as a group, and as a community, in Australian life, while at the same time permitting, indeed encouraging, the development of the community's heritage, and its desire for group survival. There are of course other alternatives, but cultural pluralism seems best suited to the demands of the Jewish community's socio-religious structure and its needs. In this way the group can continue to maintain its independent existence in all spheres, while taking up its position in society at large.

While cultural pluralism is particularly suited to the community's internal socio-religious needs, it does not exclude the possibility and the likelihood of alternative approaches existing side by side with it. Complete ghettoization and the attempt to completely ignore the external society is one such possibility. A second approach, not excluded, is the quest for complete integration into non-Jewish society by individual Jews, the attempt to completely ignore Jewish society. A third alternative is the attempt by Jews to participate as individuals in the affairs of the larger society, without either emphasizing or de-emphasizing the Jewish aspects of their participation, and without relating it to the organized affairs of the Jewish community.

What cultural pluralism does, is to enable Jewry to further and develop its own socio-religious structure and cater for its particularistic group needs, while participating in the affairs of the external society. It thus specifically seeks to avoid the extremes of ghettoization and complete integration, and the tensions between the particularistic and the general —in other words, to resist the posing of the question in terms of the polar opposites, in an either-or relationship.

While this seems to be the direction in which the Jewish community is moving, a number of obstacles present themselves. There is firstly the major question whether such a theory is, in fact, suited to Australian society. Cultural and religious pluralism are of basic importance in American society, but is this true of Australia? Many would argue that certain basic aspects of Australian society, culture and attitudes stand in strong opposition to theories of cultural pluralism.

The communal revolution which occurred in the past two generations was primarily the result of the influx of over twenty thousand Jewish migrants, the majority from eastern Europe. Many of them, strongly imbued with Jewish values, religious, cultural and Zionist, set out to fashion the community in their likeness. Not long after the war the migrants constituted nearly 60 per cent of Melbourne Jewry, giving them the numbers to support and develop existing institutions and establish new ones. This process was given tremendous impetus by the universal strengthening of Jewish consciousness resulting from the Nazi holocaust and the establishment of Israel. These served to mobilize the emotions and activities of Jews everywhere, and in particular, to arouse and attract Jews who were only marginally identified. The already strongly identified were not only reinforced in their outlooks but were now able to count upon the support of broader sections of the community. The community underwent a centripetal process, in which the ethnic survivalists—the Orthodox, the strong Zionists and the traditional-cultural-national Jews—acted as magnets for many who wished to give expression to rekindled pride by identifying with the group. As we noted, the process of engaging the loyalties of the less identified Jews and attracting the peripheral to the centre, took place in all areas of communal life. In it, the element of pride in the group is particularly vital; its absence spells the disintegration of the group, while its presence constitutes the foundation upon which a socio-religious structure can be erected.

A key role has been played by the desire of Jews to preserve their cultural heritage and group life, and the concern to establish and maintain a framework which would cater for their socio-religious needs. The simple need to belong, the quest for social cohesion and solidarity, and the security of knowing one's place have also been a significant influence in the development of the socio-religious framework. On the other hand, negative external pressures, the prejudices of the majority and discrimination against Jews seem to have had less influence on this development. Their major manifestation seems to have been in the area of opposition to intermarriage.

Without any doubt, high education and extensive social mixing with non-Jews are inversely related to Jewish identification. Education and recreation, then, seem to be the most important assimilatory factors. Economic integration, by way of contrast, seems to have had little effect (except among professionals) and levels of Jewish identification do not vary with occupational status. Education and mixing with non-Jews pose serious questions for the future development of the Jewish community, particularly as mixing with non-Jews is also a factor of migrant status. As the proportion of migrants decreases and the proportion of Australian born increases, the amount of social mixing with Gentiles seems likely to rise. Adding to this the large proportion receiving a university education, the outlook is one of decreasing Jewish identification. It is indeed a disturbing thought for a community that its most highly educated members are among the most alienated from it—with all the implications that has for the quality of communal life—and that its members most integrated in non-Jewish society are among its least identified, casting doubts upon its ability as a group to pursue the path of cultural pluralism. Does it mean that the strength of the group can be guaranteed only in the absence of higher education, and in the presence of virtual social isolation It may, of course, mean precisely that.

On the other hand, a number of factors operating in the other direction must also be considered. The pattern of identification of the highly educated was dichotomous, falling into a small group who were highly identified ('actively ethnic intellectuals') and a large majority, hardly identified ('marginally ethnic intellectuals'). There is, then, some hope for the future of the community in the maintenance of this dichotomy and an increase in the proportion of highly identified. Jewish day school education must also be borne in mind. The fact that approximately half the Jewish children in Melbourne will be educated in Jewish day schools, is perhaps the most important single determinant of the community's future development. For the eastern European Jew, university education was often an indication of a loosening of communal ties and a rejection of its values (assuming that they had, in fact, been acquired), and for the Australian Jew of the past, and many in Germany and Austria, it was accompanied by the complete absence of Jewish education. High secular education and Jewish education and identification under those conditions were alternatives. The Australian Jew of the future has the possibility of synthesizing the two; of receiving a sound Jewish education, together with a high secular education. It may well be that the future will not witness high Jewish identification and educational achievements as alternatives, but as concomitants. In other words, the proportion of 'passively' and 'actively ethnic intellectuals' is likely to increase and perhaps become the predominant mode.

The future then, will be fought between the conflicting pressures of high education and tendencies towards increased social mixing with

Gentiles on the one hand, and Jewish day schools, strengthening group identification on the other. As time moves on, the influence of Israel is likely to wane and the memories of the Nazi holocaust will become dim. The strength of Jewish identification, and its modes of expression, will have to come from internalized desires for group survival and the strength and influence of the community's socio-religious structure in communicating and reinforcing the group's norms, sentiments, values, and interests. It will depend upon these factors whether Jews will feel a need to belong to the group and search for ways to fulfil it.

ACKNOWLEDGEMENT

This chapter has been reproduced from P. Y. Medding *From Assimilation to Group Survival* by courtesy of F. W. Cheshire Publishing Pty. Ltd.

REFERENCES

1 *Jewish Herald,* 18 March 1921.

2 As distinct from individual Jews such as Sir Isaac Isaacs, then Justice of the High Court, later to become Chief Justice and finally, Governor-General of Australia, and Sir John Monash, the famous commander of the Australian forces in World War I and later head of the State Electricity Commission of Victoria.

3 According to the Commonwealth Census in 1933, 93% of Victorian Jewish females had Jewish spouses, as did 85% of Jewish males, while in 1961 this had risen to 96% for Jewish females and 91% for Jewish males. For a detailed analysis of Commonwealth Census statistics relating to Australian Jewry, see W. Lippmann, 'The Demography of Australian Jewry', *Jewish Journal of Sociology,* Vol. 8, No. 2, December 1966, pp. 213-39.

4 For more detailed analysis of Jewish demography in Australia, see C. A. Price, *Jewish Settlers in Australia,* Canberra, 1964.

5 This table is based on Price, *op. cit.,* Appendix IXa.

6 Personal communication from the Commonwealth Bureau of Census and Statistics, 30 June 1965.

7 Glazer, N. 'The American Jew and the Attainment of Middle Class Rank', in Sklare, M. (Ed.), *The Jews: Social Patterns of an American Group,* Glencoe, 1958, p. 144.

8 Kuznets, S. 'The Economic Structure and Life of the Jews', in Finkelstein, L. (Ed.), *The Jews: Their History, Culture and Religion,* London, 3rd ed., 1961, pp. 1597-622.

9 Hurvitz, N. 'Sources of Middle Class Values of American Jews', *Social Forces* 37, 1958, pp. 117-23.

10 Rosen, B. C. 'Race, Ethnicity and Achievement', *American Sociological Review* 24, 1959, pp. 47-55.

11 Thus while Melbourne Jewry doubled itself from 1947 to 1961 (14,910 to 29,932), the Greek-born increased fifteen-fold in the period 1947 to 1961 (1,965 to 28,917) and the Italian-born increased about eighteen-fold in the same period (4,277 to 73,752).

9

ITALIANS IN AUSTRALIA

J. Heiss

For the U.S.A. at least, it has long seemed obvious that immigrants living in segregated areas are less assimilated than those who live among the native population. However, there seems to be no systematic data which bear directly upon the notion. Duncan and Lieberson and others[1] provide data which supports the related hypothesis, 'Immigrant groups which are highly segregated tend to be less assimilated than those which are less segregated', but there does not seem to be any study which systematically relates the assimilation characteristics of individuals to the level of segregation in their residential area. The purpose of this brief note is to present such data and to test the limits of any generalization which emerges.

Method

The subjects of the study[2] are Italian-born male residents of Perth, Western Australia. Since no adequate listing of Italian immigrants exists, it was not possible to sample the entire group of Italians in Perth. It was necessary to limit the universe from which the sample was drawn. On the basis of practical considerations the study was limited to men who had children in the sixth or seventh grades of the local schools. A census was taken of students in these grades in a stratified random sample of state and Catholic schools, and from cards filled out by the children a list of eligible fathers was compiled. After the list was randomized, letters were sent out to the first 104 names and concerted efforts were made to obtain interviews.

These efforts were successful in ninety-four cases, giving a total non-respondent rate of about 10 per cent for the first group approached. (There were four refusals, three appeared willing but could not be interviewed in the time available, two moved and one died.) The non-respondents were replaced by ten others from the list, and all these were successfully interviewed. Thus, the sample contains 104 men.

The dependent variable, degree of assimilation, is measured by a Guttman scale which is composed of Guttman scales of satisfaction, identification with Australia, acculturation, and a single item relating to friendship with Australians of British background. The combined scale has a total coefficient of reproducibility of .92. The other requirements of Guttman scales are also met with the exception of the fact that two non-scale types have frequencies slightly above 5 per cent. For the purposes of this study, the five point scale is collapsed into a three point scale by combining scores of zero and one and scores of three and four.

Each respondent's address was noted and he was later classified as

residing in one of twelve sections of the city. These sections are natural
areas which vary in size from 1,000 to 18,000 persons. Their average
population is about 8,500. These areas were then classified into groups
depending upon the size of the ratio of Italian-born to native-born reported
in the last census. The two areas classified as most segregated have ratios
of about 0.34. The areas classified as less segregated have ratios between
.12 and .18. The non-segregated areas have ratios of .08 and below. The
ratio for the city as a whole is .09.

Before presenting data relating to these measures of assimilation and
segregation, a few general words about the Italian-born population seems
indicated. Though the largest non-British group of immigrants in the area,
the Italians represent only 3.5 per cent of the residents of the Perth
Metropolitan Area and 6.4 per cent of the population of the City of Perth.
Their total numbers are around 15,000 for the Metropolitan Area and 6,000
for the city. The vast bulk of these people are members of the post-war
immigration which reached a peak in the early fifties.

The pattern of settlement is a familiar one. The major centre of
Italian residence is across the railway tracks from the last of the three
streets which make up the central business district. This area, though by
no means a slum, is clearly below the usual standard of Perth living. Three
adjacent sections are the areas of medium-heavy Italian concentration. One

TABLE 1

*Respondents' assimilation scores by degree of segregation in
residential area*

Assimilation score	Highly segregated	Residential areas Less segregated	Non- segregated	Total
Low	18 (33%)	7 (29%)	2 (8%)	27
Medium	15 (27%)	7 (29%)	6 (24%)	28
High	22 (40%)	10 (42%)	17 (68%)	49
Total	55 (100%)	24 (100%)	25 (100%)	104

$G = .33, z = 2.27, p = .01$

TABLE 2

*Respondents' assimilation scores by degree of segregation in residential
area and length of Australian residence (post-war immigrants only)*

Assimilation score	Length of Australian residence 10 years or less Segregated areas	Non-segregated areas	11-14 years Segregated areas	Non-segregated areas
Low	14 (35%)	2 (18%)	11 (32%)	— (0%)
Medium	9 (22%)	4 (36%)	12 (35%)	2 (20%)
High	17 (42%)	5 (45%)	11 (32%)	8 (80%)
Total	40 (99%)	11 (99%)	34 (99%)	10 (100%)

$G = .18, z = .47, p > .25$ $\qquad$ $G = .81, z = 2.59, p < .01$

of these is higher in status than the central area. The non-segregated areas are found in a third tier of sections. Generally, the proportion of Italians goes down and the Socio-Economic Status goes up as one goes away from the central area. Other centres of Italian settlement are found elsewhere in the Metropolitan Area.

Results

The data presented in Table 1 indicates that those living in areas with large Italian populations tend to be less assimilated than those who live in non-segregated areas. Goodman and Kruskal's 'G', a measure of association for ordinal data, is equal to .33. An association of this magnitude would occur by chance only once in a hundred times.[3] It seems likely, therefore, that the association is reliable. It should be noted, however, that the association is almost entirely due to the high degree of assimilation in the non-segregated areas. The residents of the middle areas are not different from those who live in the most segregated areas. This point notwithstanding, the original hypothesis is borne out for a country other than America and for a small ethnic group of recent immigration.[4]

The next questions concern the stability of the relationship. Does the relationship hold up when test variables are introduced? Is the original association due to correlated biases? Is it true only for certain categories? Because of its association with the dependent and independent variables we first controlled for length of Australian residence. Table 2 shows a clear replication of the previous finding for those who are less recent arrivals. However, for those who have been in Australia for less than eleven years the association is not significant. Those in the non-segregated areas seem to be somewhat less likely to be in the lowest assimilation category, but a recent immigrant is unlikely to have achieved the highest level of assimilation regardless of where he lives. Thus we find that the original finding does not hold for all categories of people.

In Table 3 the age of the respondent is held constant, and a similar picture emerges. For older immigrants the degree of segregation is related to the degree of assimilation. In the younger group, though the same trend is observed, the association is weaker and not quite large enough to rule

TABLE 3

Respondents' assimilation scores by degree of segregation in residential area and date of birth

Assimilation score	Date of birth			
	1920 and after		Before 1920	
	Segregated areas	Non-segregated areas	Segregated areas	Non-segregated areas
Low	10 (26%)	1 (8%)	15 (37%)	1 (8%)
Medium	9 (23%)	2 (17%)	14 (34%)	3 (25%)
High	20 (51%)	9 (75%)	12 (29%)	8 (67%)
Total	39 (100%)	12 (100%)	41 (100%)	12 (100%)
	$G = .47$, $z = 1.36$, $p < .10$		$G = .63$, $z = 2.28$, $p = .01$	

out chance. Young immigrants tend to be highly assimilated, and the nature of the residential area may not make much difference.

Table 4 takes into account occupational level. Though there is a relatively narrow range of occupations in the sample it was possible to divide the group into upper and lower occupational classes. Holding this factor constant has little effect. Regardless of occupational class the segregated are less assimilated.

TABLE 4

Respondents' assimilation scores by degree of segregation in residential area and occupational level

| Assimilation score | Occupational level | | | |
| | Lower | | Higher | |
	Segregated areas	Non-segregated areas	Segregated areas	Non-segregated areas
Low	15 (45%)	1 (10%)	10 (21%)	1 (7%)
Medium	6 (18%)	3 (30%)	17 (36%)	2 (14%)
High	12 (36%)	6 (60%)	20 (43%)	11 (79%)
Total	33 (99%)	10 (100%)	47 (100%)	14 (100%)

G = .52, z = 1.64, p = .05   G = .61, z = 2.11, p < .05

Finally, a motivational variable was considered. We asked our subjects if they had wanted, when they first arrived, to become like the Australians. Though there are problems of recall in a question such as this, their responses seem to have validity. We use these responses as a control variable in Table 5. This table shows that if a person was originally ill-disposed to becoming assimilated, his place of residence is related to his present degree of assimilation. If there was a positive or neutral attitude towards assimilation, the difference between the segregated and non-segregated is small, though it is in the expected direction.

TABLE 5

Respondents' assimilation scores by degree of segregation in residential area and attitude towards acculturation at time of immigration

| Assimilation score | Attitude towards acculturation | | | |
| | Favourable or neutral | | Opposed | |
	Segregated areas	Non-segregated areas	Segregated areas	Non-segregated areas
Low	4 (15%)	1 (7%)	21 (39%)	1 (10%)
Medium	7 (27%)	3 (21%)	16 (30%)	2 (20%)
High	15 (58%)	10 (71%)	17 (32%)	7 (70%)
Total	26 (100%)	14 (99%)	54 (101%)	10 (100%)

G = .29, z = .74, p > .25   G = .64, z = 2.14, p < .05

To summarize, we have seen that Italian immigrants who live in areas of high Italian concentration are likely to be less assimilated than those who live in non-segregated areas. However, this relationship is clearly seen only for less recent immigrants, for older immigrants and for those who did not originally intend to become assimilated. Place of residence does not seem to matter as much if the respondent is a recent arrival, etc. Place of residence is significant regardless of occupation.

Discussion

It still remains for us to account for these findings. We would suggest that the original relationship results from a two-fold process. Selection is probably operating in that each type of area attracts persons of differing degree of assimilation. In addition, the area helps to 'cause' the degree of assimilation by the examples its residents provide and by the pressures they exert. The neighbours may not exert conscious pressures and their influence may be fairly small, but it should not be overlooked.

The variations in the relationship may be approached from a similar perspective. Different types of persons may show differential susceptibility to neighbourhood forces, and the selection factor may operate with differential strength for different kinds of people. To give one example: It seems probable, at least after the fact, that younger people will be less susceptible to the forces operating in segregated areas. Also, an un-assimilated young person may be less likely to go to a segregated area than is an unassimilated older person. These tendencies would produce Table 3. However, the validity of such speculations cannot be tested with the present data. A specification of the trends actually at work must await further research.

ACKNOWLEDGEMENT

This chapter is reproduced from *International Migration* Volume IV, No. 3/4, pp. 165-169, with the permission of the author.

REFERENCES

1 DUNCAN, OTIS DUDLEY and LIEBERSON, STANLEY. 'Ethnic Segregation and Assimilation', *American Journal of Sociology*, 64 (January, 1959), 364-374; LIEBERSON, STANLEY, *Ethnic Patterns in American Cities*, New York: Free Press of Glencoe, 1963

2 Previous publications of the study are: 'The Italians of Perth', *Westerly*, March, 1964, 67-69; 'Sources of Satisfaction and Assimilation Among Italian Immigrants', *Human Relations*, (Forth-coming); 'Factors Related to Immigrant Assimilation: The Early Post-Migration Situation', *Human Organization*, (Forth-coming).

3 'G' and a test of significance for it are described in FREEMAN, LINTON C., *Elementary Applied Statistics*, New York: John Wiley & Sons, 1965, pp. 79-88, 162-175. Since the direction of the association is predicted, a one-tailed test is used throughout this paper.

4 The high rate of assimilation for the respondents in the non-segregated areas cannot be explained in terms of differences between the areas in regard to average length of Australian residence. The non-segregated areas do contain a somewhat higher percentage of pre-war immigrants, but when these are removed from the analysis, G is reduced only slightly to .30. The highly segregated areas do not contain an excess of recent immigrants. However, the relatively low assimilation of the middle areas is probably due at least in part to the fact that they contain a relatively high proportion of newcomers.

10

CHINESE IN AUSTRALIA

A. Huck

It used to be commonly assumed that, given Australia's immigration policies, the non-European percentage of the population would continue to decline as it had done ever since the end of the gold rushes. In fact since 1947 the absolute number of Chinese in Australia has steadily increased.

Changes in the administrative rules governing the admittance of non-Europeans, and particularly changes in the procedures relating to naturalisation of non-Europeans or the registration of non-Europeans who are already British subjects, have allowed the permanent Chinese population to increase considerably in recent years. With the increase in the Australian born population included, the total of Chinese permanently resident has risen by about a thousand a year for a number of years. The total figure for mid-1969 can be estimated at about 23,000. (This figure does not include the large number of Chinese who are temporarily resident as students, a group which has amounted to another 9-10,000 in recent years.) There are some signs that the figure might now be tapering off somewhat, but the absolute increase and the small but distinct increase in the *proportion* of the whole population which is Chinese is undeniable. This proportion is still very small, about .15 per cent in 1961, .17 per cent in 1965, .18 per cent in 1969, but it represents a group which is larger than any other Asian group, and larger than many of the smaller groups of European settlers in Australia (Estonians, Finns, French, Swedish, Swiss, for example).[1]

What is known about this population? The general literature on the Overseas Chinese is not much help. In all the discussion about whether Australia is part of Asia, at least one set of literature is not in two minds: the writing on the Overseas Chinese rarely mentions Australia at all. The few exceptions to this are mostly in Chinese sources, but these are not up to date and tell us nothing about recent trends.

The figures used here are for Chinese permanently settled in the country. At any time the actual number is a great deal higher due to the large number of transitory people among the Chinese, visitors, seamen, and above all, students who may stay for several years but come and go in large numbers. This chapter will concentrate not on the transitory but on the permanent, who are made up of Chinese long settled here or born here, and a new wave of immigrants which has arrived since the second world war.

There has been much speculation about this new wave and it has often been assumed that they represent a very different migration stream from that which provided the prewar population. There are some differences among segments of the new arrivals, but a careful study of their known characteristics reveals many more similarities with the earlier population. Indeed it can be argued that what we have had is a limited revival, under changed conditions, of a pattern of migration with which we have been long familiar.

Most of the new arrivals have been born in China. They have come here via a stopping place like Hong Kong. Many of them have had family connections of some sort with Australia. It is not the case that in origin they are substantially different from their predecessors. In particular, it is not true that more than a small minority are Northerners; most of them still come from the traditional emigrant areas of South-East China, predominately from Kwangtung. In ordinary English usage, they are mostly Cantonese.[2]

Of the new arrivals who were born in China, over 90 per cent in Victoria and Queensland can be described as Cantonese, and over 80 per cent of those in New South Wales. Other Southerners account for an additional 10 per cent in New South Wales. The proportion of non-Southerners, people from Shanghai, the North and elsewhere account for from 3-8 per cent in different States.[3]

The following discussion of the assimilation of these people is not particularly technical. The term 'assimilation' itself is not a technical term; it is in fact notoriously ambiguous. It can be turned into a technical term by giving it an exact definition and sticking to it throughout a piece of scientific work. Such a usage, however, can have no impact beyond the circle of those willing to accept the definitional limitation. No precise definition is attempted here but one important distinction should be made. There is one sense of assimilation, which I think has often been current in Australia, which is the equivalent of absorption—the digestive metaphor it could be called. In this usage, the migrant is called upon to assimilate, to become totally absorbed in the host society and disappear from view. This makes sense if we are thinking of long term ethnic absorption in which intermarriage over a number of generations results in the disappearance of the minority ethnic group. This has occurred, for example, with many Chinese in Thailand. What is being discussed here, however, is the other sense, in which assimilation simply means *becoming similar or like the host society*.[4]

Similar in what respects? One can begin by describing some of the more easily measureable indices and then move to some that can be less easily quantified.

In the first place, where do the Chinese live? The answer is that Chinese may be found in every state and territory of the Commonwealth, but by far the greatest number live in New South Wales. Of these, by far the greatest number live in Sydney. The next most numerous group are to be found in Victoria and Melbourne. That is to say, the Chinese follow the Australian pattern of population concentration. They are a highly urbanised community, even more so than the Australian population in general, which is one of the most highly urbanised in the world. A smaller proportion of Chinese live in the country or in towns other than metropolitan cities than the general population.

Something like 70 per cent of all Chinese live in one or other of the State capital cities but it is important to realise that, within these, they do not typically live in 'China towns'. Melbourne and Sydney, in particular, have areas which can be identified as old centres of something like the China towns so well known in the United States, but these are no longer the chief centres of Chinese population even if they still have a concentration of Chinese businesses. The Chinese, like other Australians, have made the great trek to the suburbs and can be found widely distributed in both new and old suburban areas. (In a detailed study made with Michael Leigh in 1964, the changes of address of a large number of recent Chinese arriving in Melbourne were analysed: for every migrant who moved to the centre of Melbourne, three had moved out to the suburbs.)

Just as their residential patterns have changed, so have their occupations. Very few Chinese can now be found in the old occupations like market gardening which were common in the years after the gold rushes. Newer European immigrant groups have tended to take over this activity and the Chinese have moved on to other fields. Fruit and vegetable retailing still has some Chinese operation and there are important Chinese wholesale businesses, but on the whole there has been a marked shift away from primary industry. The greater gainer has been the cafe industry, and whereas Chinese restaurants were once limited to a few inner urban sites, they are now to be found in nearly every suburb of the large cities and in many smaller places as well. This has absorbed a good number of the less qualified population, but there has also been an increasing spread into white collar occupations. Levels of education of the Chinese population have been rising and they may now be found in many professional occupations, especially medicine. There are no very large Chinese businesses but many small scale ones. Generally, it can be said that the Chinese population has neither the commercially dominant position which many Chinese communities have in South-East Asia, nor the exploited poor immigrant position of the past.

It is not difficult to see some of the factors which have made it easier for the Chinese population to become more like the main population. Perhaps the most direct way of doing this is to point up the contrast with the position of the Chinese in many parts of South-East Asia. In Australia their numbers have been comparatively small. Even at the height of the gold rushes, the proportion of Chinese in the total population barely passed 3 per cent. They have never been dominant in the economy and have not been seen as an economic threat. They have suffered from very little legal discrimination. Discretionary immigration regulations have been used against them, but despite these, a Chinese population has existed in Australia since the 1840s and is now increasing again in size. The possibility of applying for citizenship after five years' residence removed the main discriminatory rule.

Chinese who have, in fact, settled in Australia have not had to face the problems of legal discrimination which have often intensified their feeling of separateness in countries in South-East Asia. The Australian society they have found themselves in has not presented insuperable problems of adaptation or understanding. Many Chinese migrants may have had rural backgrounds, but, typically, they have emerged from them some time ago; they have made the break to the city, first Chinese and then foreign. The large Australian city holds few mysteries for them. The Australian society they have found themselves in is overwhelmingly urban or suburban; it is materialistic and commercial, not obviously dominated by religious values or divided by religious barriers. In such a world Chinese immigrants can rapidly feel at home.

It is true, of course, that in the nineteenth century there was considerable anti-Chinese feeling in the country and there are memories of overt hostility, but nowadays the general atmosphere is quite different. Even in Darwin, where there has been some unease at the growth of Chinese holdings, most observers feel that the atmosphere is much more relaxed than before the war. In 1965, an Australian-born Chinese was elected President of the Northern Territory Legislative Council and in 1966 the same man became Mayor of Darwin.

The decline of ethnic organisations is, in itself, evidence of the changed situation: the old-type organisations tend to decline as the old hostilities decline; the comparative lack of ethnic organisation itself hastens the process of assimilation.

On paper, there are still many Chinese organisations of the type usual among overseas Chinese—district associations for people from the same areas, Chambers of Commerce, Chinese churches, Joss Houses—but when the actual level of activity is investigated, a fairly uniform condition is found. The district associations are considered old fashioned by the new generations. Bodies which served to unite, protect and succour people with the bond of common district origin are now social centres frequented mostly by the old. The surviving 'Joss Houses' are little used, even though one has recently been restored in Brisbane. Chinese schools have completely disappeared. Chinese language classes are occasionally conducted in churches and clubs for members who cannot read or write Chinese, but such activities are a very pale substitute for a real Chinese education, the lack of which always hastens the process of local assimilation.

The contrast with South-East Asia is perhaps most marked in the relative unimportance of the Chinese Chambers of Commerce. This key organisation in many parts of South-East Asia, in Melbourne has no permanent organisation or headquarters, and in Sydney no longer performs many of the co-operative functions it once had.

The Chinese Masonic Societies provide good examples of bodies which have lost their original point. They are descended from anti-Manchu secret societies sometimes known in English as Triad societies. It is difficult to separate fact and fiction in their histories but they certainly played some part in the overthrow of the Ch'ing dynasty. Unsuccessful rebellions in the nineteenth century led to many Triad members fleeing abroad to escape the retribution of the Ch'ing. Many went to the goldfields of America and Australia, while others went to the South Seas and Malaya. Wherever they went they remained true to the Society and set up new lodges. Sun Yat-sen is supposed to have been a Triad official and to have used their overseas organisations in his revolutionary activities. Many branches declined into more or less criminal organisations. Extortions practised in the coolie trade, which led to rioting in Hong Kong in 1886, have been charged to them. The boarding houses where the coolies stayed prior to shipment overseas were mainly controlled by Triad elements, and their owners generally acted as agents obtaining passages etc. for their guests. Opportunities for racketeering were plentiful. The societies in Australia found little scope for their programme of overthrowing the Ch'ing and restoring the Ming. As early as 1905, one observer found them 'submerged in a sea of petty local affairs'.[5] They took on the respectable

English title of Chinese Masonic Society which completely misled Lyng in his 1927 work 'Non-Britishers in Australia'. He assumed that the spread of 'Chinese branches of the Freemasonry order' was evidence of 'westernising influences' at work. In fact, members of these associations included many of the least assimilated of the old immigrants. Nowadays members apparently devote themselves to feasting, gambling and drinking without in any way disturbing the public peace. Their substantial building in Melbourne still bears, however, the mystic characters 'Hung Men' over its entrance, witness to the organisation's turbulent secret past.

Not all societies are moribund. The Melbourne Sze Yap Society, for instance, a long established association of the dominant Melbourne group, has realised that its old central city properties have greatly increased in value and, under the stimulus of a young architect, has built itself a new headquarters on one of its old sites. The Kong Chew Society has converted a North Melbourne building to house a few retired old men who are in need of a home.

The old societies, however, have mostly lost their mutual help functions and are seen by many Chinese as no longer serving any useful purpose. The associations which do flourish to some extent are more simply social. Brisbane has an active Chinese social centre and in Melbourne the Young Chinese League organises dances, an annual ball, tennis and football for members who can claim Chinese or part Chinese descent, even if the part be only one sixteenth. To visiting Chinese students it appears a very Australian organisation.

Chinese churches do exist in the big cities but their congregations are small (typically 25 to 50 for a service in Cantonese or English or both). One exception is the Sydney Presbyterian Church in Crown Street, where the congregation might number 250 and many Swatow Presbyterians are active. Increasingly, though, Chinese who are Christians take part in the activities of their ordinary local church. The Catholics in particular strive to integrate their members into their local parish.

Community politics is now distinctly muted. Whereas, at the turn of the century, a lively vernacular press discussed the great events of the day in China and the issues of Empire versus Republic, reform and revolution were hotly debated, there is now no Chinese press in Australia and few willing to engage in open debate on current matters of controversy. The political context is, of course, very different. Fifty years ago few Australians knew or cared about what was going on in China; today it is difficult to escape noticing something about it, however distant international politics are felt to be.

The formal position of the Australian government is not without ambiguity. It does not recognise the People's Republic but permits extensive trade with it; it received diplomatic and consular officials from the Republic of China but, for eighteen years until 1967, sent none in return. Many Chinese who, in other contexts, would have been regarded as 'influentials', in this situation retire into private life and say nothing. The existing branches of the Kuomintang no longer have the large following they had when they were a centre of patriotic anti-Japanese organisation. On the other hand, few who sympathise with the mainland government are prepared to engage in open activity in support of it. Those who are not yet naturalised have every reason not to do so; if they come to the attention of the Australian Security Organisation they jeopardise their chances of becoming full citizens. This is clearly understood by the organisers of one Sydney organisation sympathetic to the People's Republic; they do not expect their numbers to flourish.

Under these conditions it is impossible to obtain a reliable index of the real international political sympathies of the disparate groups which make up the different Chinese communities. There are many convinced anti-Communists, some staunch Nationalist supporters, some Communist sympathisers: probably the great majority genuinely feel that these are times in which, more than usually so, it is a good idea not to be politically involved.

To my knowledge there has only been one detailed attempt at studying the politics of Chinese in Australia. This was a survey which the Department of Political Science in Melbourne University sponsored in 1964. In this enquiry, the occasion of the state election in Victoria was used to question a sample of Melbourne voters who were Chinese and a matched sample of their non-Chinese neighbours. (The details of this are reported in *The Chinese in Australia*, Chapter 3.) There were four groups of Chinese voters who could be distinguished:—

   (i) A group of voters in a working class area who were citizens by naturalisation or registration.
   (ii) A group of Australian-born voters in the same area.
   (iii) A group of voters in a middle class area who were citizens by naturalisation or registration.
   (iv) A group of Australian-born voters in the same area.

The general picture of these Chinese voters which emerged was of people either more detached from politics or more conservative than their neighbours. Within this framework, the Australian-born groups [(ii) and (iv)] came closer to the local expectations of political behaviour, that is, half those in the working class area intended to vote Labor and more than half those in the middle class area expected to vote Liberal.

It would be wrong to suggest that there are no difficulties in the way of the assimilation of Chinese in Australia. There will clearly be a great deal of individual variation in the approach of the Chinese migrant to the country: for some it has been a refuge reluctantly chosen, for some a non-political haven, for some the promised land. We need to know a great deal more about particular family histories and individual life histories before we can generalise further. We know very little of the relations between generations, of methods of child rearing and political socialisation. The problems facing first generation migrants are obviously different from the problems facing their grandchildren.

In general, though, it can be argued that there is very little basis for the widespread belief that some special characteristics of the Chinese make them less capable than others of attaching themselves to a new country, in spite of the problems of intermarriage which often loom large in these discussions. In the past, many marriages between Australians and Chinese have occurred and there are considerable numbers of people in the country of part-Chinese descent. Attitudes opposed to intermarriage are nevertheless widespread. Indeed, they seem to be similar among the Chinese and the non-Chinese. Miss Lee Siew-eng, in a study of the Sydney Chinese, found about 64 per cent of them opposed to intermarriage. From a study of Australian attitudes carried out in the same year as the electoral study mentioned above, it can be estimated that about 69 per cent of the general Australian population would oppose intermarriage. If opposition to Asian immigration continues to decline, so, probably, will opposition to intermarriage, as the two often seem closely connected. Counter-pressures favouring intermarriage can be expected to increase in the long run but there is nothing inevitable about such a process. In the very unlikely event of a very large Chinese population building up in Australia, it is conceivable that attitudes might harden on both sides and the process of integration might be slowed down.

Even if the intermarriage rate, among newcomers especially, remains low, it does not follow that Chinese in considerable numbers cannot, in the official phrase, be 'generally integrated'. The increases in recent years have not been accompanied by any social friction and have, indeed, attracted very little attention. The process of assimilation continues, on the whole, smoothly and uneventfully.

REFERENCES

1 For details and for problems in the figures, see Huck, Arthur; *The Chinese in Australia*, Longmans, 1968, Chapter 1. I would estimate the total of Chinese permanently settled in Australia in 1969 as follows:

(a)	Australian born	9,826
(b)	Naturalised	6,551
(c)	Aliens registered	4,705
(d)	Granted citizenship by registration	1,907

Total 22,989

The source for (a) is as in Huck, *op. cit.*, Chapter 1. For (b) and (c) Department of Immigration, *Australian Immigration Consolidated Statistics*, No. 3, 1969, has been used. For (d), (b) plus (c) has been subtracted from the figure given in *Consolidated Statistics* for 'permanent and long-term arrivals'. This figure is consistent with earlier estimates of those granted citizenship by registration.

2 For a discussion of the ambiguities of this term, see Huck, *op cit.*, pp. 15-16.

3 See Huck, *op. cit.* Table VII.

4 For a comprehensive scholarly discussion of the notion of assimilation, acculturation and related topics, see the introductory article by Charles A. Price in C. A. Price (Ed.): *Australian Immigration, A Bibliography and Digest*, Canberra, 1966. Section P of the Bibliography deals with 'White Australia': Restrictive Immigration Policy and Non-Europeans. Dr. Price is working on a large study of non-European migration to Australia, New Zealand, British Columbia and California. This history of Chinese migration will play a large part in this work.
Within the Department of Demography, Australian National University, Mr. C. Y. Choi is working on a study of the assimilation of the Chinese in Melbourne.
See also Huck, Arthur. *The Chinese in Australia*, Longmans, 1968.
Inglis, C. B.: *The Darwin Chinese: A Study in Assimilation*, M.A. thesis in Sociology, Australian National University, 1967.
Lee, Siew Eng. *The Ecology of the Sydney Chinese*, B.A. Hons. thesis, Department of Geography, University of Sydney, 1963.

THE INTELLECTUAL FOUNDATION

11

RACISM AND AUSTRALIAN LITERATURE

H. O. McQueen

A marked variety of Australian Humour is the ill-treatment of Chinamen and the 'barracking' of afflicted persons. To have assaulted a Mongolian, stoned him, knocked him in the gutter, kicked him, and generally half-killed him, after probably having rifled his fruit cases, is the finest fun in the repertoire of the young Australian. It is so fine that it only has to be cleverly rendered in verse to greatly amuse the Old Australian, too.
—*Bernard O'Dowd,* 1897

It is over a decade since Bernard Smith[1] published his account of the change in European attitudes towards Australasia and its indigenous inhabitants. Partly through an examination of paintings and sketches, Smith demonstrated the replacement of a Rousseauian 'noble savage' by the harsh and degraded 'comic savage'. He thereby opened up the problems associated with the interpenetration of imperial expansion, racial notions and the creative arts. That this beginning has not been followed through into other areas such as fiction, poetry and film-making is indicated in the silence upon, or indeed the virtual denial of, the importance of racial themes in Australian life. In the brief space available here, it will be impossible to do more than point to some broad areas for research on the cultural responses to Australia's truly fateful meridian in the Anglo-Saxon-British-American-Empire sequence.

In his book, *Race and Racism*, Pierre L. van den Berghe identifies three main factors in the genesis of Western racism. Although he rightly rejects 'any simple, direct causal relationship', the impact of his analysis firmly established the consequence of economic exploitation in race prejudice. European settlement in Australia presented a conflict over land rights that was eventually resolved ideologically by the expulsion of the Aborigines from the human race and by the development of a *Herrenvolk* democracy in Australia. The physical confrontation on the expanding frontier became a stock-in-trade of nineteenth-century novelists dealing with Australia. As well as a bushfire, a flood and a lost child, there had to be an attack by Aborigines followed by a punitive expedition; Henry Kingsley's *The Recollections of Geoffrey Hamlyn* (1859) contains a typical example. Significantly, the 1928 film *History of White Australia* opens with just such an incident before proceeding to its main theme, the riots at *Lambing Flat*: the connection between fighting the blacks to gain the land and fighting the yellow hordes to retain it is quite explicit.

European penetration of the outback persisted well into the twentieth century, especially in the Northern Territory which is the setting for two of Australia's most important race novels. Mrs. Aneas Gunn's *We of the Never-Never* was first published in 1908 and, according to H. M. Green, had sold over three hundred thousand copies by 1945. There is not an unkind word about the Aborigines in Mrs. Gunn's vocabulary. There is just unadulterated maternalism. The blacks (and the Chinese) are alternatively comic, sly, affectionate, loyal and useful—indeed somewhere between children and dogs whom the 'missus' learns to manage because she is genuinely fond of them. The hundreds of thousands of Australian children who read her book in school would not have been troubled by their country's treatment of its native people. She refers to killings and theft by the whites, but suggests that these occurred before the appearance of the Law. *We of the Never-Never* provided a popular ideological foundation for the official policies of protection and preservation. What else could one do with such pets?

Certainly Mrs. Gunns' readers would have learnt little of the situation chronicled in Xavier Herbert's *Capricornia* (1937). The title of its first chapter, 'The Coming of the Dingoes', describes the arrival of the first whites and gives a good indication of Herbert's attitude and style. He is acutely aware of the frontier situation facing men 'so well equipped with lethal weapons and belief in the decency of their purpose as Anglo-Saxon builders of Empire'. There was little opportunity to develop an ideological gloss for the expropriation of these indigenes whose fierce resistance became the sufficient justification for their extermination. *Capricornia* makes it clear that race hatreds were immanent in the very act of settlement even if their articulation only appeared later. European invasion of Australia in 1788 brought its full complement of ideological reservists.

Armed invasions of Australia were later to acquire a different racial aspect and to produce their own literary genre of the Japanese horde sweeping down to rape our wives and eat our children. A good deal of this pre-1914 invason literature appeared in *The Bulletin* and its monthly companion *Lone Hand*. C. H. Kirmess's novel *The Australian Crisis* (1909) was serialised in *The Bulletin* and the continuing message of this invasion literature is epitomised in its concluding sentence: '*Australia is the precious front buckle in the white girdle of power and progress encircling the globe*'. Poets such as Bernard O'Dowd and Arthur Adams wrote of the need 'To guard the future from exotic blight' and pleaded for '*One Hour—to Arm*' since:—

> Along the frontier of our North
> The Yellow lightning shudders forth;

Henry Lawson played Cassandra with Asian invasions threats as in 'The Old, Old Story'—:

> Beware of the East, O Christian, for the sake of your fairest
>   and best;
> It is written, and written, remembered, *that the tide of invasion*
>   *goes West.*

Australia's film industry was not idle, and, in 1913, Raymond Longford directed *Australia Calls* in which twenty thousand Japanese invade New South Wales while the populace are on the beach or at the races.[2]

With the fall of Singapore, Australia passed from being the 'FRONT BUCKLE' of the British Empire to become the launching pad for United States imperialism's military push against its Japanese rival. The dark forebodings of half-a-century were fulfilled when Asian hordes swept

over New Guinea and bombed Darwin. In the midst of this race-war its
literary precursors were not forgotten:—

> That reddish veil o'er the face
> of nigh-hag East is drawn . . .
> Flames new disaster for the race?
> Or can it be the dawn?

'So wrote Bernard O'Dowd', said John Curtin. 'I see 1942 as a year in
which we will know the answer.'

Examination of the impact of the war on racial attitudes has not
begun but when it is, works such as Neville Shute's *A Town Like Alice*
and Lawson Glassop's *The Rats in New Guinea,* as well as straight
forward autobiographical accounts like Rohan Rivett's *Behind Bamboo*
should occupy a deal of attention. In the Foreword to the 1955 edition of
The Naked Island, Russell Braddon explains that 'It was written to tell
the world what sort of people the Japanese can be. It was written to
explain what they did during the war and what they might well do again'.
By 1958 when a sequel, *End of a Hate,* appeared Braddon had modified
his views:—

> 'Once I hated anyone who was Japanese simply because he came
> from Japan. Now I can no longer hate individuals. But I can still
> hate their culture . . . and I can still fear the logical outcome of
> their intense and fanatic nationalism . . . .'

It will be necessary to trace out the evolution of this response up to where
Kenneth Harrison could have *The Brave Japanese* published in 1966.
Equally important will be an investigation of the ways in which racism
has been subsumed into the legitimacy of anti-communism as in Vietnam.

Some indication of the resilience of racial imagery from the first
Pacific war can be gauged from a recent anti-Vietnam poem in the
Communist Party's paper *Tribune* (16 December 1970). The authoress
compares the war against Japan with the war in Vietnam and supports
the former because:—

> . . . then a yellow dragon clawed
> The naked shoulders of our shores;

Apart from the general point, these lines are interesting for their revival
of the Henry Lawson-Norman Lindsay imagery of Australian maiden-
hood under assault from bestial Asia. The preponderance of autobiographical over fictional accounts of Japanese prisoner-of-war camps results
from the inability of Australian authors to create Japanese guards who are
convincing characters. Either the guards lack all semblance of human
status or they are seen as the universal soldier with a wife and kids at
home, thus devoid of any Japanese content whatsoever.

Imperial chauvinism did not necessarily demand explicit denigra-
tion of non-Europeans. It could just as easily be expressed in the affirmation of the positive virtues of white, especially Anglo-Saxon, culture,
There are traces of this in the music of Percy Grainger, that paradoxically Australian-cosmopolitan; for instance his *Warrior's* suite which Roger
Covell finds suitable for a 'muscular' 'saga of particularly North European
temperament'. Subsequent pride in what O'Dowd described as the 'coming
Sun-God's Race' dominates the ballet *The Display.* In figurative drawings
it is to be found in the work of Norman Lindsay and Hugh McCrae;
Lindsay's cartoons often confronted Siegfried-style males and their
fulsome virgins with the vile oriental. Naked Anzacs, like so many anti-

podean Hectors, peopled the canvasses of the war artists after 1915. In 1931, the art critic J. S. MacDonald declared in praise of Arthur Streeton: 'If we choose we can yet be the elect of the world, the last of the pastoralists, the thoroughbred Aryans in all their nobility . . . For we are not only a nation, but a race, and both occupy a particular territory and spring from a specific soil.'

The film, *Birth of White Australia* laid great stress on the British origins of White Australia and the importance of the British race. This was underlined even more in the official New South Wales documentary, *A Nation is Built* (1938) which celebrated the 150 years of British occupation and described Sydney as 'the second white city of the Empire'. The film opens by telling the audience that Australia is a new 'anglo-Saxon empire under the Southern Cross' and ends with the singing of 'God who made thee mighty'. Identification with the higher races thus proceeded in many forms: from a submergence within the Empire to the proclamation of Australia as the final bastion and/or noblest development of the race; from accepting a tradition dating back to Athens or even Wodin, to restricting their lineage to British squires. But whatever its characteristics, a privileged position for White Australia remained its foundation.

Because of its contributions of wool and gold, nineteenth-century Australia occupied an economically advantageous position in the world capitalist system from which the labouring classes benefited, since there was also a chronic labour shortage in the colonies.[3] There can no no doubting the importance of economic competition from coloureds as a factor contributing to the intensity of anti-Asian feeling in Australia. Yet to suppose that occasional attempts to lower wages by introducing Asians 'caused' racism in Australia, would be to misunderstand totally its historic experience. Rather it was an imperial vision of a British arcady on Austral's shores that inhibited employers from attempting to increase their share of the surplus value by indenturing Asians. Where the natural increase in surplus value was small, however, as in the sugar industry, they were obliged to introduce kanakas. Chinese did come for gold and sometimes stayed to work in the pastoral industry, which absorbed a good deal of capital in the 1870s and 1880s, so that there was some necessity to keep wages down.

The activities of the Chinamen who came in the gold rushes and stayed to become market-gardeners or bush-workers permeated much Australian culture. Henry Handel Richardson's *Australia Felix* (1917) reproduces the attitudes of the diggers in Victoria and takes her account into areas of psychological fear of Chinamen in small children. In the film *History of White Australia,* the Chinese are pictured as possessing every conceivable vice. The print held in the National Library has been put together from the various reels without editing, so that its chronology is entirely absent. The resultant surrealist montage only adds to the impact of the racism which is demonstrated as Chinamen proceed to wash in the drinking water, attack a white girl, rob tents and burn down the dance hall.

Joseph Furphy's *Such is Life* (written 1897, published 1903) contains a number of derogatory remarks about Chinamen (and even more vicious comments on Aborigines) as well as a couple of long accounts of their nefarious exploits. Despite continuing references to 'Yellow agonies' and 'leprous Mongolians', Furphy treats the Chinese he encounters with a degree of amused detachment, although he makes it clear that the rest of his company take a harsher line. Also set in the Riverina was Price Warung's 'The Last of the Wombat Barge' which appeared in *The Bulletin*, 20 December 1890. It deals with Captain Kingsley who employs a Chinese crew comprising of 'Ah Fats, Ah Leans and Moy Sins', and who becomes so wealthy from the money he saves on their wages that he takes a holiday to Melbourne where his appearance on the beach reveals that he has leprosy. In case the reader has missed the moral, Warung concludes that 'When a white man clutches poles, and ropes, and fenders after Chinese paws had slimed over them, what could he expect but that some of the slime would stick?'

This connection between leprosy and Chinese labour was made in 'Banjo' Paterson's *Travelling Down the Castlereagh*:

'We shear non-union here' says he. 'I call it scab', says I,
I looked along the shearing-board before I turned to go,
There was eight or ten dashed Chinamen a-shearing in a row,
So its shift, boys shift! There wasn't the slightest doubt
It's time to make a shift with the leprosy about.

In one of the earliest urban novels of Australian life, Louis Stone's *Jonah* (1911), the combination of economic competition and disease appears when we are told that one of the characters, Chook, views the Chinese Market-gardeners as 'the scum of the earth, less than human, taking the bread out of his mouth, selling cheaply because they lived like vermin . . .'.

Chinamen were not perceived initially as low-wage workers, and only afterwards as dirty and diseased. From their arrival, they presented a total picture in which the parts complemented each other. One of these parts remains to be examined—sexual phobias and fantasies. The imbalance of the sexes in frontier Australia resulted in prostitution and homo-sexuality;[4] the alternative being 'Black Velvet', of which Herbert's *Capricornia* gives the most straightforward account:—

'Mark was trying to excuse himself for seeing beauty in a creature of a type he had been taught to look upon as a travesty of normal humanity.'

Eventually Mark chose a young Aborigine girl until 'he found (she) was with child. He sent her away, refusing to believe that the child was his . . .'.

The ballad 'Sam Holt', which was first published in *The Bulletin* on 26 March 1881, gives a popular picture:—

Oh! don't you remember Black Alice, Sam Holt—
Black Alice so dusky and dark—
That Warrego gin with a straw through her nose,
and teeth like a Moreton Bay shark;
The villainous sheep-wash tobacco she smoked . . .

The psychological inhibitions which underlay the unsatisfactory nature of interracial sexual relations are presented in Katherine Susannah Prichard's *Coonardoo* (1929) where Hugh Watt destroys himself because of the revulsion he experiences after his liaison with Coonardoo.

The essentially furtive and harsh nature of these sexual encounters should be considered in examining the idealised conception of white women that arises in the literature of the outback and in the white males' fear that coloureds, both Aborigines and Chinese, had little in their minds other than the rape of white women. It would be difficult to imagine a more explicit statement of the interplay of racial and sexual fantasies than Lawson's:—

> I see the stricken city fall . . .
> The pure girl to the leper's kiss—
> God, give us faith, for Christ's own sake,
> To kill our womankind ere this.
>
> ('To Be Amused')

The rape scene in the film *Jedda* (1955) could remain uncensored because those involved were black, for whom such behaviour was natural rather than immoral. Indeed the animalism which rape evokes in the popular consciousness could well have made the sequence highly moralistic in its appeal.

With the beginning of imperialism's defeat in the first world war, there came a change of attitudes towards coloured people, who were refusing to be ignored or over-ruled. This penetrated into Australia and found expression in the novels of Prichard and Herbert as well as Vance Palmer's *The Man Hamilton* (1928). But there still has not been a fully successful presentation of a full-blood in the fiction of a white novelist. Eleanor Dark comes close with Bennelong in *The Timeless Land* (1944) but the circumstances which make this possible are indicative of the difficulties involved. Bennelong is an historical figure from whose life Mrs. Dark could draw; the novel is set in the earliest days of settlement when the 'noble savage' concept retained influence over the colony's rulers; moreover, this is Bennelong's time and place. The result is a slightly idealised figure whose fate is nonetheless sealed as these special conditions diminish.

Alf Dubbo in Patrick White's *Riders in the Chariot* (1961) is only incidentally an aborigine whose racial origins are used as another example of being an outsider. At no point does Alf become a whole man, because he is detached from his time and his place by White's 'algebraic symbolism'. This puppet quality is equally apparent in Peter Mathers' riotously inventive *Trap* (1966).

For all his empathy with Aborigines, Donald Stuart's principal concern in *The Driven* (1961) and *Yaralie* (1962) is to show the virtues of racial mixing:—

> '. . . a generation of people with their roots in the country, people who have all the forward-thrusting attributes of the European and the wise love of the country the old blackfellow always had . . . they'll be the real people of the Nor-West.'

By accepting this as his final solution to racial conflict, Stuart denies himself the chance of writing of Aborigines as equal yet different human beings. He has had to avoid this literary problem because its resolution in Australian social practice remains remote.[5]

No matter how inadequate one considers the achievements of Australian novelists, their record of dealing with the Aborigine as an important theme in Australian life is in every way more honourable than that of the historians who, as Professor Stanner pointed out in *After the Dreaming*, have largely ignored them. Significantly, it has been that most literary of historians, Manning Clark, who has done most to restore the Aborigines to their place in the post-1788 history of Australia.

Another feature of the era of imperialist defeat has been the emergence of Aboriginal authors. The first of these needed to tell their stories through the skill of Europeans, as in Douglas Lockwood's *I the Aboriginal* (1962). More recently there have been Colin Johnston's *Wild Cat Falling* (1965) and Kath Walker's verse (1964 and 1966); both of whom are only part-Aboriginal. Unlike the people of Papua and New Guinea, the Australian indigenes have still not been permitted to speak in their own voice, to create their own written culture. It would be unwise therefore to be unduly optimistic about the state of racism in Australian culture in both senses of the word—the arts and the life-style. Some indication of the subtler persistance of racist notions can be obtained from an examination of two post-1950 examples.

As the crowning achievement of Australia's film making, *Jedda* demands detailed analysis. Despite the initial intrusiveness of a narrator, which is foreign to the dictates of a visual medium, *Jedda* quickly encompasses this distraction as it unfolds its genuinely Aristotlean dimensions. The station blacks provide an inarticulate chorus who exert their strength through the rival life-style they offer. To the European audience they are often figures of disgust and fun: one fat old gin puts a clean dress on over a dirty one. *Jedda's* white foster parents represent opposing views on the best treatment for the Aborigines. The wife believes that they *ought* to be changed—civilised—for their own good and presents a typically do-gooder mentality. The husband disagrees and, within the range of views which the film offers, has the best outlook, as he accepts the validity of tribal life, encourages walk-abouts to retain their pride of race and deprecates the fringe-dwellers.

Throughout the film, Jedda is pictured as innately non-white in her emotions and desires. When she rejects shoes and schooling, this is attributed to her 'heart being with her own people' rather than to the cross-cultural refusal of children to be restricted. In other words, a normal human attribute is invested with special racial connotations. She is taught the piano but as she plays 'In An English Country Garden', the primitive urges of her subconscious well up until the delicate melody has been transposed into a raucous tribal chant.

Enter Prometheus. A superb wild fella comes to the station. Jedda is fascinated by his physical and psychological power and he eventually sings her to his fire. But her white upbringing won't permit her to run away with him, so he takes her by force. There is no taboo—white, black or natural—that he will not break. He is the complete realisation of Camus's definition of 'man' as that force who denies Gods and defies dictators. He has escaped from prison in Darwin where he was being held for murder; armed only with a small knife he kills a crocodile; finally he defies his tribal elders for which he is sung to death. At first he rejects this as blackfellas' rubbish, but eventually succumbs and falls to his death dragging Jedda with him. The film ends with the narrator suggesting that her death was a just punishment for attempting to go against her black nature: the inelectable fate of the Greeks has become racial. Yet within this racist context, Robert Tudawalli, who played the wild fella, has created the only genuine Aboriginal human being in the entire artistic output of Australia.

Popular fiction, such as the detective novels of Arthur Upfield, can reveal two areas of information. They provide positive information of what racial ideas were receiving re-inforcement through mass culture; and negatively they show which ideas were inoffensive, that is, constituted the conventional wisdom on race. Upfield's *The Will of the Tribe* (1962) fulfils both these criteria. The half-caste Inspector Napoleon Bonaparte is described as 'the man who could think like an Aborigine and reason like a white man'. He says of himself, 'I am only half-black, and yet I too have felt the pull towards my mother's race. It's tremendously powerful, as its effects on so many promising Aborigine scholars witness.' The pre-human implications of this are spelt out when Bony says to a full-blood—'An affinity with the animal. You all have that. Even I.'

Australia's arts no longer proclaim doctrines of race-war and there are instances of real insight and some indication of expression by Aborigines themselves. But the gaps remain the dominant aspects: neither Aborigine nor European has been able to write of an Aborigine in a way that does not demean his racial integrity or diminish his humanity. To this extent, literature remains a barometer of Australian society.

REFERENCES

1 SMITH, BERNARD. *European Vision in the South Pacific, 1788-1850*, Oxford University Press, Oxford, 1960; the only exceptions to this failure have been PEARSON, W. H., *Henry Lawson Among Maoris*, A.N.U. Canberra, 1968; and RICHARDSON, B. E., 'The Aborigine in Fiction: A Survey of Attitudes Since 1900', *Armidale and District Historical Society Journal and Proceedings*, November 1969.

2 Many more instances of this kind are to be found in my *A New Britannia*, Penguin, Melbourne, 1970.

3 McFARLANE, BRUCE. 'Australia's Role in World Capitalism', PLAYFORD, JOHN and KIRSNER, DOUG (Eds.), *Australian Capitalist Society*, Penguin, Melbourne, 1971

4 In *Scribblings of an Idle Mind*, Lansdowne, Melbourne, 1966, Norman Lindsay denies the capacity for artistic fulfilment to negroes and homosexuals, pp. 131 and 50-53.

5 The Jindyworobaks advocated intellectual miscegenation.

12

RACISM AND THE PRESS

R. V. Hall

'Have they not waged unprovoked war against their fellow subjects and by doing so have they not violated the law? . . . Among the "Liberals" there is one law for the black and one for white British subjects . . . The fact is it will come to this —that the settlers, unless they witness a disposition to protect them (and that efficiently) against the aggressions of black British subjects, will take the matter into their own hands and pursue savage robbers and murderers as they would the wild beasts of the forest. And if any such calamity should unhappily come to pass, the enterprising settlers who braved the dangers of the Australian wilds will plead they were driven to extremities by the supineness or impotence of "Liberal" governments whose sympathies and charities were exclusively excited by the possessors of an Ethiopian visage.'

—Sydney Herald editorial, 21 June 1838

The editorial writer above was commenting on the murder of several squatters at Faithful Creek in Southern New South Wales, near what is now Benalla in Victoria, earlier that year. But even as he wrote, investigation was under way into an incident at Myall Creek, near the site of Inverell, which was to show that at least some residents of New South Wales needed little incitement to pursue Aborigines 'as they would the wild beasts of the forest'. On 9 June, twelve station-hands employed at Myall Creek Station massacred twenty-eight blacks. The murderers were doubtless partly inflamed by the death of five shepherds and hut-keepers in the Gwydir region since November 1837, but it is obvious that they would have been just as much influenced by the general climate of grievance expressed in the columns of the *Sydney Herald*. Some of them may have even read the indignant sarcasm of the *Herald* on 21 May when it noted that a police posse had been despatched after the murderers of the overlanders at Faithful Creek, with the comment: 'No killing of blacks however is to be allowed—they are to be treated as Her Majesty's subjects!'

The irony in the *Herald* of the time, however, was unconscious. On 28 May, it argued in favour of colonising New Zealand 'to check the spread of evil, to promote the spread of civilisation and Christianity, to open a field for British enterprise of every kind and to lay the foundation of a happy people not struggling up unassisted and unalone from barbarism to civilisation'.

The Myall Creek massacre, with its aftermath of arrests, trials and the ultimate execution of seven of the twelve station-hands, provided one of the few occasions in Australian history where white men were brought to justice for the murder of Aborigines. It also polarised the provincial white community. The *Herald* was bitterly against the trial while its rivals, the *Monitor* and *The Australian,* were for it. As was so often the case in British colonial history, the impetus for justice came from the representatives of Westminster and the countervailing pressure from settlers who invoked the cry of liberty for themselves. The Liberals in this case were Governor Gipps and his Attorney General, John Plunkett. Their crime was to bring the white man to trial and the *Herald* never forgave them. Not only that, they also attempted to implement the will of the House of Commons Select Committee on Aborigines of 1837 by the appointment of Protectors of Aborigines. The *Herald* knew what to say about that:—

> 'Judging from the outrages which for a long time past have been committed by the aborigines on Settlers, we should have thought the European colonists not the aborigines required "Protectors" ... not very many days ago we conversed with a gentleman who by permission of the Government has a sheep and cattle station somewhat beyond the boundaries of this colony ... he was right when he declared that he would shoot them as he would wild beasts, if he detected them spearing or carrying off his sheep or cattle.'

The point that it was justifiable to kill for an attack on property alone recurs often. Nothing is more blatant in the apologists for the murder of Aborigines than their failure to draw any distinction between an attack on a person or a sheep. As the last half of 1838 passed and the day of the trial of the twelve approached, the *Herald* continued its vehement language against Aborigines. On 8 October it countered a suggestion that some of the half-cast remnant of the Tasmanians should be settled near Albury with: 'We have too many of the murderous wretches about us already ... the whole gang of black animals, etc. ...'. On 19 October, it deplored the Royal Navy's failure to carry out punitive expeditions against Pacific Islanders. France, it said, 'would exterminate the murderous wretches and laugh at the hypocrites'. But on 14 November, on the eve of the trial of the white men from Myall Creek, the Sydney *Thunderer* surpassed itself with:—

> 'Protect the white settler and his wife from the filthy, brutal cannibals of New Holland. We say to the colonists, since the Government makes inadequate exertion to protect you, protect yourselves; and if the ferocious savages endeavour to plunder or destroy your property, or to murder yourselves, your families or your servants, do them as *you would do to any white robbers or murderers*—SHOOT THEM DEAD.'

It was a generous touch to include servants, most of whom were white robbers or murderers from old England where, presumably, there had not been enough rifles to hand at the time of their crimes. At least some of the jury read the *Herald,* because the twelve men were acquitted. However the Government rearrested seven and tried them on a differently worded charge. The *Herald* was furious, the more so because it had been accused of contempt of court. It argued that the law was unfair to whites because there had been fourteen white deaths at the hands of Aborigines since 1835, without the execution of a single indigene. After the seven were found guilty and executed and the fate of the others was in doubt, the *Herald* returned to argue on the value of Aboriginal testimony: 'Will any rational jury pay greater attention to it than they would to a black cockatoo . . . the possibility for white men's lives being frittered away on the statements (partial as they must be) of a young black savage possessing no more idea of ulterior responsibility—whatever he may be taught to *say*—than a baboon'. The *Herald* won. The others were never brought to trial.

This editorial outburst was important for more than local reasons. 1837 and 1838 were marked by frequent clashes between white and black. Mobs of cattle and sheep were moving south into Victoria and on to South Australia. To the north, settlement was extending past the Hunter Valley into New England and on to the Gwydir. This movement was producing a fluid frontier situation which Professor Rowley has described in *The Destruction of Aboriginal Society*. A brutalised convict class who provided the hut-keepers and shepherds of the new stations were not the men to treat anyone as brothers, let alone the black men. But more importantly for any study of the press and racism, it was at times such as this that the press noted the presence of the older inhabitants of Australia at all. The contempt of white Australians for Aborigines in the nineteenth century was so great, and their own superiority so obvious, that they hardly needed the reassurance of the pseudo-science so popular in the United States to prove that the coloured races were inferior. In July 1861, to take one example, the *Argus*, accounted a radical paper, reported a lecture by The Hon. William Hull who said of the Aborigines: 'One fact was beyond doubt, that they were very low in moral condition and intellectual power'.

There had been, at one time, optimism for the future of the Aborigines. Only a generation after the first settlement, the *Sydney Gazette* could still hope for good results from the benevolent school at Parramatta where Aboriginal children were learning the gentler pursuits of civilisation. In 1815, commenting on the annual gathering of Aborigines at Parramatta where Governor Macquarie customarily met the tribes to exhort them to improvement, the *Gazette* allowed itself a little breast-beating on the depressed state of the old Australian:—

> 'Whence have these evils originated, but in the clearing of the immense forests which formerly abounded and the wild animals they bred upon This admission certainly gives them claim on the British settler.'

But the Parramatta educational experiment failed. By January 1824, the *Gazette* was carrying a letter from 'Philanthropist', a writer, in fact, sympathetic to the Aborigines, in which he said of the group around Parramatta: 'They are still barbarians of the most unenlightened kind'. However 'Philanthropist' did go on to make a plea for the appointment of a special conciliator and stated that such a man could 'go about with perfect safety . . . from Lake Bathurst or the Five Islands to the Hunter Valley or Port Stephens, a journey of some 300 miles or so . . .'. His optimism was misplaced. Within eight months, martial law had been declared west of the Blue Mountains and the *Gazette* carried an extract of a letter from Bathurst which set the authentic tone for so many later rationalisations.

> 'No-one can feel greater antipathy, even detestation of making a deliberate and indiscriminate attack upon the unfortunate savages

of these regions than I do, but I am equally certain that the security dictated by the first law of our existence, as well as the retention of any out-stations, makes absolutely necessary the infliction of very summary and severe chastisement, such as will not only impress them with a terror of our power but keep them in such fear as will drive them to a distance from the establishment of the whites. It would be as pointless as useless to inquire at this moment into the original cause of the offence, or to argue the question of justness, of revenge, or the injustice of invading or occupying their territories. We are here forced to defend ourselves against aggressions of the most dreadful kind; and under such circumstances sometimes individual acts may occur, which a more deliberate view might stigmatise as cruel . . .'.

Alongside this letter was another from 'Philanthropist' reminding readers that the New Hollanders were human creatures. But the 'Philanthropist' lived in Sydney, and the letter writers from Bathurst more accurately reflected reality over the mountains. The Bathurst letter was characterised by the resort to euphemism which was to be all too common in the frontier situation. Instead of 'shooting down', he used the words 'very summary and severe chastisement'. He went on to invoke the magic word of 'aggression' and with a style that later propagandists might envy, brushed aside the original cause of the disorders to simply state 'we are forced to defend ourselves'.

While the out-stations and the overland drovers on the mainland were pushing out the limits of settlement, the tribes were able to retreat further west or into the mountains. But on the island of Tasmania it was not so easy. The destruction of the Tasmanian Aborigines in less than two generations was a melancholy mixture of barbarism and misplaced idealism. It has to be remembered that to the new settlers of Tasmania, the constant presence of even an Aboriginal remnant of less than a thousand blacks was a source of fear and terror.

To look through the pages of the *Colonial Times* and the *Hobart Town Courier* around 1830 is to gain the impression of a town beseiged. In September of 1830, in an editorial justifying the great drive designed to round up the Aborigines of the island, the *Hobart Town Courier* announced: 'If the outrages of the blacks are not put down at this time . . . we must abandon the island, look for safety to our ships'. The *Colonial Times* had a standard type heading 'Aborigines' under which all skirmishes were reported. In the north, the *Launceston Advertiser* in March 1830 showed its capacity for polite euphemism in reporting the killing of a number of sheep near Port Sorrell: 'Captain Smith immediately proceeded to the spot, and we have no doubt he will give a good account of them'.

As was so often the case, the press was inclined to attribute the trouble to a sinister outside influence, on this occasion a native from Sydney called Musquito, who was alleged to have stirred up the previously passive locals. In July 1830, the *Colonial Times* commented directly on 'the increased system and organisation which appear to have marked their movements . . .' The press, however, was ready to recognise the true heroes. One correspondent of the *Colonial Times* wrote with feeling of the sufferings of the bands who hunted down indigenes:—

'Was I, Mr. Editor, to supply you with a detailed account of the amazing hardships the roving parties are often obliged to endure both from hunger, cold and hard travelling'.

But the most notable contribution by the *Colonial Times* to the discussion of the Aboriginal problem that year was a long article under the title 'The Relative Situation in which the White Inhabitants of this island stand towards the aborigines'. The article set out very lucidly a rational justification for expropriation, murder and rape. It began from the proposition that all men were descended from one common stock and proceeded:—

'If then we are all descended from one common stock, we all have an equal right in the soil of the globe; but this right is never to be exercised to the prejudice of others, or in injustice—if everyone holds an inherent right in the soil of this world, we may well ask by what right do about a thousand individuals arrogate themselves a proportion of land equal in extent to Ireland, which must provide subsistence for 6 or 7 millions of people ... private property really is, or supposed to be, the reward of industry ... in all cases where the law of just necessity is in operation, the prejudices, the desires and pretensions of the few must yield to the necessity of the many ... The aborigines in the end must come to our views and that without the slightest violation of justice on our part ... so far from this (occupation) being considered an enroachment supported by unjust pretensions, it constitutes one of the chief ornaments of British character, to seek countries where millions of acres have remained for ages in unproductive idleness and to fulfil the intentions of the Creator, who did not bestow his bounties that they might be thrown away or disregarded.'

It may have been the mention of the Creator which stirred a passing misgiving on the abuse of Aboriginal women, but the writer found the argument to counter this.

'Did the black women of this island possess in the slightest degree any portion of that delicacy of sentiment which ought to be the distinguishing ornament of their sex—did they know how to set a true value on chastity—and had the aboriginal men not shared the wages of iniquity earned by their women, then indeed they would be entitled to our highest compassion ... no virtuous nor moral impression has been made on their beknighted minds ... fully associated with the grossest vices and most flagrant crimes. Such a race merits little compassion unless it might be said that the greatest degree of sin is entitled to the highest degree of compassion.'

The argument that black women and their men were vicious and degraded and that the women deserved what they got was a popular one. Almost exactly 100 years later, C. A. Jameson, a prospector, wrote an indignant letter to the Darwin newspaper, *Northern Standard*, explaining the villainy of the blacks. 'The old gag of interfering with their gins is nonsense. The black boys solicit Combos for their Comborinas; the non-payment of silver due might cause the quarrel but not the act'. This theory of degraded women travelled. The famous battle of the Wazzir celebrated by that writer of bad verse, C. J. Dennis, commemorated the application of the same principle to Wog women.

For the rest of the century, the settlers lived up to the task of fulfilling the intentions of the Creator, but as the frontier pushed farther out there was less comment in the metropolitan press. While virtual guerilla war raged on the western outskirts of Queensland, the metropolitan papers reported very little and the local papers often nothing, one suspects for very good reasons. With the growth of local responsible government, the Aboriginal problem became a matter for sporadic consideration by parliamentary committees. In 1859, a committee reported pessimistically to the Victorian Parliament but created very little interest in the press. The *Argus* noted even-handedly 'that the blacks themselves were treacherous and dangerous neighbours to the pioneers of settlement we suppose cannot be disputed; but it will forever remain an open question how far this was the result of original provocation, and of the first impression left on the native mind by oppression and injustice', and then spoke carelessly of 'the processes of extirpation to which they seemed doomed'. That being so, the *Argus* went back to the discussion of railways, the foreshadowed universal panacea of the day.

In 1861, however, another committee, this time in Queensland, achieved rather more impact. After some complaints, the Parliament had approved investigation into the Queensland Native Police. This notorious body, with a rank and file of detribalised Aborigines and with white officers, was an instrument of a conscious policy of what was called 'dispersal'. In justification of the activities of the Native Police, emphasis was laid upon their capacities to track down tribal Aborigines. Not only were they very effective in killing off those who were taken on the tracks, but also as Professor Rowley pointed out, the policy of dispersal probably did more to destroy the fabric of aboriginal society than the random killings of the settlers.

'Dispersal' was a useful word in the euphemism which letter writers and editorialists employed to cover the ugly reality. The Native Police inevitably had their defenders. In May 1861, a letter writer to the *Brisbane Courier* made it clear that they could be tactfully used:—

> 'On the occurrence of any robbery or attempt to intimidate the shepherds, the police are quickly sent for, and the punishment is quick, short and decisive—the officers of the police letting them know what the punishment is for, while the settlers keep aloof from all personal quarrels ... possessed of a Police Force which is doing so well, I hope every friend of humanity and peaceful colonialism will exert his energies to prevent the mischief that may be done by the interference of factitious ignorance and conceit'.

However, the *Courier* did show some uneasiness as the inquiries proceeded. In early July its leader writer said 'that there were blacks who were troublesome and dangerous, the police would only be acting with merciful severity by shooting down any caught in the very act of violence or depredation, we are prepared to admit', but he then went on to warn against indiscriminate slaughter. A few weeks later the *Courier* invoked the argument from efficiency;

> 'the fact of inexcusable violence having been employed for the purpose of quieting the blacks is comparatively of small importance; for if inefficient, the evils which they face may yet entail upon the white settlers and the heartless atrocities they may yet

commit on their fellow natives can hardly be contemplated without a shudder—for efficiency implies discipline'.

The opinions expressed show how, even in metropolitan public opinion, the blacks were not subjects equal before the law. Although the Native Police came badly out of the committee report, they stayed in being until 1896. Indeed, in the rest of Australia they were cited as a kind of model. By the 1880s, the frontier in the Eastern States had receded, but the new settlement in the Northern Territory was still as beleaguered in the minds of its inhabitants as was Hobart in 1830.

The settlers only newspaper, the *Northern Territory Times and Gazette* published at Palmerston (now Darwin) faithfully echoed the arguments of an earlier generation of apologists in the south. In June 1882, the blacks murdered two Chinese carriers. The response of the *Times and Gazette* was clear. 'We think therefore that the late sad occurrence shows the necessity of at once repressing the murderous proclivity of the natives with a firm hand, and giving them a lesson they will not be likely to forget . . .'

> 'The paper rejected the idea of giving natives any trial: 'the lesson would be thrown away on the up-country natives. In the interests of public safety we hope that such severe punishment will be dealt out to them as will strike terror into the hearts of all marauding tribes and deter them from perpetuating in such horrible atrocities in the future . . .'

Stimulated by the editorial, a public meeting was convened. Again the word 'dispersal' was the keynote. Two local Chinese, Ping Que and Sun Wal Loung, gave £20 each 'towards fitting out a party to disperse the blacks'. A letter writer after the meeting scorned pretence when he wrote 'any natives found on the tracks might justly be put down as the offenders, without losing time on the results of inquests etc', and then went on to articulate another ever popular argument, the case from International Law.

> 'Moreover considering the doings of the natives during the past few weeks all about one tract of our country, I consider we may fairly look upon the blacks of that part as aggressors and so have placed themselves beyond the jurisdiction of the police which is the civil power and should be dealt with by International Law'.

These were the familiar arguments, whether in New South Wales, in Tasmania, in Queensland or in the Northern Territory: the divinely appointed right of settlement; the sacred nature of property, the outlawing of Aborigines by threat of their aggression; the moral vileness of the black race, its treachery and immorality. Very rarely was the press as open as the *Sydney Herald* in its indignation at the Myall Creek Trial. The euphemisms of 'dispersal, quick and decisive punishment, a firm hand' served very well to screening the doings of the nineteenth century Calleys.

But as the frontier continued to recede, so too did the obtrusiveness of the dying minority of Aborigines. One can scan the pages of the press of the early twentieth century for years without finding any reference to the nation's first inhabitants. Comment, when it did come in a more enlightened and polite generation, was cautious or simply pseudo-scientific. The Aborigines, it was understood, were dying out. Half-castes remained a problem.

A letter writer in the *Northern Standard* in September 1932 could attack the notion that half-castes should be allowed to attend the same school as whites with: 'facts have proved that the average half-caste individual slips back to the characteristics of the native parent'. Probably a major contribution to continuing degradation of the Aborigine in the twentieth century has been in humour. The historian of *Smith's Weekly,* in a casual aside, refers to one artist as being in charge of 'Abo humour'. Long before Smith's, *The Bulletin,* that very accurate mirror of Australian prejudices, had set the style with 'Aboriginalities', which included many a paragraph illustrating the essential stupidity of the black remnant. (Paradoxically the same column also ran some useful observations of Aboriginal culture.)

The level of the wit is perhaps best illustrated from *The Bulletin* of July 30, 1898. A photograph of an old, ugly and thick-lipped aboriginal woman is captioned 'A KANOWA BELLE . . . Take oh! Take those lips away!' The end of open war with the blacks left them as figures of fun.

There was never open war between the Chinese minority and the white Australians, although some of the mining riots were on the edge of becoming massacres. If one were to accept the communal mythology about Chinese in the nineteenth century, one would have to categorise it as xenophobic rather than racist. The apologia follows the line that the White Australia policy and its main stimulus, anti-Chinese feeling, were the products of economic forces, a response to the necessity to stop wage levels being destroyed. This rationalisation simply will not stand up.

Any scrutiny of press writing and reporting on Chinese shows a strong under-current of sexual jealousy and fear, as strong as the tensions that stimulated the Klu Klux Klan lynch mobs in the southern United States. In June 1861, Henry Parkes' Sydney newspaper, *The Empire,* ran a story on Chinese charcoal burners living near Sydney. Noting that a white woman was living with one of the Chinese and had given him several children, *The Empire* unleashed itself:—

'One could see at a glance that there has been blending of Caucasian and Mongolian blood—the former asserting its natural superiority . . . there is a good deal of the animal about the Chinaman, and his passions must be gratified, it should be made imperative for every male immigrant to bring with him a female . . . by degrees they have demoralised many of the white women . . . the white population is becoming demoralised by the presence of hordes of idolatrist barbarians, destitute of religion and morality, as well as every social virtue which makes us proud of our Anglo-Saxon race and institutions.'

If *The Empire* was interested in morals, the *Brisbane Courier* took a more cosmic view in July 1861 when it said: 'In the competition between our countrymen and the worthless hordes of China, it may be that the latter, by force of overwhelming numbers, will in the end come forth triumphant, the victory however will not be yielded without a struggle'. For the rest of the century the verbal onslaught continued while the urban pushes bashed the Chinese and the rural miners made them their scapegoats for failure. Humphrey McQueen has drawn attention to the racism of that curious figure, William Lane, and other leaders of the embryonic Labor movement. *The Worker,* on 1 April 1890, summed it up with 'For the truth is, if we can't get along without these low-lived aliens we deserve to starve, every man Jack of us'. However during the great strike, *The Worker's* attack was always levelled at the capitalists. Even when, on 21 March 1891, the whole front page was given over to a cartoon showing a Chinese-faced spider about to devour the honest white working man, it was made clear that the Chinese spider was only a tool of the capitalists.

For the frankest exposition of popular prejudice in the 1890s, inevitably we have to turn to *The Bulletin*. Its technique of filling the substantial segment of its pages under the various headings of Aboriginalities, Society, Political Points, made it the voice of hundreds if not thousands of Australians. If there was a kind of jocular patronage towards the Aborigine, there was no quarter for the Chinese. The dominant themes of the paragraphs are Hygiene, Leprosy, Sexual Jealousy and Fear. They reveal a curious view of the white woman. It seems that only a touch of yellow fingers is needed to send them into a swoon of surrender. Missionaries who take an interest in the Chinese get the same contemptuous treatment as the *Sydney Herald* gave to the Aboriginal Protectors sixty years previously.

On 16 July 1898 T.D. wrote:—

'What disgusts me more than anything else about Chinese gambling shops is the regular indulgence by whites in tea from pots or cups previously mouthed by Chows, kanakas, niggers and the whole motley crew . . . ugh!'

Not only were the Chinese devils in Australia, but also at home. On 23 July 1898, *The Bulletin* carried a harrowing story from an unnamed London paper on the fate of lone girl missionaries in China.

'She lands in Shanghai fresh from home, roses on her cheeks, a heart full of enthusiasm and a determination to do good, clean clothes, spotless linen and a skin pure, clean and soft as velvet . . . likely she does not yet know enough of Chinese to understand the foul remarks made about her by the swarming almond-eyed celestials on either side . . . one point I have not yet more than hinted at, but one which I feel I must be more explicit. Often these girls are alone and utterly without protection in the midst of lewd coolies and debauched, brutal and almost all powerful soldiery. When the opportunity arises of gratifying their desire —practically without risk—why they gratify it. And the poor girl is powerless to resist, and her overwhelming shame will not let her proclaim the outrage afterwards.'

In August, another contributor told the story of the governesses in China:—

'Women must have some association of some kind with males of her species from time to time. In the larger parts of China the ordinary run of white girls are all right . . . but the poor governess in the big parts and the girl in the part where whites are few and far between have but a slack time. Then the quiet cat-like, purring houseboy, who is always about and who recognises the right moment, has his innings.'

Not only governesses can fall. Another contributor in the same issue writes of Australia:—

'The chow vegetable vendor is the refuge and asylum for ugly servant girls . . . the butcher and the baker shy with true Australian rudeness from this amorous and unfortunate female, but the Asiatic squints loving compliments from his almond eyes, etc. . . .'

Next week it printed a paragraph from the *Maryborough Patriot* 'The children of white settlers are being continually followed by Hindus and Japs who make indecent overtures to them. Leperland, [i.e. Queensland] wallows in the mire it loves.'

K.K. contributed a new line on the Chinese in November:—

> 'The European's dislike to the Chinaman is not a matter of taste, but a healthy racial instinct. It is the same survival of an out-of-date instinct that is evidenced in a horses' instinctive dread at the smell of tigers . . . In the case of chinkies, this out-of-date instinctive dislike has lasted long enough to be useful again as a protection against a race that is more dangerous to civilisation than a savage with a club is to a fellow savage.'

Next month one cartoonist caught the spirit of the times with a drawing captioned 'It is feared that the bubonic plague will be introduced here through rats' which showed a stream of rats with Chinese and Kanaka faces coming ashore.

In 1899, *The Bulletin* was still sounding the tocsin. A poem from Vot Kotze printed on the editorial rather than on The Red Page opened;

> 'To your arms! The countless hordes of Asia
> Are a-swarm, a demon world released!
> From the camps of Zhengis Khan and Jubal
> Filthy scouring of the putrid East'

and ended:

> 'White man's land, you cowards, is in danger
> White man's land is calling you to arms.'

Leprosy was something of an obsession with *The Bulletin* contributors. In May, one of them told, as a curiosity, how lepers were brought south to Brisbane Leprosarium.

> 'The lepers are carried in a packing case fixture, secured as a temporary deck-house. This is lined with tin, having a small sliding window through which food was received in a tin dish. Water is supplied through a funnel which communicates with a bucket outside.'

There was a lot more to anti-Chinese feeling than mere economics. In a way, the Japanese got more respect. They came later to Queensland than the Chinese and *The Bulletin's* contributors liked to lay stress on the fact that the Japanese brought their own prostitutes. Still, at the end of 1898, *The Bulletin* printed what it called 'A bitter wail' from Thursday Island, tracing the growth in Japanese population from 22 in 1890 to 619, thus outnumbering the 608 whites. As well there were 575 other aliens.

The Kanakas provided another scapegoat. Although the importation of South Sea Islanders was always a matter of controversy, there does not seem to have been a great deal of passion and bitterness until the 1890s. The only substantial known kanaka-white clash, the Mackay races riot in December 1883, was reported with bias but not fanaticism. The riot began when a time-expired Kanaka was refused a drink at the races in one of those sporadic outbursts of barman's morality. The local newspaper, the *Mackay Mercury,* saw something sinister in the immediate aftermath:—

> 'Simultaneously (and as if by preconceived arrangement) other Kanakas hidden in the cane sprang up and discharged missiles in every direction. For a few moments the Europeans on the course seemed well-nigh panic-stricken (the whites rallied). Immediately on their appearance the rebellious Kanakas tried to make their escape ... small mercy befell those who were caught ...'

One Kanaka was killed and many others injured. The riot was one of the factors leading to a stringent tightening up of the regulations covering the recruitment of islanders. By the 1890s the Kanakas had become pawns in the manoeuverings for and against Federation. One aspect of the Kanaka population was the number who had been able to acquire some property. At the time of deportation after 1904, there were, according to Edward Docker, some 317 Kanakas farming on a leasehold basis. There were a number of inter-marriages and in the '90s similar tensions of sexual jealousy to those felt towards the Chinese began to show up in *The Bulletin.* That journal's correspondents in North Queensland did have some cause for insecurity. Nine out of twenty men in North Queensland were Kanakas, Chinese or other coloured aliens. In September 1898, *The Bulletin* reminded its readers of what the Kanakas were up to with 'a white female outcast was lately taken from the Kanaka quarters at Isis Scrub where our black and tan brothers went shares in her society'. In November it reported the case of Mrs. O'Donoghue who shot a Kanaka who was trying to break in to her house at Mosman. She had been charged with shooting and given bail. But the correspondent went on:—

> 'If the local authorities don't show a lot more tact in dealing with white women, especially miners' wives, under such circumstances there will probably be niggers dangling at the end of a string'.

In April 1899, *The Bulletin* quoted with approval an article by J. B. Drake, M.L.A. in the periodical *Progress* on the 'Danger of the Kanaka becoming a permanent curse', particularly the time-expired:—

> 'who work for the highest wages they can get, take occasional holidays at Kanaka boarding houses and ape all the vices of the white man. These are the men who lease land, marry white women ... it is an army of semi-civilised barbarians who have settled down in Queensland and who are continually tightening their hold ... it is mud and filth entering into the stream of a nation's pure life-blood'.

In June 1899, *The Bulletin* followed up with a question:—

> 'It would be interesting to know how many white women are living on the proceeds of Tommy Tanna's labour—also how many half-castes are added annually to the population of Mongrelia'.

Federation and White Australia removed some of the internal sources of friction concerning the Chinese and Kanaka issues. By the twentieth century the conflict with Aborigines had been brushed to the edge of the frontier. The victory of Japan over Russia in 1904 showed up a new menace. Humphrey McQueen in *New Britannia* has traced very well the influence of race-fear of Japan in the earlier years of this century.

This huge topic is beyond the scope of this present article, as also is the press and propaganda style in World War Two after Pearl Harbour. The domestic anti-German frenzy of the First World War must be put aside on the grounds that it was closer to xenophobia than racism, although Christopher Brennan's *Chant of Doom* crosses this dividing line.

Likewise anti-semitism, while present on the bogus economic argument and joke level, never really reached the scale of racism (although *The Bulletin* continued to believe Dreyfus was guilty even after Esterhazy's guilt was admitted). Apart from some negro soldier—Australian clashes during World War II, perhaps only once in this century did the black or negro become an issue—the Jack Johnson v. Tommy Burns world title fight at Sydney in 1908. Johnson won, even though the Australian crowd was against him. The Sydney *Daily Telegraph* summed things up in a caption to a cartoon:—

> 'And yet for all we know and feel,
> For Christ and Shakespeare, knowledge, love,
> We watch a white man bleeding reel,
> We cheer a black with blooded glove.'

But such a tone was to fade as the press became blander, except in one chain, that owned by Ezra Norton. No study of racism in Australian press is complete without citation from the gentleman who inherited the *Truth* chain of newspapers from his notorious father, John Norton, characteristically after a legal battle. Ezra Norton played a decisive and dominant policy role in his newspapers. He was a short, unhappy, almost pathetic man who loved animals and feared Asians. On 27 March 1949 he summed up his philosophy succinctly in an editorial in *Truth* (he wrote most of them in an unmistakable style):—

> 'The White Australia policy', it said, 'like chastity admits of no degree. We cannot be moderately white, since white means white.'

The editorial was in fervent support of the then Minister for Immigration, Mr. A. A. Calwell, who had advised deportation of a Filipino who had married an Australian woman. As *Truth* put it,

> 'Maudlin sympathisers are moved at the plight of white women who have married these prohibited immigrants regardless of the possible consequences to themselves. If a woman is silly enough to contract such a marriage in defiance of the law she has made a choice which must be regarded as deliberate, and she must be prepared to accept the consequences.'

Only a few weeks previously, travel-writer Frank Clune was brought in to tell the readers of *Truth*:—

> 'the overpopulation of Asia is a result of reckless breeding. They merely reproduce to indulge their interests and do nothing or very little to assure that their offspring will have the necessities of life ... Our aim is to make Australia a home for the White Race!'

The year before, Mr. Norton had warned

> 'These Asiatic Communists have a fifth column already established in the country, actively tampering with our national bulwark, the White Australia policy!'

Not surprisingly his sub-editors had got the message. In 1949 they put a heading on the report of the Aly Khan-Hayworth wedding

'Disgusting vulgarity, at Rita-Aly wedding ... Black, white and brindle join orgy'. This sort of reporting continued until Norton sold out in 1959.

How much of the post-war political propaganda and comment on Communist threat can be called racist is a matter for debate. In the judgment of this writer, most of it manages to stay on the side of shoddiness rather than outright racism. The colour of the enemy is usually hinted at rather than explicitly named. There have been a few exceptions. During the Indonesian-Dutch war, the *News-Weekly*, organ of the extreme right in the Australian Labour Party, supported the Dutch on the ground that they would be 'some small barrier against the ever rising flood of colour and communism to the north of Australia.'

It has become unfashionable to be so overt. To make this point is rather important. The spectacular manifestations of racism in the press is no longer fashionable. An example of patronising 'Abo humour', however, still is. We don't have Norton's fulmination against the Asians, but we have urbane indifference to Asian deaths, whether by war or famine. We don't have overt opposition to development aid, but we have the presupposition that Asian's don't know how to spend it.

Finally, the silence of the city press and the editorial quietness of the provincial press have meant that the squalid living conditions of Aborigines in country towns have gone unacknowledged. It is a question of some moment to contemplate whether apathy in the face of such scandalous conditions is not the by-product of communal education on the race issue, by the popular Press, over the last one hundred years. Certainly their previous commitment has shown little concern as to the fate of the nation's original inhabitants. It rests at about the same level as their concern for the human misfortunes of the country's foreign policy.

13

THE WHITE AUSTRALIA POLICY

A. C. Palfreeman

The White Australia policy is a much-abused term in urgent need of precise definition. It is used variously to describe a national ideal, a statutory requirement, an unwritten administrative procedure, a national aberration, a journalistic catchcry or a traditional myth.

It is, of course, to some extent all these things. Definitions are not of vital importance in political evaluations, but since the implications of the policy in its current context are, we should perhaps make the attempt.

From one point of view, the White Australia policy exists on two levels. On one, it is the government's *response* to a general consensus—to keep Australia white and racially homogeneous. In this sense it is a fixed, unquestioned objective of Australian society. But on the other level, the White Australia policy is the difficult and complex business of *implementing* the consensus. Clearly the complete exclusion of non-Europeans has never been and can never be possible. An accommodation, which has no place in the statutes, has occurred from the beginning. It was left to the discretion of the administrator to effect a compromise. This he has done under the umbrella of the legislation, while exercising his discretion well away from public scrutiny.

In this chapter I propose to look at firstly the *statutes,* in so far as they underpin the objective of a White Australia; secondly, at the government's *policy,* in the strict sense of the term, i.e. how it has gone about implementing this objective; thirdly, at the quantitative and qualitative success of the policies over seventy years; and finally, at the arguments for and against change and reform.

The Law

There is no White Australia Act. There is no law which excludes non-Europeans from entering Australia. There is no statute which discriminates between intending immigrants on the ground of race. The closest that Parliament has come to prescribing the exclusion of certain categories of persons by reason of their race have been the Pacific Islands Labourers' Act of 1906 and the Wartime Refugees Removal Act of 1949. But the exclusion policy itself has not been enshrined as such in any legislation. The trick is done, so to speak, with mirrors.

The need for common action on immigration by the six colonies was one of the more urgent reasons for their federation in 1901. The federal constitution gave the Federal Parliament competence in the field of immigration and one of its first laws was the Immigration Restriction Act which came into force in December, 1901. It became known as the

Immigration Act, and remained in force until 1959 when it was entirely replaced by the Migration Act. These two Acts constitute the basic statutory authority for the White Australia policy.

During the 1901 debate in Parliament on the Immigration Restriction Bill, it became quite clear that the overwhelming majority of members wanted the complete exclusion of non-Europeans from permanent settlement in Australia. But at the same time, cabinet ministers explained to Parliament that any racially discriminatory legislation would be strongly resisted by the British government, itself very conscious of the multi-racial character of the Empire and of its new relations with Japan and China.

Parliamentary opinion was almost unanimously in favour of exclusion. 'I do not think', said the Prime Minister, 'that the doctrine of the equality of man was really ever intended to include racial equality'.[1] 'The objection I have', offered the Labor Party leader, J. C. Watson, 'to the mixing of the coloured people with the white people of Australia— although I admit it is to a large extent tinged with considerations of an industrial nature—lies in the main in the possibility and probability of racial contamination'.[2] The need was, in the words of Wilkinson, a Protectionist, to 'preserve Australia for all future time to the best races of the world and not to the servile races of Asia'.[3]

But in spite of all this, the *machinery* of exclusion needed to be racially neutral. Thus it was decided to borrow the dictation test method of *exclusion* from the South African Natal Act of 1897, together with exemption certificates and deportation procedure as the methods of *control*.

Section Four of the Immigration Act reads:—

> Any person who when asked to do so by an officer fails to write out at dictation and sign in the presence of the officer a passage of fifty words in length in any European language directed by the officer (is a prohibited immigrant).

Of course, only those whom the officer intended to exclude were given the test and the 'European language' chosen was one which the immigrant could not possibly know. In one case, the Transylvanian dialect of Rumanian was used. In the course of debate, Parliament was assured by the Government not only that the dictation test method would quite effectively keep out non-Europeans, but also that it would not be used to discourage European migration.

The highly discriminatory nature of Parliament's intentions was not lost on the governments of China, India and Japan; they all protested in one way or the other. The Japanese, for example, diplomatically attacking the letter rather than the spirit of the Act, complained that using a 'European' language for the dictation test was discriminatory. With magnanimity, Parliament amended the clause in 1904 to read 'any prescribed language'. But no non-European language was ever prescribed.

The dictation test then was the method of *exclusion*, but there needed to be also a means of *controlling* the temporary entry of non-Europeans. After all, there were, in 1901, about 47,000 Non-Europeans in Australia. They could not all be persuaded to leave. Their wives and families living outside Australia could not totally be prevented from visiting them. Trade and other contacts with Asia were growing and the visits of merchants, students, interpreters and so on were inevitable.

So the Immigration Act included machinery to meet this need. The Minister was empowered to grant 'certificates of exemption' from the dictation test. The policy was to grant these certificates to non-Europeans who were given permission to come in temporarily, for periods up to seven years, for specific purposes such as study, business, family reasons, or to work in a local business of 'community value', where for example the services of a Chinese or Japanese were essential—such as a cook for a Chinese restaurant, or a diver for the pearling industry. If the immigrant violated the conditions of his entry by, for example, changing his employment to something not acceptable to the Immigration Department, then the Minister could simply cancel his certificate of exemption and submit him to a dictation test. Upon failing it, he would be declared a prohibited immigrant and deported.

This system of control was used with great effectiveness for nearly sixty years. In 1958, the Immigration Act was repealed and with it, into history, went the dictation test and its attendant machinery. In its place, Parliament passed the Migration Act, which greatly simplified the procedure. It gives the Minister the power to issue a 'temporary entry permit' to an immigrant who is not permitted to settle permanently. If necessary he can cancel this permit, after which the holder becomes a prohibited immigrant and can be deported.

As before, therefore, the Minister has an almost absolute discretion to decide who should and who should not enter Australia, and under what conditions.

There have, from time to time, been amendments to the basic Act and also supporting legislation to reinforce the extension policy. The Pacific Island Labourers' Act of 1906 was designed to repatriate islanders from the Queensland sugar plantations. The Wartime Refugees Removal Act of 1949 was an extraordinary legislative attempt to insist on a White Australia, coming as a climax to probably the most controversial period in the policy's history. It came about in this way.

The Minister for Immigration in the post-war Labor Government, Mr. A. A. Calwell, had set himself two complementary tasks. One, of immense significance for Australia, was the introduction and development of a massive programme to recruit immigrants from Britain and Europe, a programme which, to 1971, has brought over two million European settlers to Australia.

But his other task was to maintain, as steadfastly as possible, the traditional exclusion of non-Europeans, permitting only their temporary entry for specific purposes. In addition he also proposed to repatriate some thousands of non-European refugees who had found their way into Australia during the war.

The exclusion policy, he very competently managed by using the Immigration Act in the way we have described. Even the Japanese wives of Australian servicemen were refused entry. They were the subject of one of Mr. Calwell's more notorious remarks, albeit in the heat of debate, that Japanese women should never be allowed to pollute our shores, and that this view would be supported by all Australians who had suffered at the hands of the Japanese.[4]

But the repatriation of the wartime refugees was more difficult. While most of them returned to their countries of origin voluntarily, a residue of some nine hundred, mostly Chinese, refused to go, claiming they had made their homes in Australia and that they could expect no warm welcome in Communist China.

Mr. Calwell was adamant they should go, but then found the Immigration Act inadequate for his purpose. His attempt to deport an Indonesian refugee, Mrs. O'Keefe, the wife of a British subject, failed when the High Court ruled that since she had not been issued with a certificate of exemption on entry (and this was the case with most of the refugees) it could not be cancelled and she could not be made a prohibited immigrant.[5]

Calwells' reaction was to have Parliament very quickly pass the Wartime Refugee Removal Act in July 1949. Section 4 of this Act defined the people affected. These were every person 'who entered Australia during the period of hostilities and is an alien; (and) who, during the period of hostilities, entered Australia as a place of refuge, by reason of the occupation ... of any place by an enemy, and has not left Australia since.'

The Act was directed at both aliens and British subjects. The Minister needed only to certify in writing that a person was a wartime refugee and then make an order for his deportation. The Act was tested almost immediately before the High Court, which recognized its constitutional validity.[6]

However, public criticism and attacks by the Parliamentary Opposition on the legislation were effective enough to persuade the Government to stay its hand and await the outcome of the general election of December 1949, before proceeding with any deportations. As a result of that election, the Liberal-Country Party coalition was returned to power and honoured its election promise not to implement the Act. The refugees stayed and eventually were granted permanent residence.

Another use of legislation to ensure the White Australia objective was to deny naturalisation rights to non-Europeans. If they were not permitted permanent settlement, they could clearly not be allowed naturalisation. Not until 1956 was this privilege extended to non-Europeans. The legislative authority for this policy was originally the Naturalization Act of 1903 which, surprisingly in the circumstances, specifically excluded from naturalisation the 'aboriginal nations of Asia, Africa or the Islands of the Pacific, excepting New Zealand.' Non-European British subjects were not included.

In 1920, a new Nationalisation Act was substituted and the racial references dropped. From 1948, British subjects could become Australian citizens only if they registered as such, but the Minister reserved the right to refuse such registration. The Act, as amended in 1958, now excludes from citizenship prohibited immigrants, and persons holding temporary entry permits. Before they can apply for naturalisation or registration they need to be granted permanent residence, whether they are British subjects, Commonwealth citizens or aliens.

It can be seen then, that while White Australia cannot be discovered in any Act of Parliament, the discretionary power of the Minister is firmly anchored in the legislation, and has allowed his officers to administer a policy of near-exclusion for over half a century, and for the last few years, one of very limited entry. This has meant that successive Ministers, in delimiting the objectives of White Australia and unable to find guidance in the statutes, have had to interpret the intentions of

Parliament and people as best they could. The tendency has been, therefore, to exercise this discretion with the optimum degree of secrecy. Only very recently has the Government begun to make public the details of the policy's administration.

The Policy

As we have intimated, the objective of the White Australia policy, as established in 1901, and as implemented for over half a century, was quite simply to keep Australia white by preventing persons of non-European race from settling. It was, to repeat, a policy of exclusion and it was very effectively carried out.

There were a few exceptions. The foreign-born children of Australian citizens were, in some cases, allowed in; so were the wives and children of some Indian residents, by arrangement with the Indian government in 1919. Generally speaking, Maoris have been admitted, as a concession to the feelings of New Zealand. As we have seen, there has always been some provision for the temporary entry of some non-Europeans. Merchants, students, assistants to Chinese businessmen, cooks, market gardeners, pearlers, refugees and people in other assorted categories have been admitted for specific periods to engage in specific work. Great care was taken to ensure they remained in their prescribed occupation and to ensure their departure when it became due.

Some face saving concessions were made to foreign governments. For example, until the Second War, 'Gentlemen's Agreements' with China and Japan allowed businessmen and students to come in for short periods without being subjected to the dictation test.

The political and economic transformations brought about by the Pacific War and with them the new ideologies and attitudes toward racialism, may have led one to expect a radical reappraisal of the exclusion policy. But instead, it was pursued with even greater single-mindedness by Mr. Calwell with a good deal of embarrassing publicity. At one stage in 1949, the Philippines government threatened to break off diplomatic relations with Australia over the exclusion of Sergeant Gamboa, a Filipino in the United States army.

From 1950, the policy was implemented with much more circumspection, but exclusion from permanent settlement remained the touchstone. Not until 1956 did the first crack appear. For the first time the Department of Immigration issued a statement of the conditions of non-European entry, which included the possibility of permanent residence and naturalization to Asians who

> 'have resided in Australia for a minimum period of fifteen years, who have abided by the conditions of their admission, are of good character and have an adequate knowledge of English, may now be permitted to remain in Australia for permanent residence. Once permanent residence is granted to an Asian he may then apply for naturalization or registration as an Australian citizen.'

In addition, some 'Distinguished or Highly Qualified Asians' were to be admitted for 'extended stay', for example those 'fitted to fill professional or high grade technical positions'; or with 'outstanding cultural attainments'; or those with 'substantial capital which they are prepared to invest in Australian commerce or industry'.

But except for the very close relatives of Australian citizens and the spouses of white British subjects, the entry of non-Europeans for permanent settlement was still not officially countenanced, and this remained the case until new regulations were announced in March 1966. Not until then could it be said that the foundation pillars of the sixty-five year old White Australia policy began, itself, to be 'white-anted', to use the colourful language of those long-ago debates which laid them.

Now for the first time, non-Europeans were to be officially admitted as settlers. They included:—

'Persons with specialized technical skills for appointments for which local residents are not available.

'Persons of high attainment in the arts and sciences, or of prominent achievement in other ways.

'Persons nominated by responsible authorities or institutions for specific important professional appointments, which otherwise would remain unfilled.

'Executives, technicians, and other specialists who have spent substantial periods in Australia—for example with the branches here of large Asian companies—and who have qualifications or experience in positive demand here.

'Businessmen who in their own countries have been engaged in substantial international trading and would be able to carry on such trade from Australia.

'Persons who have been of particular and lasting help to Australia's interest abroad in trade, or in other ways.

'Persons who by former residence in Australia or by association with us have demonstrated an interest in or identification with Australia that should make their future residence here feasible.'

As a further concession, non-Europeans could apply for naturalisation or registration after the same length of residence and under the same conditions as aliens and British subjects of European race.

1966, therefore, marked the formal end of the exclusion policy and the beginning of limited entry. We need now to examine the record of the last five years in order to evaluate how limited the entry has been and what the signs are for the future. While we are playing with numbers, why not look at the whole picture?

The Arithmetic[7]

In 1901 when the Immigration Restriction Act was passed, there were about 47,000 foreign-born Asians and Polynesians in Australia, representing about 1.25 per cent of the total population. In 1947, there were 22,000, but only 6,400 were foreign-born residents. The rest were Australian-born, both full and mixed-blood, and 'migratory'. Together they represented only 0.21 per cent of the population, and if the foreign-born only are considered, the figure becomes only 0.07 per cent: the policy had successfully rendered the population almost whiter than white.

Since 1947 there has been a gradual increase in the percentage. By June 1970, there were about 46,000 non-Europeans in Australia, excluding persons of mixed blood. Of these, 11,200 were Australian-born, about 18,800 were foreign-born permanent residents, and some 15,400 were students and other temporary residents. Taking the permanent residents, both Australian and foreign-born together, about 30,000, they represent about 0.24 per cent of the total population. This figure may validly be taken as the measure of the success of the White Australia policy in seventy years of operation.

Insofar as the future intake of non-Europeans is concerned, the figures show a gathering momentum. Between March 1966 and September 1970, 6,342 'well-qualified' non-Europeans, including dependant, were admitted for settlement. Nearly half of these (2,933) were approved in the twelve months prior to September 1970, so the 'approval rate' is now about 2,200 p.a., although the rate of actual arrivals is lagging behind.

In addition, from January 1966 to June 1970, 4,192 close relatives were admitted as permanent residents, and 5,471 non-Europeans, who had arrived as temporary immigrants, were granted permanent residence. In addition, 18,487 persons of mixed racial descent migrated to Australia.

On the basis of these figures, it is likely that some 4,000 non-Europeans will acquire permanent residence in 1971 and the annual rate will increase over the next few years. But even at this rate it will be a long time before the percentage of non-Europeans in the population reaches the figure it was in 1901.

Public Opinion

Few, if any, Australians want to 'open the floodgates', or to include non-Europeans in the immigration programme on the same basis as that of Europeans. It is generally agreed that restrictions of some kind must be applied to non-European immigration.

The debate concerns the stringency of these restrictions. Those who continue to advocate severe curbs on permanent residence for non-Europeans claim that the policy has proved eminently successful in preventing racial conflict in Australia. They point to the incidence of racial strife in many corners of the globe—the United States, South Africa, Britain, Malaysia, for example. It may be unfortunate that people of difference race find it so difficult to live together, but since this is in the nature of man and of human society, it makes sense to preserve a racially homogenous society. Why allow the problem to develop? The British did but now clearly regret it, and have had to impose severe restrictions.

Other traditional arguments are still put forward. Economically there is no place in the Australian economy for cheap unskilled labour from Asia; socially, culturally and morally we cannot permit the existence of second class citizens who will be the hewers of wood and drawers of water; it leads to a master/servant class structure which is degrading to all. Politically their tradition and values are so far removed from our own that they cannot be expected to understand and participate in the Australian body politic.

On the other hand, those who believe the restrictions should be relaxed, argue just as persuasively that our exclusionist policies have been and are based largely on racial prejudice. This is a most unhealthy characteristic of any society, especially in today's multi-racial world. The way to break it down is through the controlled entry of non-Europeans for permanent residence, together with their controlled assimilation, so that by living together the prejudice will disappear.

Economically, it is claimed, there is plenty of room for tens of thousands of skilled and semi-skilled workers, not to mention professional people, from all over South-east Asia, India and even Japan, who find the opportunities very limited in their own countries. They would be integrated into the Australian wage structure and their contribution to the Australian economy would be much greater than it would be in their own.

Culturally, we must benefit from an infusion of new values and new approaches, although it is often pointed out in this regard that many educated Asians from, for example, Malaysia, Singapore and Hong Kong, are much more attuned to the values of Australian society than are many southern European migrants. Morally, we must make some attempt to share our natural bounty with our neighbours, even if it is with very few of them. But most importantly, some would argue, it is our political and diplomatic standing in the world which is at stake. If the administration of our immigration policy labels us throughout the world as a narrow, racist, exclusivist people, as for example South Africa and Rhodesia have been labelled, then, at best, we can never grow in stature as a member of the international community, at worst, we put our future security in jeopardy.

The contribution we can make to that community, the benefits we can expect, the influence we can exert, will be severely limited by a narrow and prejudiced domestic policy. If modifications to that policy can kill the stigma of White Australia, then the benefits in terms of long term goodwill and acceptance, especially by our near neighbours, will be incalculable.

These then are the two sides of the continuing argument. Meanwhile, the great majority of Australians seem content to accept the Government's gradual relaxation of the entry policy. Very little, if any, criticism followed the announcement in January 1971 by the Minister for Immigration that 1,400 qualified non-European settlers and their families had been admitted during the previous financial year, as well as 780 relatives of non-Europeans already in Australia. If this was increased over the next few years to say, 10,000 a year, it would probably continue to find acceptance by most Australians and would still represent a very small fraction of the country's total population.

The groups which have achieved more than any other in bringing about the relaxation of the restrictions in the last six years have been the Immigration Reform Associations. By clarifying the issues and developing moderate objectives based on a small balanced annual intake of non-European migrants, the Associations have earned public support on one hand and reached the ear of the Minister for Immigration on the other. The result is that public debate on the issue is more moderate and constructive than it has ever been; and the administration of the restrictive policy, while still anchored in ministerial discretion, is much more frank and open.

The Government believes that these entry provisions will be enough to convince the world that the White Australia policy is dead, and that we are not a prejudiced, backward-looking white island. But the fact remains that non-Europeans will not be admitted to Australia on the same basis as European settlers for a very long time to come. World opinion is unpredictable and it may force Australia to institute much wider reforms than now seem necessary.

REFERENCES

1 *Commonwealth Parliamentary Debates*, Vol. 4, p. 5233.

2 *Ibid*, Vol. 4, p. 4633.

3 *Ibid*, Vol. 4, p. 4648.

4 *Ibid*, Vol. 198, p. 1281.

5 O'Keefe v. Calwell (1949) 77. *Commonwealth Law Report*, p. 274

6 Koon Wing Lau v. Calwell (1949) 80. *Commonwealth Law Report*, p. 533.

7 The figures in this section are derived from the Commonwealth Census Report and from the Department of Inmigration.

14

ATTITUDES TOWARDS NON-EUROPEAN MIGRANTS

A. T. Yarwood

When the Australian colonies joined together to form the Commonwealth on 1 January 1901, it appeared not unrealistic for the makers of national policy to talk seriously of a 'White Australia' as a realizable goal. The Aborigines of the mainland appeared to be rapidly following their Tasmanian counterparts to extinction. Immigrant non-European races, of which the most numerously represented were the Chinese, Pacific Islanders, Japanese, Indians, and Syrians, made up a total of only about 49,000 people, or 1.2 per cent of the whole population. They too, it was expected, would fade into numerical insignificance, provided that a total bar was placed on the entry of fresh non-European immigrants. The aims of this chapter are to consider the origins of this policy in the colonial period, and to examine its implementation by the Commonwealth during the first two decades of this century.

The first phase of the debate over non-European immigration was prompted by the attempts of New South Wales squatters to recruit a labour force for their vast inland sheep runs. From the time of the appointment of the Molesworth Committee on Transportation in 1837, it appeared evident that the convict assignment system was doomed. Abolition occurred in 1840, but before and after that date, graziers experimented with indentured labourers from India, China and the Pacific Islands. John Mackay, an ex-Indian planter, initiated proposals for a government assisted indenture scheme in October 1836. He wrote again in May 1837 to Governor Sir Richard Bourke, quoting in support a Mauritius planter's letter which described his experiment with Indian coolies as 'a complete success ... a cargo is at this moment coming up the harbour, and two thousand men more are on their passage. They are quiet, docile, and industrious', and their total cost over a five years' indenture would average out at five shillings a week, 'which you will allow is cheap labour in any country'.

To John Mackay and other graziers who followed him in the traffic with coloured labour, its special virtue resided not so much in its cheapness as in its anticipated 'reliability'. Their great problem in finding a substitute for convict labour, which perforce had to go and stay where it was sent, lay in the fact that immigrant workers from Britain were repelled by the loneliness of the Australian bush and by the association of shepherding with convictism. Vital to the success of the indenture system was the active support of the State, both in providing administrative machinery and financial assistance in the experimental phase, and in underpinning it with penal sanctions that could enforce labour contracts. It seems that not one of these supports was available: the importation of coloured labour in the era before gold was numerically insignificant, and, for the employers, financially disastrous.

Why were the British government and its servants in New South Wales so hostile to the labour proposals of the squatters? We find a continuity of opposition from Secretaries of State Glenelg and Stanley, and from Governors Bourke and Gipps. The key to the question appears to lie in their common concern to preserve the colonies as repositories for future generations of emigrant Britishers, who would find in their adopted country conditions that were congenial to the recreation of the best features of British society itself. This conservationist view was expressed by Sir James Stephen, Permanent Under Secretary for the Colonies from 1836 to 1847, who stated the case for exclusion of non-Europeans in a minute of 12 September 1843, which anticipates many of the later arguments for a 'White Australia':—

> It being the most arduous, if not the first, duty of a Government to consult for the permanent interest of society as opposed to the immediate interests of the most active and powerful of its members, and to watch over the welfare of the many rather than the present advantage of the few, and to protect those whose only property is in the power of labour against the rapacity of the rich, it is, in my mind, the evident duty of the British Government to oppose the application of any part of the revenue of New South Wales to the introduction of coolies. They would debase by their intermixture the noble European race. They would introduce caste with all its evils. They would bring with them the idolatry and debasing habits of their country. They would beat down the wages of the poor labouring Europeans until the poor became wholly dependent on the rich—the opposite state of society, namely, the dependence of the rich on the poor, being the happiest state of society wherever it exists. They would cut off the resource for many of our own distressed people. To introduce them [i.e., the coolies] at the public expense would be to countenance and affirm the favourite theory of all colonies that the first settlers in a new country become the proprietors of it all; and that the affairs of it are to be conducted for their benefit rather than for the benefit of the metropolitan state. For these and similar reasons my opinion is that this is a proposal to be negatived and discountenanced.

James Stephen's minute combined idealism, a hard headed pursuit of British imperial interests, and a belief in the superiority of the 'noble European race'. It belongs to an era in which the values of middle and upper class evangelists and humanitarians found notable expression, as in the abolition of slavery and the formation of the Aborigines' Protection Society. Their opposition to the creation in the colonies suited to white settlement of a plantation type society based on coolie labour expressed what Stephen saw as the natural compatability of British morality, religion, and profit. Much the same amalgam of motives survived, with a heavier leavening of racial intolerance, into a later period, in which the Australian colonists formed their immigration policies.

The decade of the 1850s conferred on the eastern Australian colonies gold, self-government, the adult male franchise, and a massive inflow of migrants, including a high proportion of Chinese. What concerns us here is the character of the Chinese migration, the violent antipathy they encountered, the motivation of the restrictive measures placed thereon, and the long term effect of this experience on the dominant white population.

By 1859 there were about 42,000 Chinese in Victoria, comprising perhaps one fourteenth of the total population. A small proportion of the Chinese had been brought under indentures arranged by the chronically labour-starved pastoralists. The great majority, almost exclusively natives of Kwangtung province, came to what they called the 'New Golden Mountain' under engagement to Chinese and European capitalists. They were drawn or impelled by a variety of motives. Emigration brokers told stories of fantastic alluvial golden wealth that could be won by adventurous peasants and then brought back to inject prosperity and prestige to the family and clan in Canton. Redundancy of population in many districts and depression of the rural industries at the time gave a keener edge to these acquisitive and clan-patriotic motives.

Europeans on the gold fields observed and resented the clannishness and solidarity of the Chinese communities. This derived from many causes, including, no doubt, a natural cleaving together of strangers in an alien cultural environment. But the solidarity had, as well, a more purposeful and positive element. From the moment the peasant left his village to the expiry of the passage money bond, he was under the control of a headman who acted as agent for the entrepreneur. Armed guards supervised the emigrants in the ships' holds and, in the colony itself, they were formed into highly disciplined gangs. For virtually all their economic, social and political purposes, the Chinese in Australia, as in California, were a state within a state. Transportation, the supply of food, the observance of law and religion and decisions about where, when and under what conditions work should be done—all were subject to pervasive and detailed control by regional associations. The final sanction against absconders was the threat of retaliation by the association upon the relatives in China.

The close-knit organization of the Chinese on Australian gold fields may have deferred, briefly, the inevitable collisions with the majority of European diggers, both by offering the protection of numbers and by imposing rules designed to reduce the likelihood of offending the latters' susceptibilities. But this very organization, by emphasizing the size and separateness of the Chinese camps, probably ensured that altercations, when they occurred, were of serious dimensions, involving necessarily large-scale assaults by white miners. Another factor making for early peace was the tendency for Chinese to work abandoned diggings, which yielded satisfactory returns to the disciplined and frugal exertions of large gangs. Trouble was narrowly averted at Bendigo in July 1854 when, in the face of allegedly declining yields, agitators called for attacks on the Chinese, as a means *inter alia* of forcing the Victorian Government to restrict their immigration.

The first major riot aimed at the Chinese in Victoria occurred on the Buckland River, where, according to Geoffrey Serle, some 2,000 Chinese had established themselves, in an unaccustomed majority, on new ground. The Legislative Council had earlier, in June 1855, passed legislation introduced by Governor Hotham, which imposed a poll tax of £10 on Chinese immigrants and limited the numbers that could be carried by any one ship. Large numbers evaded the Act, by disembarking in South Australia and proceeding overland to the diggings, so that in mid-1857 there were 35,000 in Victoria. At Buckland River, a meeting of eighty diggers determined on expelling the Chinese 'because they were "robbing us of our goldfields" and because of their "gross and beastly practices"'. As Westgarth describes the ensuing riot, it was intended as a further warning to the government that effective restrictions were required. The camp was pillaged and burnt, and its occupants put to flight, some of them dying from wounds and from drowning. Leading rioters were tried at Beechworth, but juries sympathised with the accused and the more serious charges were not sheeted home.

Dr. Serle's explanation for the brutal treatment of the Chinese notices the range of allegations urged against them, including misuse of scarce water, exportation of gold earnings, and offences against prevailing customs of morality, hygiene and religion. But he concludes that 'the main ones are all aspects of economic competition . . . the basic complaint was that the Chinese were reducing the European digger's opportunities and earnings.'

Why were the Chinese the sole recipients of economically based reprisals on a large scale? The answer to this crucial question appears to be that the Chinese were readily, indeed dramatically, identifiable as an 'out-group', and as a threat to the rest of the diggers at times of hardship. This was so, because they differed from the European majority in physique, dress, and custom and because they formed distinct enclaves. It seems quite likely that, at this stage in a spasmodic exclusionist movement, race hatred was not of primary importance in initiating discriminatory actions.

Legislation by the parliaments of Victoria and New South Wales for the restriction of Chinese immigration was, in its early phase, a reaction to the problem of maintaining law and order on the gold fields. In speaking to the bills, members traversed the diggers' familiar complaints, although here, as in the press, there were many appeals to liberal concepts of freedom of movement and to the principle that the stranger within the gates should be protected from injury. True, the inferiority of the Chinese race was freely assumed, and comparisons were made with the social evils that had attended convict transportation. But, remembering that well-to-do parliamentarians had no clear economic interest in excluding the Chinese, it appears probable that they were concerned mainly with preventing breaches of the peace.

The pragmatism of the early legislation against the Chinese appears to be confirmed by the fact that the laws were repealed between 1861 and 1867, with the rapid dwindling of the Chinese minorities as alluvial mining declined. However, the next phase of the anti-Chinese movement, which came to a head with the inter-colonial conferences of 1881 and 1888, was strongly doctrinaire and based on concepts of an ideal society, in which the Chinese were seen as having no place.

Revival of Australian fears of Chinese migration occurred with the rush to the Palmer River diggings in Queensland, where in 1877 they outnumbered European miners by 17,000 to 14,000. In this situation, resentment at the export of Chinese earnings made a good deal of sense and the question appeared to be seriously posed as to whether the colony would remain substantially of British stock. Severe restrictions were placed on the entry of Chinese and they were virtually excluded from gold mining. This was to be the pattern for Western Australia from the very beginning of its major gold strikes.

The growth of organized labour was probably the greatest single influence on this phase of the anti-Chinese movement. Trades and Labour Councils were established in Sydney and Melbourne in 1871 and 1874, and inter-colonial links were formed between workers, particularly those involved in shearing, mining and shipping. The importance of this development lay in its tendency to co-ordinate and give continuity to action against the Chinese who, in this period, if they remained in Australia, were leaving gold mining for alternative occupations such as market gardening, furniture making, storekeeping, pastoral work and eventually shipping. In the fight for improved conditions of labour, and for the recognition of unionism itself, the worker saw the non-unionist Chinese as a hated ally of the employers and as a competitor whose lower standard of living, lack of dependents and tireless application made him trebly dangerous.

Trouble occurred at a number of shearing sheds and injected what has been seen as a virulent racialist strain into some of the ballads of the period. But the most significant collision took place during the three months from November 1878, when the Australian Steam Navigation Company began to employ Chinese seamen at rates of £2.15.0 per month, compared with the hard-won, unionist rate of £6.8.0. Support for the striking seamen extended throughout the colonies and to New Zealand. An important factor in the virtual capitulation of the company was the Queensland government's decision to withdraw its mail subsidy and to make its future award conditional upon the exclusive employment of white labour. This was to form the pattern for Commonwealth policy from 1901, because governments accepted the unionists' proposition that the matter went beyond the simple question of rates and conditions, to include the issue of the survival of a locally manned shipping industry.

Meanwhile, the lessons of the seamen's strike were discussed at the first inter-colonial Trade Union Congress at Sydney in 1879, when a motion against 'Asiatic Immigration' was carried unanimously. The incident was important for its impact on a body of men who would increasingly influence public policy, particularly after the formation of the first Parliamentary Labour Party in New South Wales in 1891.

Trade unionists may have been the best organized and most vocal 'ginger group' in campaigning for the exclusion of Chinese, but they had as allies a majority of the old style politicians such as Parkes in New South Wales, Griffith in Queensland and Duffy in Victoria. These men not only conceded the workers' right to protection from unfair competition, which non-European labour almost invariably constituted in the employment context of the late nineteenth century, when perhaps no more than one worker in ten was a unionist. They accepted as well the view that all of society's greater interests were deeply involved in decisions about Chinese immigration. Believing this, Parkes and his fellow premiers set up inter-colonial conferences in 1881 and 1888, from which emerged draft exclusion bills that were designed to enforce a uniform and almost prohibitive policy throughout Australia.

Attempts by the British government to temper colonial action with a regard for the Crown's treaty obligations to the Chinese Empire accelerated, if anything, intransigent action by the Australian premiers. The arrival of successive vessels containing smallpox cases amongst Chinese passengers and the discovery of a high proportion of forged naturalization certificates galvanized Parkes into pushing emergency measures through the New South Wales parliament. His speech on 16 May 1888 represents well the state of public opinion:—

> I contend that if this young nation is to maintain the fabric of its liberties unassailed and unimpaired, it cannot admit into its population any element that of necessity must be of an inferior nature and character. In other words, I have maintained at all times that we should not encourage or admit amongst us any class of persons whatever whom we are not prepared to advance to all our franchises, to all our privileges as citizens, and all our social rights, including the right of marriage. I maintain that no class of persons should be admitted here, so far as we can reasonably exclude them, who cannot come amongst us, take up all our rights, perform on a ground of equality all our duties, and share in our august and lofty work of founding a free nation.

Sir Samuel Griffith's letter of 24 March 1888 to the Governor of Queensland expresses views which, like those of Sir Henry Parkes, are strongly reminiscent of Stephen's minute of 1843. In each there is a basic assumption of the superiority of the 'European race', and a belief that intermarriage with other races, whether 'different' or 'inferior' would cause rapid degeneration. However, we can also discern responsible and mature judgement as to the dangers which non-European immigration posed for the development of democratic institutions in a new country.

Rootedly opposed as they were to Chinese immigration, Queenslanders remained unconvinced until 1901 on the matter of indentured coloured labour, on which their great sugar industry was based. With federation, the majority decision against all forms of non-European labour was imposed on a reluctant Queensland government. Till then, the colony followed the pattern of Natal, with its implications for the indefinite subjection of voteless coloured mass to a white élite.

For most of the last twenty years of the nineteenth century, the sugar plantations had employed up to 10,000 Pacific Island labourers, of whom between 5 and 10 per cent were females. Importation of the islanders, who were known as Kanakas, began in 1863, when Captain Robert Towns brought sixty-seven labourers to Moreton Bay to establish a cotton plantation on the Logan River. From the outset, the government had its critics, who accused it of winking at the introduction of a *de facto* slave trade. But the traffic flourished, as southern capitalists followed the example of the Hon. Louis Hope, who employed islanders on three year indentures to clear and cultivate land for sugar growing. Against their critics, the planters urged the formidable arguments that the industry could not be pioneered without cheap, 'reliable' labour and that even if white men were physically capable of performing field labour in the tropics, they could not be attracted to the work at economically viable rates.

The forty years' agony of the Pacific Islanders in Queensland pioneered a great industry, founded some impressive fortunes and enabled a leisured class to build a graceful life upon the model of the defunct American slave colonies. It produced also some notable scandals especially associated with the blackbirders' recruitment methods and with the notoriously high mortality rate of the islanders during their period of unaccustomed labour on the plantations. A *Herald* investigator estimated in 1901 that, of the 50,500 Kanakas imported up to 1895, at least 10,000, in the prime of their lives, had died in Queensland, at a rate over three times the colony's average.

Over the years, the system of recruitment and employment came under more beneficient regulation, inspired by humanitarian concern and by threat of abolitionist pressure that fed upon scandalous exposures. For twenty years, Queenslanders negotiated with the Government of India for an alternative supply of labour, but the conditions and guarantees offered always fell short of the latter's minimum demands. In 1885 the Griffith government gave the planters five years to adjust to white labour and attempted to set up a financial and administrative framework within which a conversion of plantations to family based farms might be effected. But in the 1890s, financial depression and competition from European beet sugar forced a deferment. The end came only when Queensland's narrow vote for federation put Premier Philp and the sugar industry in the hands of an overwhelmingly abolitionist Commonwealth Parliament.

The first session of the first Federal Parliament passed two measures that were designed to secure a 'White Australia', the Pacific Island Labourers' Act and the Immigration Restriction Act. The former prohibited the introduction of Pacific Islanders after 31 March 1904 and required repatriation by the end of 1906, of those remaining, with the exception of a few who were deemed to have achieved domicile in Australia.

In spite of protests and talk of secession by the Philp government, this Act faithfully carried out the mandate of Queensland voters in the first federal elections, which had been fought in that state almost exclusively on the issue of coloured labour. A victory for the Protectionist Party did not imply, however, the destruction of the sugar industry. Edmund Barton had promised and he quickly implemented, a customs duty that shielded Queensland sugar producers from cheap imports, while at the same time the Constitution guaranteed free access to the whole Australian market. Adjustment to white labour was eased by the increase of the world price for sugar, by technological improvements and by the movement of labour from the dying mining fields.

Complementary to the legislation on Pacific Islanders was the Commonwealth Parliament's Immigration Restriction Act, which instituted the dictation test as a device for excluding non-European immigrants. Unlike the Kanaka issue in Queensland, the reservation of the privilege of immigration for white men aroused no public or parliamentary controversy, except on the question of how it was to be effected. The choice lay between direct legislation that defined non-Europeans as prohibited immigrants and what was seen as the more courteous approach of prohibiting the entry of persons who failed in a given language test. After lengthy debate and sustained diplomatic pressure, the parliament chose the latter method.

It remains now to consider the motivation of this final phase of the exclusionist movement. From 1896, several colonial parliaments passed legislation which set the pattern for Commonwealth action in two ways, by establishing barriers against *all* non-European immigrants and by employing, in place of the blunt language of the anti-Chinese Acts, the more diplomatically acceptable device of the dictation test. It is evident, when we notice the tiny scale of Japanese and Indian settlement, that the bills of the 1890s were of a preventive character. They were devised to meet a potential influx made possible, in part, by the opening up of regular steamship communication between Japan and Australia and by the beginnings of Japanese labour recruitment for the Australian tropics. In spite of the arguments of a few powerful advocates who applauded the marvellous advances of the Japanese nation and who pointed to rich trading prospects, the view that won general acceptance was that Japanese, being of non-European race, would not be assimilated into Australian society. For the same reason the people of India, though British subjects, were to be excluded.

As George Reid, Premier of New South Wales, expressed the point in moving the second reading of the Coloured Races Restriction and Regulation Bill of 1896, which was subsequently refused Royal Assent, '... I do not think it necessary to make a very long speech ... much of what was said in 1881 and 1888 on the question of restricting the immigration of Chinese is applicable to this bill; in fact it was simply an extension of the views which were held at that time in connection with the Chinese.'

This, it must be recalled, was a time in world history in which the theories of the Social Darwinists combined with the military, technical, and administrative pre-eminence of the white races to confirm Europeans in their assumption of an intrinsic superiority over the coloured races. In Australia, the popular mood was expressed by the Brisbane *Worker,* which welcomed the proclamation of the new Commonwealth and the beginning of the twentieth Century with an editorial that called on the federated colonies to form a society free from the 'class distinctions, traditions, superstitions and sanctified fables and fallacies of the older nations', free also from the extremes of wealth and poverty, a 'state built up of a multitude of perfect human units'. In the racially homogeneous utopia of the Australian nationalist there was to be no place for the coloured man.

George Reid made a vital contribution to the movement that culminated in the Commonwealth's Immigration Restriction Act of 1901, both in calling the intercolonial conferences of 1896 and 1898 that sought to evolve a common policy on non-European immigration, and in insisting on diplomatic arguments for excluding Japanese. In his own parliament and at the London premiers' conference of 1897, he warned of the danger of permitting the development of a 'uitlander' situation that might give the Japanese government a pretext for intervening in Australia, as Britain was shortly to intervene in the Transvaal, on behalf of its distressed nationals. Striking vindication for this policy was soon afforded by Queensland's experience of diplomatic protests against her discriminatory treatment of Japanese, and by the bitterness injected into Japanese-American relations for three decades by the disputes over the disabilities suffered by the Japanese residents of California.

Reid's apprehension of the new kind of danger that might be posed by a sizeable Japanese minority bore immediate fruit in the 1896 bills, excluding the coloured races in unambiguous terms. In company with his fellow premiers at the London conference of 1897, Reid heard Mr. Chamberlain's appeal for the self-governing colonies to refrain from legislation that offered a gratuitous insult to the Indian and other coloured races which comprised a large portion of the British Empire. The Secretary of State for the Colonies recommended instead action on the lines of Natal's Immigration Restriction Act of 1897, which required a modest standard of literacy in a European language. This device was not at first acceptable to Reid, who wanted to legislate in clear and unmistakable terms. But the diplomatic pressure mounted by the Japanese government, directly through its consular staff and indirectly through the Foreign Office, at length persuaded the Australian premiers of the expediency of using the Natal device. Western Australia, New South Wales and Tasmania did so in 1897 and 1898. The Commonwealth followed their lead in 1901 with the Immigration Restriction Act, establishing a dictation test in any European language chosen by the administering officer that was to prove capable of excluding any immigrant to whom it was applied.

Within six months of its introduction by the Commonwealth, the dictation test had proved capable of the severity promised by the Barton government. The administering officers, originally men from the Customs Department who searched ships for contraband and Chinese stowaways, were made to realize that the test should be applied only to non-Europeans and in such a form as to ensure failure. Test passages were changed from month to month; they were chosen for their difficulty, and it was within the officer's power to apply the test in a language other than English when the immigrant appeared to be conversant with that language. In effect, the shipping companies became the first line of White Australia's defence, because they faced heavy penalties for carrying to Australia people who were later deemed by courts to be prohibited immigrants, on the basis of their failure in the test.

During the Commonwealth's first two decades, the Immigration Restriction Act was frequently amended and its impact was modified by administrative decision. These changes were all in harmony with the basic policy of excluding non-European settlement. Legislative loopholes were blocked, as immigrants explored the Act's deficiencies and the work of detection was improved both at the ports and in the areas of Chinese residence. But the major change was the suspension in March 1903 of the exemption offered by section 3 (m) of the Act to the wives and minor children of domiciled non-Europeans. The Commonwealth's greatest asset in pursuing the 'White Australia' policy, was the overwhelming masculinity of the immigrant non-white population, which in 1901 ranged from, approximately, 62 per cent for the Syrians, to 93.4 per cent for Japanese, 98.5 per cent for Chinese and 99.2 per cent for Indians. Apart from the Syrians, who gradually came to be regarded as Europeans, the minority races faced certain decline, provided that their immigration was totally stopped.

Concern about relations with Japan prompted the second major change in the 1901 Act and its administration—the provision of specific facilities for the temporary entry of merchants, students and tourists who had passports verifying their status. Prime Minister Alfred Deakin initiated the negotiations that produced the passport arrangement of 1904 in the belief that the Japanese government and people had been deeply offended by Australia's exclusive legislation. He tried without success to bring into being a formal treaty by which both Australia and Japan recognized the other party's migration policies, while providing for temporary visits in a courteous fashion. Failing in this, the Deakin government and its successors attempted to conciliate Japan in every way, short of admitting her settlers.

Trade prospects had a place in Deakin's thinking, but his great object was to reduce sources of friction with the only Asian power that loomed as a threat to Australian security. Fears of a terrible Japanese revenge and of designs on 'empty spaces' underlay some of the Commonwealth's major policies in these decades. The encouragement of European immigration and the establishment of an Australian navy and of compulsory military training, were dimensions of this fear. Towards the close of the period came anxieties about Japan's territorial gains from the Treaty of Versailles, which brought her closer to Australian soil. W. M. Hughes insisted on Australia's receiving New Guinea, as a barrier to invasion, and he led the opposition to the insertion in the League of Nations' Covenant of the Japanese-proposed 'racial equality' clause, which he regarded as a first step in forcing the admission of Japanese settlers.

The 'white outpost' mentality influenced greatly Hughes' attitude to the empire and helped to form policies towards India. Fear of Japan was a factor in Hughes' insistence on conscripting Australians for service in the Empire's war, as a means of ensuring Imperial and Indian support in the event of an attack by Japan. It produced also the reciprocal arrangements with India that promised temporary admission to Indians on even more favourable terms than Japanese and allowed the entry of the families of domiciled Indians. An understanding was eventually made and carried out, to remove the statutory disabilities suffered by Indian residents in Australia. The first hesitant steps were being taken in the direction of liberalizing the ' "White Australia" Policy'.

It is apparent that the arrangements for temporary visits by Asians and the concession to the families of domiciled Indians, who numbered little more than 2,000 in 1921, amounted to no major breach in the policy of exclusion. 'White Australia' remained a settled national policy, an article of faith that encountered virtually no criticism from within Australia and little challenge from outside. Apologists for the doctrine had changed their ground, however, in urging the *differences* between races, cultures and political institutions rather than the superiority of the white race. This change was influenced greatly by the dramatic progress of the Japanese in terms meaningful to Europeans, but offsetting this example was the condition of much of Asia and Africa, which remained subject to the European colonial empires. This is not to suggest that emanicipation of the coloured races would cause an immediate revision of Australian policy, for belief in the eugenic and political virtues of race homogeneity would die hard.

ACKNOWLEDGEMENTS

I especially wish to acknowledge my indebtedness to several scholars on whose unpublished work I lean heavily in dealing with the anti-Chinese movements. They are Mr. Tony Ohlsson, Mr. Sing Wu Wang and Mr. Choi Ching Yan. The firm of Cassell Australia Ltd. was kind enough to allow me to use again small portions of the text in my *Attitudes to Non-European Immigration*.

I depend greatly, of course, on pioneering students of the period, such as Sir Timothy Coghlan, Myra Willard, Bede Nairn, Geoffrey Bolton and Geoffrey Serle.

REFERENCES

BOOKS:

BOLTON, GEOFFREY. *A Thousand Miles Away; A History of North Queensland to 1929*, Brisbane, 1963.

SERLE, GEOFFREY. Chapter on 'The Chinese Minority' in his *The Golden Age; A History of the Colony of Victoria, 1851-1861*, Melbourne, 1963.

WILLARD, MYRA. *History of the White Australia Policy*, Melbourne, 1923.

YARWOOD, A. T. *Asian Migration to Australia; The Background to Exclusion, 1896-1923*, Melbourne, 1964.

YARWOOD, A. T. (ed.). *Attitudes to Non-European Immigration*, Melbourne, 1968

ARTICLES:

DALLAS, K. M. "The Origins of "White Australia"", *Australian Quarterly*, Vol. xxvii, March, 1955.

MANSFIELD, B. C. 'The Origins of "White Australia"', *ibid*, Vol. xxvi, December, 1954.

NAIRN, N. B. 'A Survey of the History of the White Australia Policy in the 19th Century', *ibid*, Vol. xxviii, September, 1956.

THESES:

CHOI, C. Y. 'Chinese Migration and Settlement in Australia with special reference to the Chinese in Melbourne'.

WANG, SING WU. 'The organisation of Chinese Emigration, 1848-1888 with special reference to Chinese Emigration to Australia', M.A. thesis, A.N.U,, 1968.

THE MORAL FOUNDATION

15

RACISM, THE CHURCH AND AUSTRALIA

R. G. Nettheim

Racism: Words v. Actions

It is probably true to say that almost everyone in the Australian community is opposed to racism and racial discrimination, just as almost everyone would be in favour of motherhood. Even letters to editors from Australian supporters of Ian Smith and Mr. Vorster (the *Rhodesia Lobby* and the *Pretorian Guard*) commonly commence with such phrases as 'I am not a racist, but . . .' or 'I disapprove of *apartheid*, however . . .'.

The Australian electorate, by a 90 per cent majority, approved the 1967 referendum to amend the Commonwealth Constitution so as to give the Commonwealth Parliament power to make laws for Aborigines and to include Aborigines in the census. In fact, no party or group opposed the proposals. This referendum could be interpreted as a massive gesture of white goodwill towards the long-neglected black Australians.

But gestures do not feed the hungry, educate the illiterate, or change the deep-rooted prejudices of many white townsfolk against black shanty-dwellers. What people say, and even what they believe, may have little relevance to how they feel, or what they would do in a particular situation. Professor Charles Glock, a sociologist from Berkeley, told the 1969 London Consultation on Racism about a Californian survey which was conducted to test the effect of church teachings on the actual conduct of white Christians in the sample area—well over 90 per cent of those interviewed accepted the brotherhood of man as Christian teaching; but when asked what they would do if a black family moved next door, a significant number indicated that they would move away. The traditional Australian approach to the problem of choice in such a situation has been to avoid the situation altogether by ensuring that blacks do not move next door.

The significance of 1971: for the United Nations

On 11 December, 1969, the General Assembly of the United Nations, by Resolution 2544 (XXIV), designated 1971 as International Year for Action to Combat Racism and Racial Discrimination. There have been International Years before, (for example, Human Rights Year in 1968) and it has been difficult to perceive any drastic improvement in the human condition as a result. Conferences and seminars are held, books are published, resolutions are passed, sermons are delivered—all with the utmost sincerity, conviction and sense of achievement—but the hearts and the actions of the majority of mankind remain unreached and unreformed.

It was probably in recognition of this truism that the General Assembly included in the title for the 1971 year the word 'Action'. Human attitudes are the issue, and attitudes are not changed by platitudes. 'Action' is specifically called for if the Year is to have any significance whatever.

In particular, Resolution 2544 (XXIV) called for action by the governments of member nations. It called 'upon all States to co-operate in every possible way in (the) implementation' of the programme for the observance of the International Year prepared by the Secretary-General. And it 'urgently appeal(ed) to all States to intensify and expand their efforts at the national and the international level towards ensuring the rapid and total eradication of racial discrimination'.

For the Australian Government

In reply to a question in the House of Representatives, the Minister for External Affairs (as he then was), Mr. McMahon, indicated on 30 October, 1970, that the Federal Government was doing little more than giving 'careful consideration' to a 'suitable programme' to observe the International Year, and he referred the questioner to 'celebration' of the Year at the non-governmental level. With 1971 already well under way, the Government has revealed nothing further as to any plans which it may have to observe the Year even in words, let alone in action.[1] Indeed, as far as Australia's international posture is concerned, the Government commenced the year with its stance of 'neutrality' at the Commonwealth Conference in Singapore on the proposed British arms sales to South Africa,[2] and with a studied rebuke to the British Race Relations Board for questioning Australia's policy of offering assisted passages only to white immigrants.[3]

For Australian citizens

Any initiatives, then, seem to be left to private organizations. These, of course, do not command the powers of government which are essential for most of the conceivable forms of 'action' required to implement the purposes of the International Year in Australia. They can, however, if they proceed effectively, help to mobilise political pressures of one sort or another to persuade Federal and State governments to action.

Early in 1970 a number of interested individuals and organizations did come together to attempt to instigate some Australian observance of the International Year. The catalyst was the able Dennis Brutus[4] who, on a brief visit en route from America to Britain brought with him from U.N. headquarters the message of 1971. These individuals and organizations formed an *ad hoc* committee which immediately contacted the United Nations Association of Australia with a view to its spearheading national and state committees for the observance of 1971. The U.N.A.A. is in good standing with the Federal Government,[5] and the effectiveness of any Australian programme for the International Year will partly depend on the work of the committees which it convenes. Its work is to be co-ordinated through a special Melbourne-based committee called CARRD (Committee for Action against Racism and Racial Discrimination) but, at the time of going to press, it is not yet clear what action is intended. At the same time, of course, a number of the supporting organizations (and others) have planned their own individual programmes for action for 1971—and beyond.

Involved in all this activity have been a number of members, lay and clerical, of various Australian religious faiths.

The position of the Church

It is probably misleading to attempt to identify a Christian position on race relations as distinct from a secular 'liberal' position. It is true that Christians (and Jews) can produce textual support from the Old Testament for the notion of the essential unity of mankind, and Christians can rely particularly on the teachings of the New Testament.

But theologians, like lawyers, will agree that it is frequently possible to discover, from any substantial body of textual authority, support for totally conflicting propositions. Segregationist churches in the southern United States and the Dutch Reformed Church in South Africa claim to find Biblical support for racist attitudes. And, of course, the 'liberal' texts existed 300, 200 and 100 years ago when Christianity generally was prepared to countenance the subjugation of 'pagan' races, even if only for the purposes of religious conversion. The irony of the current situation, as Shaw predicted,[6] is that the converted black peoples are now in a position to judge the converting white societies in accordance with their own teachings.

If churchmen are now to be found in the forefront of the struggle against racism and racial discrimination,[7] it seems too simple to attribute the fact to Church teaching alone. Such men and women appear, rather, to have responded as Christians to a broader movement against racism which has been developing in the world especially since the First World War. On the other hand, 'rationalists', 'humanitarians' and other secular 'liberals' from the Western world can scarcely help but to have been influenced by the Christian ethic which is still (if only in theory) the accepted basis of human relations in their cultures. Their idealism has today been linked with the much more pragmatic motivations of the peoples of the Third World who, now articulate, claim the benefit of the moral teachings of their former masters. In some cases, of course, Third World leaders are themselves committed Christians, such as President Julius Nyerere of Tanzania (a Roman Catholic) and President Kenneth Kaunda of Zambia (a Presbyterian).

It has, it is suggested, been in response to (and as part of) this much broader movement that the organized church has now (if belatedly) rallied behind those of its ministers who have hitherto borne Christian witness as individuals in courageous opposition to racism.[8]

The final statement of the 1969 London Consultation on Racism made this point: 'If the churches are to have any relevance in these critical times, it is imperative that they no longer concentrate their attention on the individual actions of individual Christians who are fighting racism. To the majority of Christians, the Church is a community, a group—perhaps even a movement—and it is therefore necessary that issues of racism be addressed by a group. Individual commitment is commendable —but not enough.'

The question remains whether, in the 1970s, the Church has any significant role to play in changing the racist and discriminating attitudes of people who may have only a tenuous connection (if that) with organized religion and who have become accustomed to the notion that Christian teaching (beyond a possible passive hour or two on Sunday) has nothing to do with actual living.

The World Council of Churches

For the 232 churches represented in the World Council of Churches,[9] 1969 must be regarded as a watershed year in the matter of race relations. Although the primary concern of the WCC is the ecumenical movement in all its aspects,[10] it is only natural that it should have become a spokesman for the Church on issues of broad common concern in an increasingly secular age. Racism and racial discrimination constitute one of those issues.

The issue has been the subject of resolutions and other activity by the ecumenical movement over a number of years. But Dr. W. A. Visser 't Hooft, General Secretary of the WCC from 1948 until 1967, and now its Honorary President, in reviewing the record at the 1969 London Consultation on Racism, concluded that the Church had done 'too little, too late'. He went on to summarise particular points of criticism:—

(i) We have believed too much in persuasion by declarations and not been sufficiently aware of the irrational factors in the situation.

(ii) We have not given adequate attention to the economic factors making for racial injustice.

(iii) We have insisted too little on the very considerable sacrifices which have to be made if racial justice is to prevail.

(iv) We have not yet found common answers to the problem of violence and non-violence as methods of transforming present patterns and present structures.

By 1968 two things had become clearly apparent. One was that past activity by the WCC had had little or no significant effect. The other was that racial antagonism was emerging, with frightening rapidity, as, arguably, the most dangerous and divisive issue in the modern world. So the Fourth Assembly of the WCC meeting in Uppsala, Sweden, in July 1968 decided not just to pass more resolutions but, as a prelude to possible action, to seek advice.

The Central Committee of the WCC subsequently authorised its Geneva staff to convene a Consultation on Racism. This was eventually held at the Ecumenical Centre in Notting Hill, London from 19-24 May, 1969. Those involved were asked to examine the issue of racism and to report back to the World Council 'proposals for an ecumenical programme of education *and action* for the World Council and its member churches'.

Consultation

The Consultation took the form of a gathering of about forty participants, twenty-five Consultants and several Observers, together with members of the World Council staff, under the chairmanship of U.S. Senator George McGovern, a Methodist layman. The Participants were all committed Christians (four of them Roman Catholics). The Consultants were not necessarily Christian at all and represented a range, from conservative to radical, of people with experience in racial confrontations in many parts of the world. All they shared in common was an opposition to racism and sufficient belief in the possible relevance of the Church to the issue at this time (though some clearly had their doubts) to make it worthwhile to take part. They came from France, Germany, Holland, Hungary, Sweden, Switzerland, the U.S.S.R., the U.K., Egypt, Algeria, Kenya, Sierra Leone, Cameroun, Rhodesia, South Africa, Japan, India, Ceylon, Indonesia, Australia, New Zealand, Fiji, Peru, Trinidad-Tobago, Canada and the U.S.A.; and from organizations such as UNESCO, YMCA and YWCA.

It had been requested that emphasis be placed on white racism—not that whites have a monopoly of racism, but, rather, because the attitude of whites to non-whites was conceded to be the most serious current form of racism, coinciding largely as it does with the dividing line between the haves and the have-nots.[11] And, of course, the Christian church has been the religion of the whites.

If anyone had expected the Consultation to be an occasion of the Church looking in sorrow on the sinfulness of the outside world, he was in for a shock. The Church itself came in for bitter attack. Frequently it had been the ally of white supremacy—not only in the distant past when conquest and conversion went hand in hand to destroy entire cultures (as in the Americas, the Pacific and Australia) but even today, in more subtle ways. As the final statement of the Consultation put it: 'The identification of the churches with the *status quo* means today, as before, that it has remained, in effect, part of the racial problem and not a means of eliminating it'.

It is rare to find a Church explicitly preaching white supremacy.[12] But the charges were made from all parts of the world that the Church had said nothing; or the Church had spoken but done nothing; or, more seriously, that the Church had condoned racism, profited from racism, or even practised racism. Churchmen themselves made the charges. The Church itself was brought to confession of its sins, in recommendations and resolutions noted below.

The institutional church, however, was only a peripheral target. It was the conduct and attitudes of white society as a whole that came under scrutiny, and though many basic elements of white society may derive from church teachings,[13] they now have their own momentum while the role of the Church continues to contract.

Although the geographical range of representation at the Consultation was broad, attention was focused primarily on three areas—Southern Africa, the United Kingdom and the U.S.A.

Southern Africa

Actually not a great deal was said about Southern Africa. Little needed to be said as the situation there is so explicit. It became even more explicit during the Consultation itself with the announcement of Ian Smith's proposed new constitution for Rhodesia. Invitees from South Africa were 'unable to attend', but the region had ample witnesses in Garfield Todd, Rev. Herbert Chikomo, Bishop Trevor Huddleston, Rev. Michael Scott, Oliver Tambo and Joseph Matthews.

Britain

Britain having provided the venue for the Consultation, there were several discussions on race relations in Britain.[14] After one such panel, Roy Sawh, militant chairman of the Black Power Party, described the experience of listening to a statement given by Merlyn Rees, M.P. (then the Home Office minister with special responsibility for race relations) as like listening to Enoch Powell. But he then observed that there was little point in putting his question as Mr. Rees had been called away. Taking him at his word, the Archbishop of Canterbury, Dr. Ramsey, as chairman of the panel, called on the next speaker. Mr. Sawh who *had* intended to speak on, walked out in protest, and subsequently received the Archbishop's apology. This was merely one of several 'black power confrontations' picked up by the Press. A more significant one was an interruption of the final stages of the Consultation by a group of young black militants who presented certain demands as a 'Declaration of Revolution'.

U.S.A.

But the Americans dominated the Consultation. What they (white and black) had to say and to propose largely set the tone for the mood of urgency attending the meeting. The sophistication of American 'black power' techniques already has influence elsewhere, and will certainly continue to do so. Gradualism, patience, charity, even integration are now at a discount among black Americans. Instead there is growing demand for separatism (especially in colleges and churches),[15] not, apparently, as any long-term solution but simply as a short-term withdrawal from white society in order to establish a strong sense of identity within the black community itself. Superficially, this resurgent black consciousness may seem to have many things in common with precisely that white racism against which it is reacting. But while black Americans are bitter in their assertions that white society must be remade, at least on a non-racist basis, (and possibly by fundamental changes in traditional 'bourgeois' structures and traditions) most of the speakers still saw this as a worthwhile goal which a cohesive black community might help to achieve.

Australia

Although attention was directed mainly to these three parts of the world, problems elsewhere also received mention. Australia, for example, had Kath Walker and Don Dunstan to demonstrate that, in the matter of white contempt for black, Australia should not be regarded as lagging more than its customary distance behind its great and powerful friends. Mr. Dunstan spoke of his South Australian Aboriginal Land Trust Act of 1966 to vest land ownership in trust for the Aborigines, and regretted that other Australian governments had not yet seen fit to take similar action to remedy this ancient grievance.[16] Mrs. Walker, Aboriginal leader and poet, spoke movingly about the destruction of the sacred places of the Yirrkala people by the aluminium consortium. (A suitable analogy for the occasion might have been to invite Christians to contemplate open-cut coal mining in Jerusalem.) She also had much to say about the Gurindjis and the Vestey meat interests.

Power

This stress on land rights, in the Australian context, simply echoed a general theme of the Consultation—the need for power, and primarily economic power.[17] Ideology, as such, was treated as virtually irrelevant. Christianity, itself, had not prevented racism. (On the other hand,

Communism scarcely rated a mention.) What counts now in an age of disillusion is action, not words; power, not ideology. If power is not accessible to people, for no other reason than that they are black, it will be striven for by them on the basis of their blackness. 'Black power', if you like. Despite scare headlines, the phrase primarily indicates nothing more than the antithesis of black powerlessness.

It was made quite clear that black people do not want things done *for* them, as charity (and little of significance has ever been done for them on that basis). Rather, they insist, as a matter of justice, on the right to win some command over their own destiny. Access to economic power is regarded as critical. Only with economic power will they be treated with human respect by a white society which tends to worship Mammon before God. (Even white South Africans do business with Japanese as 'honorary whites'.) Only with economic power can political and social equality be achieved in terms of housing, education, skills and so on. Only with economic power can they recapture self-respect as peoples. Trade rather than aid. Employment rather than hand-outs. Justice rather than charity. And action rather than words.

The message certainly got through to all those at the Consultation. The World Council's General Secretary, Dr. Eugene Carson Blake, described the Consultation in his subsequent report as 'an event . . . a happening'. 'By this,' he added, 'I mean that no person who went through the experience came out unaffected. We all learned'.

The chairman of the Consultation, Senator McGovern, described it as 'a memorable and significant experience in human dynamics marked by love and anger, hope and despair, bitter realism and sweet pieties, succinct insights and rambling oratory. It was a week of blunt confrontation, surprising turbulence, and outspoken condemnations, as well as of tedium, frustration and intellectual posturing. But above all, it was a week in which a diverse group of human beings grappled seriously and sometimes painfully with the terrible sin of racism'.

Senator McGovern went on to stress the sense of urgency which was the overwhelming impression to emerge from the Consultation. Nothing highlighted this urgency more than the one public meeting of the week held in Church House next to Westminster Abbey. The floor of the hall and the galleries were well filled to hear addresses by Bishop Huddleston and Oliver Tambo. But no sooner had the Bishop mentioned the name of Enoch Powell (unfavourably) than some dozens of people in the gallery burst into chants of 'Enoch! Enoch!' and 'Blacks Out!' It was Britain's National Front using its familiar technique of disruption. And although they were gradually ushered out, courteously, by the police, enough remained to keep up heckling throughout the evening. The National Front represents only hundreds in a population of some 50 million. But the less blatant expressions of racism in Britain are the more dangerous because more widespread—job discrimination, excessive rentals for slum housing, and so on. It has, in the last few years, become only too apparent what too many otherwise decent Britons would do if a black family moved next door.

Recommendations

The Consultation, seized with this sense of urgency, produced a number of resolutions. One of them concerned racism in the Church itself and some extracts are worth quoting. The churches, it said, should 'confess their involvement in the perpetuation of racism'. They should 'make full and open disclosure of their assets, income, investments, land-holdings and financial involvements' so that it may be seen how 'the churches' financial practices, both domestic and international, contribute to the support of racially oppressive governments, discriminatory industries and inhuman working conditions'. 'Christians should develop strategies aimed at the disengagement of the Church from the support of racial oppression'.

In consequence, the Consultation endorsed the principle of reparation:—[18]

> 'Religious institutions of the white northern world have acquired excessively enormous wealth both in collusion with and as a consequence of racially exploitative economic systems. The forces seeking to liberate coloured peoples from the oppressive yoke of white domination have appropriately demanded the participation of religious institutions in restoring wealth and power to people. We urge religious institutions to divest themselves of their excessive material wealth by immediately allocating a significant portion of their total resources, without employing any mechanism of control, to organizations of the racially oppressed'.

The Consultation also expressed its deep concern at the proposed new Constitution for Rhodesia and, amongst other things, called on Britain to withdraw her earlier assurance that force would not be used in resolving the conflict.

Amongst a number of powerful recommendations by Working Group B were two to this effect:—

> 'The churches should support the organizations of the victims of white racism by publicly endorsing these movements and by providing funds, personnel and other resources to promote the success of their efforts'.
> 'The churches should support movements for the political liberation of oppressed racial groups'.

Not surprisingly, some of the Press had a field day, presenting an image of the Church Militant invading Rhodesia, aiding terrorists and so on. They overlooked that the Consultation was not the Church and that its resolutions and recommendations had yet to be considered by 120 delegates to the World Council's Central Committee meeting in Canterbury in August, 1969.

Decisions

That meeting was stormy. Much of the meat offered by the Consultation was too strong for the more conservative clerics and heated debates took place between them and the 'progressives'. The Central Committee finally accepted a modified form of the resolutions on racism in the church which allotted guilt only to individual churches (unspecified) and rejected reparation at least as a concept. And the Committee drew up a Five-Year Programme of 'study, consultation and information' to be run by an executive staff unit of three advised by an International Advisory Committee of twenty. More words?

But it did also propose that a special fund be set up ($US200,000 from WCC reserves, $US300,000 to come from member churches) to 'be distributed to organizations of oppressed racial groups or organizations supporting victims of racial injustice whose purposes are not inconsistent with the general purposes of the World Council'. It went on to propose that 'the Executive Committee be authorised to decide, on recommendations from the International Advisory Committee, the organizations to which the Special Fund shall be distributed'.

The International Advisory Committee for the WCC's Programme to Combat Racism, when established, developed criteria to govern its recommendations for grants from the Special Fund. On the basis of those criteria it recommended the immediate distribution of the $200,000 from WCC reserves to nineteen organizations engaged in combating racism in twelve countries. The WCC's Executive Committee adopted the recommendations in September 1970 without dissenting votes. It noted that the organizations which had appealed for grants had given assurances that they would not use the funds for military purposes but for activities in harmony with the purposes of the WCC and its divisions. All the applications were for social, health and educational purposes and for legal aid.

Repercussions

At this point, an international storm of controversy descended on the World Council. Most of the grants passed without comment. In Australia, for example, there was no suggestion that Federal Council for the Advancement of Aborigines and Torres Strait Islanders and the National Tribal Council ought not have been beneficiaries, though some church spokesmen did dub the latter organization as 'radical' and protested that they were not consulted about the distribution. (Is this very protest a claim to racial superiority?) But it was the grants amounting to $120,000 to the eleven liberation movements for Southern Africa which caused trouble. Even though the grants were for non-military purposes, they were made to organizations which had eschewed non-violence. The reaction in Black Africa was, predictably, favourable, even enthusiastic.[19] The reaction in South Africa was, equally predictably, hostile and the Prime Minister, Mr. Vorster, warned South African churches that if they did not sever their links with the WCC he would be forced to act against them. Two British Anglican priests were that month deported for supporting the WCC's action.[20] More recently, the Anglican Dean of Capetown has been detained incommunicado under the Terrorism Act.[21] Churches and churchmen in South Africa divided on the issue.

But the debate was world-wide. The WCC received a vast volume of mail, some in protest, some in commendation. The Australian Council of Churches had a similar experience. The WCC itself, in a letter sent to those who had written about the grants, included the following points:—

'2. Grants from the Special Fund to Combat Racism do not constitute an unqualified endorsement of specific tactics employed by the recipient organizations. They do represent general support from the WCC for the long-term goals towards which the organizations are working. They also imply that anti-racist organizations which believe they have no other option but to resort to violence, are no longer to be automatically excluded from the possibility of moral and practical support from the WCC. The WCC has not opted for violence, in spite of the fact that during World War II

European Christians resisted foreign domination with violence and in spite of the fact that most newly independent countries liberated themselves from oppression by violence and not without moral support from the churches. It will continue to work for reconciliation, for an end to the violence of the oppressors as well as the violence of the oppressed.

'3. $120,000 (out of $200,000) goes to liberation movements in Southern Africa. They have given the assurance that the funds allocated to them will be used for their social welfare, health, educational and legal aid programmes and not for military purposes. Some will use it for development programmes inside liberated territory, others for programmes to counter the propaganda of white apartheid regimes and to inform international public opinion about the plight of the racially oppressed. There is every reason to trust the assurances given by those movements. Of course, there are risks involved in the decision. The churches have taken risks in similar situations before. Would funds for Arab refugees in the Middle East be used by Palestinian freedom fighters? Would support to the Red Cross for medical work in North Vietnam be used by the liberation front to attack villages in South Vietnam?

'4. In the past, church support has been mainly to white liberal groups. The newly created Ecumenical Programme to Combat Racism must give priority to solidarity with the racially oppressed. The WCC cannot any longer ignore the growing number of voices among the racially oppressed asking the churches to make their stand unmistakably clear. It is encouraging, therefore, to know that more and more churches are deciding openly to support the non-violent parts of liberation movements and other groups combating racism.

'5. From the preceding points it is clear that the decision does not represent anything basically new for the WCC. The same could be said of the member churches individually. Many churches committed themselves to programmes of massive humanitarian aid for the victims of the civil war in Nigeria. This was a clear form of support to a liberation movement (Biafra) which was using violent methods. At that time the question of support to a liberation movement did not present any problem. Human suffering was the issue. Are these churches now using different criteria? Could it be that a war between black and black is valued in a different way from a war between black and white? If that is the case black Christians have every right to ask for further explanations.

'8. Many people in the West are asking whether this decision will not damage relationships within the ecumenical fellowship in general and with the white member churches in Southern Africa in particular. It is, of course, possible that some churches may leave the WCC over the issue of race as has happened in the past (two Dutch Reformed Churches in South Africa left the Council in 1960). It is painful but perhaps inevitable that this action will cause trouble and perhaps even physical suffering for some among the WCC's constituency with whom it has had a long and close relationship. It is significant to note that voices of protest against the decision are coming almost exclusively from one side: the white West. But the WCC cannot listen to its white constituency only. It cannot turn a deaf ear to its constituency in Africa, Asia and Latin America and indeed to the plight of all the oppressed.

'9. Finally, the debate about this decision has only started and it will, no doubt, continue for some time. We are not asking for unconditional support, but we are asking that any discussion within the ecumenical fellowship takes place on the basis of the long-standing commitment by the WCC to struggle for racial justice. That struggle has now entered a new phase. It is therefore more urgent than ever before that the Church be clear in its stand.'

At the Central Committee meeting held in January, 1971, in Addis Ababa, the WCC's Secretary-General, Dr. Eugene Carson Blake stated his belief that the decision for the anti-racism programme had been right and that some good things had come out of the controversy. But he had to concede some losses: 'The controversy has been the occasion for people within and outside the Churches to separate themselves and their churches from the World Council as if "Geneva" was fundamentally something other than a fellowship of all churches'. He went on to say that the decision had made more difficult Christian work in South Africa, and had put under new pressures ecumenical work in such other nations as Portugal, Ireland, Greece, Britain and Germany.[22]

Action in Australia? . . . Issues

What, if any, of all this activity at the highest ecclesiastical levels percolates down to Australian churches? The question is relevant, for Australia cannot be regarded as exempt from concern with issues of racism. This country has to face questions of race relations, both within its borders and beyond them. It has to face these questions in response to both internal and external pressures.

Internally, Australia is, of course, itself a multi-racial society. Its population contains as high a percentage of non-whites as does that of Britain (about 2 per cent). Of these, the Aborigines (about 1 per cent of the population, but increasing) are no longer prepared to be left forgotten on the rubbish dumps. They are moving into the towns and cities. They know what is happening elsewhere in the world. And they want the same opportunities in Australian society that the rest have. Eventually they will have those opportunities. The question is whether their needs are to be foreseen, taken seriously, and met by white Australians *now*, or whether they are finally to be achieved only after decades of struggle, producing a legacy of bitterness for generations to come? Already the black militants of yesterday are regarded as today's 'Uncle Toms'. American society left remedial action too late. In Britain, where a great deal is being done, there is still some chance of achieving broad racial harmony. In Australia, little is being done, and time is not on our side.

Externally, Australia is at test in its relationships—political, economic, social—with the peoples of Papua-New Guinea.[23] It will also be increasingly challenged in its relationships with Pacific Island peoples,[24] especially the people of Fiji which for generations has been virtually an economic colony of Australia.[25]

Australia is particularly vulnerable to world criticism in regard to its attitudes to and relationships with the white minority governments of

Southern Africa. South Africa clearly places a high value on strengthening its links with Australia in such matters as commerce, defence[26] and sport.[27] Rhodesia hopes, for the moment, for a purely formal Australian observance of United Nations sanctions while seeking to develop, through 'kith and kin' arguments and the powerful Rhodesia lobby in this country, Australian sympathy for its 'special problems'.[28] It is already apparent that Australia is increasingly regarded as a racist nation because of its links with these two countries.

But the main basis for Australia's international reputation for racism continues to be its immigration policy. It may be fair to say that the White Australia Policy no longer exists as such, especially in view of increased non-white immigration since 1966. It may also be fair to say that other nations also restrict the intake of peoples of other races. And no-one, black or white, advocates any 'opening of floodgates'. But it only requires one well-published incident, especially if handled with the clumsiness and insensitivity which seems to be characteristic of Australian official action in this area—such as the repercussions resulting from the refusal in 1970 of an assisted passage to a non-white British immigrant, Mr. Jan Allen—to bring Australia once again into world contempt. The only people abroad who react favourably to such incidents (apart from South Africans who are happy to share some of their odium) are white racists, some of whom respond by themselves migrating to Australia as a last haven of white supremacy. Australians do not need such reinforcement to be at least as capable (if only latently) of racism as Britons; and their presence makes more difficult the task of educating Australians to accept people of other races (and the nation is surrounded by them) as fellow humans.

But who is to do this educating? No-one is making any serious attempt yet. Obviously the critical areas of action can only be taken by governments, Federal and State and local. But members of governments are Australians and represent Australians. If Australians generally are not alive to these critical issues of racial justice, nothing will be done. It is not enough to make grudging concessions to international pressures (as often seems to be the case in Australian voting at the United Nations); there must also be developed pressures from within the Australian community. The various private organizations represent relatively small numbers and command relatively small influence, though they may gain greater impact through the Australian Citizens' Campaign to Overcome Racial Discrimination (ACCORD). If a wider section of the community is to be won to non-racist attitudes, this must be done through channels which command a wider reach. Leadership initiatives are required. Here the Australian churches can play a part. Will they?

The Australian Council of Churches

Whatever the past record of the Australian churches may have been, some at least appear now to be committed to the achievement of racial justice.

WCC resolutions and statements are transmitted directly to the national denominations. Few if any of them seem to seep down to individual members of Australian congregations, though the Australian Council of Churches does attempt to follow up.

The ACC followed up the dramatic World Council developments of

1969-70 at the Annual Meeting of its eleven member churches held in Sydney in August, 1970. Race relations was one of the themes of the meeting, and a number of people personally involved in race relations issues were invited to take part in a preliminary panel discussion. Subsequently the Council passed a number of resolutions. It requested the Australian Government to assist Pacific territories facing problems of over-population (including Tonga, Fiji and the Gilbert and Ellice Islands) by permitting the initial immigration of 1,000 settlers per year, by offering assistance with family-planning services, and by offering various forms of development aid. The Council requested the Government to extend control of exports to Rhodesia, to use its diplomatic procedures with a view to changing Rhodesian policies, and to offer educational assistance to African refugees from Rhodesia in neighbouring countries. It called upon the Rugby Union of Australian and the Australian Cricket Board of Control to cancel proposed Springbok tours of Australia, and called on all Australian sporting bodies to sever relations with South Africa until that country ceases to apply *apartheid* in sport. It condemned Britains' proposed sale of arms to South Africa, called upon the Australian Government to speak out against the proposal, and requested Heads of Churches and others to urge church members to take political action to these ends. It urged Churches at State and local level to participate fully in events to mark the International Year. It called on all Christians to work to make the question of Aboriginal land rights a major issue in the Senate Elections. And it established Commissions on Aboriginal Development and on Race Relations to advise and assist the Australian Council of Churches.

All this may seem nothing more than words. But words represent at least a start. If taken seriously they can create awareness, and awareness, on this issue, is a commodity sorely lacking in Australia. Awareness may eventually lead to action.

The Churches, in Australia as well as internationally, are finally coming to grips with the issue of racism, at least at the higher institutional levels. The resolutions being passed leave little to be desired. Where action is taken (as in the WCC grants and the Australian churches' support of Aboriginal land rights), this can be of more direct value to black people seeking the achievement of racial justice.

The question remains, how wide and how deep will be the effectiveness of the churches' commitment against racism? Will the Church be simply another organization, making its valuable but limited contribution? Or can it hope to reach down to individual ministers and, through them, out to the hearts and minds of their congregations and the wider community (and, ultimately, their elected representatives)? The Church as an *institution* is becoming mobilized on this issue. But what of the Church as *community*? *Is* the Church in Australia a community in anything other than the immediate spiritual and social concerns of individual congregations? In those parishes where racial antipathies may be overt (e.g. country towns), how can the Church provide a lead without sacrificing its following?

1971 provides an opportunity for the Australian churches to attempt to find the answers to such questions. The answer will be relevant not only to the question of racism, but also to the question of the position of the Church itself in Australian society. 1971 not only provides *an* opportunity but, possibly, *the* last opportunity both for the Church and for Australia as a whole to come to grips with the issue of racism. Any later may well be too late. In the age of McLuhan's 'global village', Australia is isolated from the wider world not geographically but only mentally. Black people *are* living next door. Black people are themselves Australians. And white Australia cannot move elsewhere.

Apart from the distinguished men and women attending the 1969 London Consultation on Racism, one was aware of the invisible presence of three men. One was white—Enoch Powell, who, whatever his purposes, made it acceptable in England to speak the unspeakable. The other two are both black, both Christian, both dead. From Southern Africa one felt the spirit of Albert Luthuli who, from his own greatness of soul, kept the African National Congress so long committed to its historical policy of non-violence. From the United States, one sensed the presence of Martin Luther King, who likewise espoused non-violence and attempted to transcend race by making his campaign one against poverty in general. Luthuli and King were allowed by white society to fail, and their places have been taken by angrier and more determined men. Some telling words of Dr. King's, written shortly before his assassination, were quoted more than once at the Consultation. 'What has counted,' he said, 'has been less the deeds of evil men than the appalling silence of good men.'

These words must be heard, even in Australia. And heeded. It is already too late for good men merely to break their silence by words. Actions alone can speak in 1971.

REFERENCES

1 The Prime Minister (as he then was), Mr. Gorton, did pledge in January, 1970, that the Commonwealth would override discriminatory provisions in Aboriginal legislation in Western Australia and Queensland if those States themselves failed to repeal them. The pledge was not made with any reference to the International Year. *Sydney Morning Herald*, 21st January, 1971.

2 *The Australian*, 23rd December, 1970.

3 *The Australian*, 8th January, 1971.

4 See his 'Sport and Apartheid', *Current Affairs Bulletin*, Vol. 46, No. 12. No. 2, 1970.

5 The U.N.A.A. requested a grant of $20,000 for the purposes of the Year. The Federal Government has granted $12,000. *The Australian*, 21st January, 1971.

6 In his Preface to his play, 'The Black Girl in Search of God'.

7 A few names immediately come to mind from particular crisis situations of recent years, for example, Martin Luther King, Chief Albert Luthuli, Bishop Trevor Huddleston, Bishop Ambrose Reeves, Canon John Collins.

8 For those of the Jewish faith it has, of course, been easier to identify with victims of oppression. At the same time, some blacks now view Jews as among the oppressors, mainly in view of the Middle East situation but also, in the U.S.A., in view of recent troubles in the Ocean Hills-Brownsville school system in New York.

9 The Roman Catholic Church, which is not a member of the WCC, has of course also spoken out against racism, notably at Vatican II. *The Documents of Vatican II*, ed. W. M. Abbott, S. J. (Chapman), The Essential Equality of Men and Social Justice, p. 227, para. 29; Non-Christians, pp. 667-8, para. 5. In Australia, the Episcopal Conference spoke out on racial matters in January, 1971—*Sydney Morning Herald*, 23rd January, 1971. The emphasis in this

paper on the WCC churches at the international and national levels is not intended to suggest that other religious denominations have shown any less concern.

10 'The Many Faces of Ecumenism', *Current Affairs Bulletin*, Vol. 43, No. 8, March 10, 1969.

11 'It is the coincidence, however, of an accumulation of wealth and power in the hands of the white peoples, following upon their historical and economic progress during the past 400 years, which is the reason for a focus on the various forms of *white* racism in the different parts of the world.' Statement from meeting of the WCC Central Committee, Canterbury, 1969.

12 The major exception, the Dutch Reformed Church of South Africa ('the Nationalist Party at prayer') had led a Dutch anthropologist at the Consultation, Professor J. P. Feddema, to study it virtually as an exercise in religious pathology.

13 The Puritan ethic, for example, has commonly been regarded as a factor in the growth of acquisitive capitalism.

14 See ' "Race" in British Politics', *Current Affairs Bulletin*, Vol. 42, No. 12, Nov. 4, 1968.

15 A sort of black ecumenical power movement, co-ordinating the efforts of black clergy in various U.S. denominations, was established in 1967 as the National Committee of Black Churchmen. One of the aims of the movement is the need to 'brown Jesus Christ up a bit'.

16 The Victorian Government announced similar plans in April, 1970, in respect of two reserve areas. *The Australian*, 11th April, 1970.

17 The 'Background Statement on White Racism' presented to the Uppsala Assembly of the WCC stated: '. . . . confrontation arises from the fact that oppressed people realise increasingly that unless they share fully in all of the instruments of power, they will be unable to free themselves from the effects of social exploitation'.

18 The demand for financial reparation from white American churches and synagogues first achieved prominence in a manifesto presented by James Forman to, and adopted by, the National Black Economic Development Conference in Detroit on the 26th April, 1969. The sum then demanded was $500,000,000 or, as Forman put it, '15 dollars per nigger'.

19 The All Africa Conference of Church meeting in Lome, Togo, in September, 1970, unanimously welcomed the WCC action.

20 The warning was immediately defied by the General Assembly of the Presbyterian Church in Capetown—*International Herald Tribune*, 25th September, 1970, and by the South African Council of Churches—*Church Times*, 25th September, 1970. Two Dutch Reformed Churches in South Africa had left the WCC in 1960.

21 The *Daily Telegraph* (London), 26th September, 1970.

22 *Sydney Morning Herald*, 22nd January, 1971.

23 *Sydney Morning Herald*, 12th January, 1971.

24 See 'Race Relations in New Guinea', *Current Affairs Bulletin*, Vol. 44, No. 3, June 30, 1969; 'Bougainville Copper', *Current Affairs Bulletin*, Vol. 45, No. 3, December 29, 1969.

25 See 'Pacific Island Peoples', *Current Affairs Bulletin*, Vol. 44, No. 6, August 11, 1969.

26 On the context for the current dispute over proposed British arms sales to South Africa, see 'U.S.S.R.—and the Indian Ocean', *Current Affairs Bulletin*, Vol. 45, No. 10, April 6, 1970.

27 Dennis Brutus, 'Sport and Aparthied', *Current Affairs Bulletin,* Vol. 46, No. 12, Nov. 2, 1970.

28 Judith Todd, 'The Rhodesia of Mr. Smith', *Current Affairs Bulletin,* Vol. 45, No. 12.

16

THE PROTESTANT CHURCH AND RACE PREJUDICE

F. Engel

No decision of the World Council of Churches, or of the Australian Council of Churches, has aroused so much controversy as the action of the Executive Committee of the W.C.C., in September 1970, in authorising grants totalling $200,000 to nineteen organizations combating racism in twelve countries, including Australia. In this country, there were raised eyebrows that two Australian organizations were included, some ruffled tempers at the grants to African liberation movements, and a flurry of enquiries as to whether the W.C.C. had the power to make the grants (which in fact it clearly did have). Whatever the reasons for the various Australian reactions, it was clear that the W.C.C.'s action had touched Australian churches on a sensitive spot.

Prior to that, in August, the A.C.C. had itself gone on public record at its General Annual Meeting, with a series of statements against the sale of arms to South Africa, racism in sport, trade with Rhodesia and in favour of land rights for the Aborigines.

The flow of correspondence into the A.C.C. office, on both counts, showed that racism had become an issue. It also revealed the division between those who were prepared to accept it as an issue of importance here, as well as abroad, and those who continued to regard it as a foreign imposition.

Significantly, one objection was to Australia being given 'foreign aid'. We are, after all, an affluent country quite capable of financing our own affairs. By implication, it was suggested that the W.C.C. had been ill-advised, extravagant or trouble-making. Such criticism was ignorant of, or over-looked the fact that the Federal Council for the Advancment of Aborigines and Torres Strait Islanders has never had an adequate budget and has rarely had even one full-time secretary during the thirteen years of its existence. The newly-formed National Tribal Council was beginning its search for resources in an atmosphere of suspicion that it might be a 'radical' group.

In Queensland, in fact, there was objection to the N.T.C. being assisted. Such questions were asked as to why the money was not given to churches or missions. In raising questions like these, the grant was making the real issue a living one, namely that the bonds of paternalism should be severed by placing resources and decisions in the hands of an Aboriginal organization organized on a national level. The time had come

for helping these Aborigines to continue the decision-making responsi-
bility and initiative which had been begun by the formation of the
N.T.C. This body had, in fact, come into existence to ensure that
Aboriginal votes determined Aboriginal organizational policy and plans.

Paternalism is the chief form of racism in terms of relations between
Whites and Aborigines. It is not recognized as being racist, or even as
existing, because it is motivated by kindness and by concern for the
well-being of Aborigines. Such motives are transparently good, even
Christian. But what few people have learnt is that the form in which the
motive finds expression is important. One form can be oppressive,
another liberating. Kindness can be lethal or life-giving—in the fullest
sense of either term—depending on the organizational, structural or legal
arrangements. If these do not provide means for the expression of the
personality and rights of Aborigines, and if they do not provide means
for the assumption of responsibility and of decision-making by
Aborigines, they become instruments of oppression no matter how sugar-
coated or 'necessary' they may appear. Genuine kindness becomes the
kindness-that-killed-the-cat type, because it never found the practical
means of transforming paternalistic care into partnership in development.
The Queensland Act (the Aborigines' and Torres Strait Islanders' Affairs
Act of 1965, and its Regulations), with the continued emphasis on the
assistance and close supervision of Aborigines, perpetuates authoritarian
paternalism, and reflects a general attitude in that State which is highly
critical of any Aborigine who is out-spoken or of any action which
implies criticism of the existing state of affairs.

In such a situation, it is not surprising if church members and some
leaders reflect similar attitudes—that Aborigines are in need of assistance
and that it is the responsibility of Church and State to provide it. This
remains the general climate of opinion there and elsewhere, even though
in some places a change has appeared as to the meaning and means of
assistance. A welcome feature of that change has been the initiative in
leadership taken by the National Missionary Council of Australia, the
Australian Council of Churches, and several of its member churches.

But before such changes are considered, it is desirable to recognize
that the Churches in Australia have been largely conditioned in the past
by the prevailing climate of public opinion. They accepted the attitudes
of white, western superiority and supremacy which soon developed after
the early encounters, in and around Sydney, between 1788 and the end of
that century.[1] Such attitudes were based on the obvious facts of
European technological advancement, financial resources, military power
and organizational experience as contrasted with the 'apparent' lack of
Aboriginal equivalents. These contrasts coupled with the often grim
struggle for survival in an inhospitable land of droughts and floods led
quickly to the assumption of racial superiority and the suppression of the
black minority, except in so far as use could be made of them to find water
in the interests of white survival. For example, Ernest Giles, in his
exploration of the Pitjantjatjara country of Central Australia, in 1872,
recorded that 'he wished that he "could catch a native" to lead him to
waters that must have been close by'.[2] Later, having discovered some
small water-holes in rock, he wrote that the Aborigines were 'no doubt
... dreadfully annoyed to find their little reservoirs discovered by such
water-swallowing wretches as they doubtless thought white men to be; I

could only console myself with the reflection, that in such a region as this we must be prepared to lay down our lives at any moment in our attempts to procure water and we must take it when we find it at any price, as life and water are synonymous terms'.[3] The white man in his determined, fear-ridden quest for new and more lands for pasture, again and again bought his own survival at the price of Aboriginal lives for whom life and water were just as vitally linked. This was, in part, due to the white man's ruthless drive for economic wealth and, in part, to his inability to comprehend or appreciate a way of life so different from his own.[4]

Ambition to establish himself in a way of life which was impossible for him in Great Britain, determination to survive, consciousness of technical superiority, and incomprehension of a different culture were fortified by inculcated ideas of Western superiority which had arisen from the conquests of North America and India. These were further strengthened in the latter half of the nineteenth century by the confidence in progress born of the Industrial Revolution and scientific discoveries. So, for example, Ernest Giles wrote in Central Australia:—

'The great Designer of the universe, in the long past periods of creation, permitted a fiat to be recorded, that the beings whom it was His pleasure in the first instance to place amidst these lovely scenes, must eventually be swept from the face of the earth by others more intellectual, more dearly beloved and more gifted than they'.[5]

The language of this essay into theology, in 1873, smacks rather of eighteenth century Deism than of Christianity—which perhaps indicates how long it takes for theological ideas to percolate from academic cloister to lay mind—or it may represent a compromise position between Christianity and the rising scientific humanism of the day. In any case, it expresses a strong and fairly widespread conviction in the superiority of the 'more intellectual, more dearly beloved and gifted' white man from Europe, and the bolstering of this conviction with illegitimate theological arguments.

It has recently been claimed by Hartz, Bastide and others that white racism[6] has been encouraged by Calvinism. While there may be some grounds for this in the case of the distorted Calvinism of the Dutch Reformed Church in South Africa and of some of the churches in the Southern States of the U.S.A., it is doubtful whether it played any direct part in Australian racialism. The latter seems to be due, chiefly, to the bases of Australian colonization—the convict system, the clearing of the Scottish Highlands, the Irish famine, the poverty caused by English industrialization, and the discoveries of gold. Hence the ruthlessness of Australian settlement based as it was on the experience in Britain of cruelty, dispossession and dire necessity. It was not unnatural that such characteristics should mark the advance of white men in Australia, especially as there was no major religious factor or event which made any formative impact on the new colonies. It was pragmatism rather than Puritanism that was decisive.

The indictment of the Churches, then, in the first century or more of Australian settlement, was not that they provided theological grounds and religious motivations for white superiority, but that they did so little to challenge the prevailing mood and actions. It was that they mirrored society too much and Christ too little or too vaguely. Their efforts were pastoral and priestly, rather than prophetic, institution-building rather than policy-making.

Consequently, their chief contribution was to care for the Aborigines by taking to them the Gospel, by translating the Bible into their languages, by establishing schools and nursing services. It was the straight-forward response of concerned Christians desiring to help defeated minorities who were fast disappearing and dying out. In the South, this process of death was rapid for most groups of Aborigines. But in the North, the churches have continued their mission stations, and in several areas added new ones in the twentieth century. In doing so, they have provided a notable service, often involving hardship and sacrifice, which has contributed to the survival of the Aborigines. But the pattern has usually been of white supremacy exercised through a missionary staff—devoted but paternalistic.

Until recent times, there was little attention to problems of malnutrition, to leadership training or to the spiritual awareness and heritage of Aborigines. In other words, until thirty or forty years ago, the missions were limited in their approach by the prevailing conviction that the Aborigines were a dying race, and by the slowness of Australian acceptance of dietetics and sociology as important fields of knowledge.

On the other hand, the Churches operated, almost unwittingly, a bi-racial policy: Missions in remote places for the Aborigines and separate missions to the remote white settler. So, to take one of several examples, the Presbyterian Church, in 1912, began the Australian Inland Mission to cattle stations throughout the outback. It has provided a remarkable service to white cattlemen and their families. But for many years it accepted the cattleman's attitudes toward the Aborigines—namely indifference, condescension and exploitation. Other Churches had similar activities which again reflected the racial apathy, contempt or intolerance of the white settler. It is an irony of history that the A.I.M.'s nursing homes are now busy treating Aboriginal patients. The policy towards Aborigines has had to be re-thought. It has become evident that the Aborigine is here to stay and is increasing rapidly in numbers, that in the northern part of Australia the majority of the population is black and that we are in fact a bi-racial country. The call to the Churches, as to the nation, is to ensure that there develops a multi-racial society based on mutual respect, confidence and acceptance of one another as made equally in the image of God.

Here we come to the basic Christian convictions about race which should have formed the grounds for the Churches' criticism and reformation of the commonly accepted social attitudes of the Australian society. They spring directly from two of the central elements of the Christian faith—the crucifixion and the gift of the Holy Spirit.

St. Paul states the first of these in writing as a Jew to Gentile Ephesians (Ephesians 2:11-22). Seeing the crucifixion as a defeat which had become a victory, a revelation of God's love and power, he recognized it also as the point where the racial separatism of Judaism was broken down. He wrote to Gentile Christians:—

> 'Now in union with Christ Jesus you who once were far off have been brought near through the shedding of Christ's blood. For he is himself our peace. Gentiles and Jews, he has made the two one,

and in his own body of flesh and blood has broken down the emnity which stood like a dividing wall between them; for he annulled the law with its rules and regulations, so as to create out of the two a single new humanity in himself, thereby making peace. This was his purpose, to reconcile the two in a single body to God through the cross, on which he killed the enmity. So he came and proclaimed the good news: peace to you who were far off, and peace to those who were near by; for through him we both alike have access to the Father in the one Spirit.' (Ephesians 2:13-18. N.E.B.)

In the experience of St. Peter, it was the realization of unity 'in the one Spirit' which transformed his attitude. When it became clear to him that, as he put it, 'God has no favourites' and that Romans were as able to receive the Holy Spirit as were Jews, he took the initiative in agreeing to, and arranging for, their baptism, saying: 'Is anyone prepared to with-hold the water for baptism from these persons, who have received the Holy Spirit just as we did ourselves?' (Acts 10:47. N.E.B.) Then he stayed with them for sometime, although, as he had said earlier, he knew 'that a Jew is forbidden by his religion to visit or associate with a man of another race'. Subsequently, he successfully defended his action and change of views before the Church in Jerusalem. The verdict being 'This means that God has granted life-giving repentance to the Gentiles also'. (Acts 11:18.)

Further, baptism is the sacrament of admission into membership of the Church. This alone is the basis of fellowship in the Church, the bond of oneness in Christ. In it a person of whatever race, culture or education receives his identity as a Christian and this identity is shared with all who are baptized into Christ.

There can be no question then that racism is outlawed in the New Testament; and that this is done in terms of central doctrines, not of incidental or peripheral teaching.

This has been recognized by the Churches in that they have taken the good news of Christ to people of all races and have baptized them. But, in most cases, there has been extraordinary slowness on the part of white leadership in Asia, Africa and the Pacific, to be rid of that form of racism which is paternalism.

At the same time, in white societies, there has been too little said or done to bring social morality nearer the higher levels of Christian conviction. Religion has remained too much a 'private matter', and organized society has taken pains for the sake of its own comfort 'to keep religion out of politics'. So we have the phenomenon which Reinhold Niebuhr described as 'moral man and immoral society', 'the constant and seemingly irreconcilable conflict between the needs of society and the imperatives of a sensitive conscience'. He continues: 'This conflict, which could be most briefly defined as the conflict between ethics and politics, is made inevitable by the double focus of the moral life. One focus is in the inner life of the individual, and the other in the necessities of man's social life. From the perspective of society the highest moral ideal is justice. From the perspective of the individual the highest ideal is unselfishness. Society must strive for justice even if it is forced to use means, such as self-assertion, resistance, coercion and perhaps resentment, which cannot gain the moral sanction of the most sensitive moral spirit.

The individual must strive to realise his life by losing and finding himself in something greater than himself.'

'These two moral perspectives are not mutually exclusive and the contradiction between them is not absolute. But neither are they easily harmonised'.[8]

It has, therefore, been easier for the Churches to concentrate on racial harmony as expressed through its missionary movement and through its sense of fellowship with 'the Church overseas' or 'the World Church', than to act for racial equality in society. But, to quote Niebuhr again:—

> 'We can no longer buy the highest satisfactions of the individual life at the expense of social injustice. We cannot build our individual ladders to heaven and leave the total human enterprise unredeemed of its excesses and corruptions'.[9]

It is easier to talk of the need for reconciliation than of justice. It can even be said, with a measure of truth, that the Christian is called to love all men including the Afrikaaner and that, therefore, we should not 'isolate' South Africa. The first part of that statement is unquestionably true. The latter overlooks the fact that justice is a public form of love. Therefore, where injustice exists, as in the case of the suppression of the majority of a population by a small white minority, love is called to act in social and political ways in order that it may find adequate expression of its concern for the welfare of both black and white. If international isolation is the only way left, since forty years of continued contact and consultation have resulted in no response or improvement, then the Christian must face the challenge, even the agony, of incarnating religious ideals in practical policies. It is not for nothing that he himself is a Christian because of the Incarnation—the fact of the Word made flesh that, through His love and suffering, men might be liberated and find both self-realization and universal unity in Him.

In commenting appreciatively on Niebuhr's 'significant and brilliantly developed idea', Kyle Heselden has written:—

> 'but what now needs to be emphasized is not merely the absence of ethical sensitivity in social groups but the ability of the individual Christian to exempt himself from all sense of personal responsibility for the actions of his group and from his own involvement in its failings and to do so on the basis of what he considers to be the prior claims of his religion and by the substituting of personal piety for social justice'.
>
> 'At bottom the question for the church as it faces the racial evils of our day is not whether man is moral and society immoral, but whether the whole formula by which Christians test rightness and wrongness in man and in society is itself corrupt.'[10]

In Australia, it has been corrupted by the secular tradition, by the ignorance, inertia and indifferentism of a conformist and now affluent society, and by a concentration in the Churches on personal piety to the exclusion of clear theological thinking about the meaning of the Gospel and Christian social responsibility. By and large, the popularity of the Church has been more important than the reformation of society, except that some churches have conceived the latter only in terms of the prohibition of alcohol and gambling. In such a situation, it is perhaps not surprising that the Rev. R. J. Jepsen, Presbyterian minister of Walgett,

New South Wales, was forced out of that pulpit and town, in 1970, because he attempted to take Aborigines seriously as human beings under his pastoral care. It is, nevertheless, an indictment of the laity of a church that they have understood so little of the Gospel that their racial attitudes are simply those of the secular white community.

On the other hand, as indicated earlier, there has been at least the beginning of important changes in thought and action in some Church circles. In 1963, the National Missionary Council of Australia, not for the first time, gave significant leadership in a statement called 'The Meaning of Assimilation' which was, in fact, a re-interpretation of that unfortunate word. It set out five principles which must be regarded as fundamental to any policy related to the Aborigines:—

'1. The Aborigines form a distinct ethnic group within the Commonwealth of Australia, biologically and intellectually equal with other ethnic groups. They have rights, as a responsible people, which must be recognised and fully safeguarded.

'2. No law which limits the political or social rights of certain inhabitants on the sole grounds of race or culture can be tolerated.

'3. The assimilation of Aborigines into the life of the community must be subject to their consent. The principle must be recognised that the existence of distinctively Aboriginal groups, at the wish of the Aborigines themselves, need not be detrimental to national well-being. Opportunity for assimilation may be offered, but acceptance must not be forced.

'4. The Aborigines must have the opportunity to participate freely in drawing up plans and executing policies which concern their welfare, whether initiated by Government, Mission, or local community. Assimilation cannot be accomplished quickly or by short cuts: a forced pace, or the too early withdrawal of necessary assistance, would hinder Aboriginal initiative and responsibility.

'5. Because of their prior occupation of the land, the Aborigines have a just claim to adequate provision for their economic, social and educational advancement; and such provision must be made.'

The statement went on to urge that the Government's policy of assimilation be based on the voluntary acceptance of it by Aborigines. It spoke of them as a people with rights, and the need for social equality, assent, participation and economic justice.[11]

At the same time, the N.M.C.A. issued 'Four Major Issues in Assimilation' which were Land, Language, Law and Political Education and Development. Here, for the first time, it was proposed that the 'corporate freehold ownership of remaining reserves' be guaranteed 'as the rightful heritage of certain tribes'; and that a National Aborigines Capital Fund be set up by the Federal Government, 'not as an act of generosity, but as the discharge of an obligation' to make economic assistance available to corporate groups or individuals for the purchase of land or the establishment of industries.

When the N.M.C.A. was integrated with the Australian Council of Churches, the latter took up and publicly advocated this land rights policy. Copies of its two basic documents[12] were circulated widely, including to all members of Australia's seven parliaments. A further statement 'The Future of Aboriginal Missions' issued by the Division of Mission (successor to N.M.C.A.) in 1967 also bore on this subject of land.

In 1969 and 1970, the A.C.C. retained the services of a public relations consultant in Canberra to advocate its policy in the Federal Parliament. In the process, a further and more detailed proposal was agreed on by the A.C.C.'s Executive Committee, in part as follows:—

'1. We want Aboriginal affairs given a higher priority by the Government and the Parliament. We want the Commonwealth to take more initiative on its own account rather than depend so greatly upon state agreement. The Council believes that the measures set out below would help speed up the pace of Aboriginal advancement and eventual assimilation.

'2. The Office of Aboriginal Affairs should be made a Department of State with a full time Minister of Cabinet rank.

'3. Assimilation must be the eventual goal—but assimilation based on choice. Aborigines will choose to assimilate when they enjoy the same rights, social and economic equality and the same sense of participation and belonging as others. The greatest step towards encouraging these qualities is the grant of land rights. The Council believes the Government should grant Aborigines corporate ownership and control of existing reserves in the Northern Territory along the lines laid down in the South Australian 'Aboriginal Land Trusts Act 1966' and should encourage state governments to do likewise.

'4. Control of reserves should include control over mining rights so that mining companies will need to make the same reasonable arrangements with the local inhabitants to obtain mining rights as Broken Hill Proprietary Ltd. made to obtain concessions at Groote Eylandt.

'5. New reserves should be created after a survey by an appropriate authority to establish Aboriginal needs.'

At the beginning of 1970, the A.C.C. Executive wrote to all the Premiers and Leaders of Oppositions (except in South Australia) urging the passing of legislation to provide for land rights.[13]

In 1968, 1969 and 1970, the A.C.C. took action to press the claim of the Gurindji tribe for 500 square miles of the Wave Hill lease in the Northern Territory by two approaches to Lord Vestey, by protests to the Federal Government, and by joining in a joint discussion with the Australian management of the Vestey interests and in the public demonstrations and publicity of the Gurindji Campaign.

In the early 1960s, the Church Missionary Society took out mining rights for Groote Eylandt which enabled them to bargain, subsequently, with Broken Hill Proprietary Ltd. for royalties and other benefits for the Aborigines. Later a trust fund was established under Aboriginal control for the receipt and management of the royalties.

In 1968, due to the initiative of the Christian Citizenship Committee of the Methodist Church of Victoria, legal action was instituted in the Supreme Court of the Northern Territory to establish the ownership of Aboriginal tribes in Arnhem Land to the land which the Federal Government had excised from the Reserve and leased to Nabalco, a bauxite mining company. The A.C.C. contributed a substantial sum towards the legal costs.

In September 1970, the General Assembly of the Presbyterian Church of Australia passed an important resolution on Aboriginal land rights in which the Assembly declared:—

'1 (a) That it is essential for Australian Aborigines to be granted independent corporate ownership of all lands at present and in the future designated as Aboriginal Reserves.

'(b) That special concurrent State and Federal legislation should be introduced to provide such corporate ownership of land and also to provide for corporate commercial and industrial enterprises.

'(c) That it appears the most appropriate form of corporate structure should be on the shire corporation model rather than current Company structures.

'(d) That such corporations should be granted Federal Income Tax relief.

'(e) That all Aboriginal Reserve Land should be exempted from the operation of the provisions of the relevant State or Federal Mining Acts.

'2. That there should be no further alienation of Reserve Land and land previously alienated should be returned or if impracticable the equivalent area be declared Reserve. For instance the area excised in 1955 at Wingellina should be returned.

'3 (a) That where appropriate, land other than reserve land traditionally occupied by Aboriginal groups should be declared Aboriginal Reserves.

'(b) That it gives support to the Gurindji tribe in their request for 500 square miles of the Wave Hill land *and* also supports the claims for land and control of land by the various groups of Aborigines in Arnhem Land.

'4. That the compensation so far given to the Weipa people is completely inadequate having regard to the immense mineral wealth extracted, and despite the promises made to the Church's representatives, no programme has yet been forthcoming to educate and train the people for employment in and about that great industrial undertaking.

'5. That because of past appropriation of Aboriginal tribal land, there is a moral obligation on the Australian nation through Governmental action, to set up an adequate National Aborigines Capital Fund and that such Fund be set up and administered in accordance with the recommendation made by the Division of Mission of the Australian Council of Churches in 1965.

'6. That the foregoing resolutions be communicated to the Federal and State Governments and that all church members be encouraged to make personal representations to their State and Federal Members of Parliament with a view to the implementation of the above policies.'[14]

The Churches have also been active in their opposition to the racial basis of Australia's immigration policy. For example, in the mid-1940s, the Presbyterian Church of Victoria attacked it, as did the National Missionary Council in 1948 and the A.C.C. in the 1950s. In January 1966, the A.C.C.'s Annual Meeting called on the Federal Government *inter alia*:—

'1. To remove as soon as possible the racial discrimination

involved in the rule that non-Europeans may not normally be naturalized in less than fifteen years.

'2. To raise the number of non-Europeans granted permanent residence to some 1500 a year.

'3. To reconsider Australia's policy concerning the entry of skilled and professional people of non-European race.'[15]

H. I. London, in commenting on this in his book 'Non-White Immigration and the "White Australia" Policy', suggested the possibility of some connection with the announcement by the Hon. H. Opperman, Minister for Immigration, in March 1966, of a change in policy: 'The Church Council did not have a direct line to government circles through the Immigration Advisory Committee or the Cabinet. It is therefore highly unlikely that its proposals affected the Opperman announcement directly. But it may have been significant that the Council's resolution was quite similar to the Immigration Department's proposals.'[16]

More recently, the A.C.C. has been concerned that Australia is being identified abroad as an ally of South Africa and Rhodesia, and described as a third white racist country of the South. It has sought to awaken Church opinion on this matter. It has also established a Commission on Race Relations which issued a call to Churches to observe March 21, 1971, the anniversary of Sharpeville, as the beginning of the U.N. Year for Action to Combat Racism and Racial Discrimination.

In that connection, it published a leaflet, 'Racism 1971' which was distributed to the congregations of all its member churches. This was an attempt to overcome the unfortunate gap which exists between pronouncements of ecclesiastical assemblies or ecumenical councils and the habits of thought of the local congregation, or the gap between many clergy and their laity. Here the churches are caught in a double stance and it is of urgent importance that the stance of the leadership become that of the membership also, that the policies and attitudes of the official pronouncements be understood, accepted and advocated by the body of the local clergy and laity. Not because the top leadership is always to be obeyed, but because, in this matter, they point to the regeneration of the Church and without that there is little hope of the transformation of society.

If, however, there is to be a sustained and effective contribution from the Churches, there needs also to be some strenuous theological thinking about such basic issues as the clash between reconciliation and justice, as has been indicated, for example, by the Faith and Order Commission of the World Council of Churches:—

'How can one and the same community embody the priestly mission of reconciliation among men and the prophetic mission of rebuking evil and making militant cause against its attack upon God's creatures and upon the People of God in particular? The agony of the Church lies in the tension which she must share between openness to sinners and the struggle against sin. To the degree that she embraces the diversities of mankind in a catholic unity, to that degree she must also have the courage to embrace and purify and make fruitful the controversies among men, always with the aim of concentrating the attack upon the real evil. At one level this may mean strengthening her practice of Church discipline to make it clear that catholicity does not mean indifferentism and relativism about the ethical and doctrinal implications of authentic unity. On another level, it may mean insisting that those Christians who differ profoundly, particularly on issues of social and political importance, should learn what it means to have vigorous and productive controversy ("speaking the truth in love," Eph. 4), and to commune with each other responsibly as witnesses and brothers of Christ. Again, could it not mean that congregations associate themselves for corporate witness in the world, if necessary on differing sides of the same controversy? This question of how the Church militant unites reconciliation and prophetic action is, as we see it, the most searching challenge to the universal claims of Christian unity in our day.'[17]

In drawing attention to this statement, Professor John Deschner, in an important article in the International Review of Mission, underlined the last sentence and added: '... when reconciliation does not imply liberation, or liberation reconciliation, both are false'.[18]

Australian Churches must also discover that reconciliation between races does not mean that other races are merely permanent paying guests, that is, minorities who are absorbed into and exist at the fringes of the family circle. This is the paternalistic view of the affirmation that 'we are all one in Christ'—a view that is naturally wide-spread in a country in which other races are very small minorities.

John Deschner, in the article already referred to, has pointed to the need for an understanding of baptism in relation to the race problem. Describing baptism as 'the sacrament of Christian identity, the occasion out of which we learn who *we really are*', he asks:—

'But have we adequately grasped the richness of this Christian identity? . . . The identity we receive in baptism is the shared identity of Christ, the New Man. And his humanity is concrete. As the Notting Hill Consultation (of the World Council of Churches) put it:

'Our Lord became incarnate as a member of a particular people, and as such became the New Man and the brother of all men; His Jewishness is inseparable from his representative and universal humanity in the same sense that the Old Testament is inseparable from the New.

'The concreteness is the basis for the universality; Christ is the faithful Jew for all men, the one in whom the ancient vocation of Israel as the Suffering Servant of the nations is truly fulfilled. In Christ it becomes clear that Jewishness is not primarily a "racial identity", but primarily a vocation to be the People of God. In this way He is the universal Christ: The Christ for Indians or for blacks or for outcastes or for whites, only as He is and remains the faithful Jew, fulfilling the covenant for all men.'[19]

Deschner goes on to ask, 'What can all that mean for our problem of "racial identity"?' He answers, 'Certainly not that we ignore it in the name of some universal "humanum". Certainly, the Christian's support of the universality of man and his human rights must never fail! But the Christian knows that the truly universal is the truly concrete, and he will welcome whatever exalts the authentic diversity and richness of human community. He will also be alert to the danger that superficial integrations can mean the universalizing of one particular style and way, and will work for truly diversified, enriched integrations.'[20]

He concludes, 'Ecumenical theology has focused almost exclusively on the light which Christian baptism sheds on the problem of church unity. Is it not time to recognize the light it also throws on our understanding of man and the richness of the diversity which is united in Christ?'[21]

Australian Churches are called to serious study—theological and sociological—and to social and political action to identify racism wherever it exists and to overcome it in the name of Christ. The action cannot await the completion of the study. Nor can the study be of any relevance without involvement in action. Both must go on simultaneously, one refining the other in a continuous encounter with the evil that is racism.

As long ago as 1924, J. H. Oldham wrote in one of the earliest modern books on racism, 'Christianity and the Race Problem':—

> 'Christianity is not primarily a philosophy but a crusade. As Christ was sent by the Father, so He sends His disciples to set up in the world the Kingdom of God. His coming was a declaration of war —a war to the death against the powers of darkness. He was manifested to destroy the works of the devil. Hence when Christians find in the world a state of things that is not in accord with the truth which they have learned from Christ, their concern is not that it should be explained but that it should be ended. In that temper we must approach everything in the relations between races that cannot be reconciled with the Christian ideal.'[22]

In contrast to that, many Australian church people insist that it can all be 'explained'. 'Don't rock the boat. Things will gradually improve if we are not interfered with by outsiders'. In our geographical isolation, it is hard for many to realise that 'gradualism' has had more than enough time, that time has run out, that urgency is the key note of the day.

REFERENCES

1 For a treatment of the changing attitudes of Governor Phillip, see STANNER, W. E. H., 'After the Dreaming', Sydney: Australian Broadcasting Commission, 1968.

2 GILES, E., 'Australia Twice Traversed', Vol. 1, p. 83, quoted by W. Hilliard, *The People in Between,* London: Hodder and Stoughton, 1968.

3 GILES, E., *op. cit.,* Vol. 1, p. 212, quoted in W. Hilliard, *op. cit.,* p. 42.

4 The fact that some white men acted differently is recorded by MARY DUROCK in *Kings in Grass Castles,* London: Constable and Co., 1959, p. 71.
'One of the party, about to move on, dipped his leather water bag into the well. Instantly there were lowered brows and upraised spears, for the blacks were masters still in this timeless country where life was sustained by a stern discipline of mind and body uncomprehended by the white. These little reservoirs in an arid land had succoured the traveller from time beyond memory and were a sacred tribal trust, not to be camped on for unnecessary time, their contents never to be carried away. The water was tipped back and following the example of the blacks, the whitemen placed pebbles under their tongues.'
And yet she has to add of the same men at another place when the blacks had vanished: '. . . . the water in their canteens was low and when these were filled and the horses watered for the return journey, the little native well was

drained dry. And already men were saying of a people whose lives had been pared and restrained to a system of survival remarkable among all races on earth—"The blacks have no thought for tomorrow" '.

5 GILES, *op. cit.*, p. 184.

6 White racism was defined by the Uppsala Assembly of the World Council of Churches as follows:—

'By white racism we mean the conscious or unconscious belief in the inherent superiority of persons of European ancestry (particularly those of Northern European origin), which entitles all white peoples to a position of dominance and privilege, coupled with the belief in the innate inferiority of all darker peoples, especially those of African ancestry, which justifies their subordination and exploitation. By focusing upon white racism, we are not unaware of other forms of ethnocentrism which produce inter-ethnic and inter-tribal tensions and conflicts throughout the world today.' The Uppsala 1968 Report (W.C.C., Geneva, 1968), p. 241.

7 There could, therefore, be no greater distortion of Christianity than the attempt made to justify apartheid by reference to an Old Testament passage which speaks of black people being 'hewers of wood and drawers of water', for it denies the centrality of Christ in the Bible and the need to re-interpret all that went before him in the light of his fulfilment of the law and the prophets.

8 NIEBUHR, REINHOLD, *Moral Man and Immoral Society*, New York, Charles Scribner's Sons, 1941, p. 257.

9 *Ibid*, p. 277.

10 HASELDEN, KYLE, *The Racial Problem in Christian Perspective*, London, Lutterworth Press, 1959, p. 62.

11 National Missionary Council of Australia, Sydney, 1963. 'The Meaning of Assimilation', continued:—

'THE MEANING OF VOLUNTARY ASSIMILATION

The foregoing fundamental principles must colour our understanding of the purposes of the policy of assimilation, the means whereby the legal equality of the Aborigines is to be assured and the manner in which economic and social equality, whether in the mainstream of society or outside it, is to be offered.

1. A PEOPLE WITH RIGHTS:

The policy of assimilation should be interpreted in terms of voluntary, not compulsory, assimilation and should aim at granting Aborigines the opportunity to take their places in Australian society if they so wish.

Voluntary assimilation implies freedom of movement for Aborigines from State to State and from district to district. It also implies full access to all Australian institutions on the same conditions as those pertaining to other Australians.

2. SOCIAL EQUALITY:

It is recognised that assimilation is a two-way process and the greater initiative rests with the white Australian. Every effort needs to be made by responsible authorities, and particularly within the Churches, to encourage in the general public an attitude of acceptance of the Aborigines as full and worthy citizens of Australia, and to discourage all discrimination against them.

Christian people should have a sense of deep obligation to share their fellowship, their faith and their society with the Aborigines.

3. THE NEED FOR ASSENT:

The policy of voluntary assimilation requires the provision of alternatives to participation in the mainstream of Australian life, an opportunity to remain outside it if desired.

Provision must be made by Governments to assist the progress of such groups as remain unassimilated by giving adequate financial assistance for their community development, including joint economic enterprises capable of sustaining the community whose members wish to maintain their community's independent identity.

Insistence on the inevitability of assimilation can defeat assimilation by creating feelings of anxiety, resentment and resistance, with the rejection of new ideas and institutions; therefore, administration of the policy must be in the hands of adequately trained persons who understand the importance of voluntary acceptance of the policy and participation in it.

4. PARTICIPATION:

Independent Aboriginal communities will require the development of leadership; and this must be encouraged through adequate training and practical opportunities.

5. ECONOMIC JUSTICE:

Assimilation requires that there be access to education comparable to that available to other Australians.

It requires economic assistance. Aborigines can exercise a genuine choice between isolation and assimilation only if they are economically able to do so. Opportunity to be assimilated, if they wish, is not opportunity to be absorbed into the labour pool of the general community, but equality of opportunity to participate independently in free enterprise, to train for and enter the professions, and to learn useful skills and trades.'

12 *The Land Rights of Australian Aborigines* (1965) and *Turning Land into Hope* (1968), both by FRANK ENGEL.

13 The South Australian Parliament enacted its Aboriginal Land Trust Act in December, 1966. It is interesting to note that while the Victorian Government replied to the A.C.C. with arguments against the proposal, it shortly afterwards took steps to transfer title to Aborigines in respect of the Lake Tyers and Framlingham reserves.

14 Minutes of Proceedings of the Thirty-Second General Assembly of the Presbyterian Church of Australia, Sydney, September, 1970, Minute 75.

15 A.C.C. Annual Meeting Minutes, January, 1966, Minute 59.

16 LONDON, H. I. *Non-White Immigration and 'White Australia Policy'*, Sydney University Press, 1970, p. 39.

17 Faith and Order Paper No. 54, pp. 17-18, quoted in *International Review of Mission*, Vol. LIX, No. 235, July, 1970, pp. 292-3.

18 DESCHNER, JOHN, Ecclesiological Aspects of the Race Problem, *International Review of Mission*, July 1970, p. 293.

19 *Ibid*, pp. 287-8.

20 *Ibid*, p. 289.

21 *Ibid*, p. 290.

22 OLDHAM, J. H. *Christianity and the Race Problem*, London, SCM Press, 1924, p. 26.

17

THE CATHOLIC CHURCH AND RACE PREJUDICE

R. A. Mulkearns

In an independent African country last year, I spoke to a young coloured girl who was awaiting a passage to England, where she hoped to start a new life. She was born in Africa, but her parents were from Goa and hence she was not an African citizen. She had been told that she must leave the country in which she had been born, the only country she had ever known. Aware that those who were not citizens had been given the opportunity to apply for citizenship after her country had achieved its independence, I asked her why she had not taken advantage of this offer whilst it was open. 'We just could not foresee, at that time, what the future would be like here', she replied. 'And now we are very glad that we did not accept citizenship because those of our background who did so are now being discriminated against here and they are unable to leave'. Why choose England for a new start in life? 'My parents, coming from Goa, hold Portuguese Passports. If we return to Goa, these Passports will be destroyed and we will automatically become Indian citizens. But Goans are allegedly being discriminated against in their own country by those who "liberated" them. The only opportunity open to us appears to be that of travelling to England on Portugese Passports and endeavouring to settle there'.

In an adjoining independent African country, I asked an American missionary if there was a barber in the town in which I was staying. He replied that there was, but that he would have to find out his new location. The barber, an Indian, had had a shop in the main street. A law was then passed declaring this street to be an 'African Street'—nobody but an African was permitted to trade in it. The Indian barber thus had to sell his shop—and he was obviously in no position to bargain over the price, since he was forbidden by law to retain it—and seek alternative premises in a side street, where I ultimately found him.

These instances, which may appear to have little bearing on the Australian scene, are mentioned in order to try to place the issue of Racism and Racial Discrimination in perspective. Racism is not a prejudice peculiar to white people. It is unfortunately to be found in almost all communities. Harsh discriminatory laws are on the books in South Africa, for example, but in other parts of that continent African discriminates against Indian and against European, as surely as the European and Indian discriminate against African. Economic arguments brought forward to justify the expulsion of non-citizens from the African countries of their birth are the same arguments as those used by Australians to justify keeping Australia white. But added to these arguments, which may sometimes have a certain validity, is almost always a measure of prejudice or of bitterness. What most people who protest that they are 'as good as anyone else' really mean is that they are better!

Nor is racial discrimination easily identified or isolated. Within races, there can and does exist tribal and class prejudice. In *An African Autobiography*, South African born Ezekiel Mphahlele writes:—

'I have no romantic ideas about Africans or Nigerians, only a vague feeling that where race conflicts are negligible, Africans can treat one another decently. I have no illusions about the fact that the problem of haves and have-nots is a universal one (and that in Southern Africa it is only magnified by colour prejudice). But I was not prepared for the rude shock that assailed me. I saw times without number the manner in which Nigerians treated their domestic servants, chauffeurs, and other workers. A man who considers his social or economic status to be high, whether he is literate or not, treats his domestics in a way I have come to associate only with the white man in the south.'

(Quoted in *African Writing Today*, Penguin Books, 1967, p. 259.)

In the same anthology, Ake Loba, of the Ivory Coast, has one of his characters utter a significant comment when he says: 'Can you give me the name of a single educated African who doesn't want to go into politics? Doesn't Kocoumbo sleep and eat and complain about life? Doesn't he bear grudges against other people? Well, that's politics!' (*op. cit.* p. 215).

That racial, tribal or class discrimination is divisive of the human family is both un-Christian and clear. But it would be extremely difficult for the objective observer, if such there be, to single out any race, tribe or class that would be justified in casting the first stone.

The second reason for mentioning the two victims of prejudice, amongst many encountered last year, is to recall a fundamental fact that, in speaking of racial relations and of Christian attitudes, there is a dangerous tendency to think of the inhabitants of our world, especially of the more populous nations, in terms of 'masses' of people, without due consideration of the fact that it is individuals who go to make up these masses. The two mentioned are individuals who are affected by the decisions of governments and the attitudes and prejudices of their neighbours. They are people who share the same hopes and who suffer the same pain, anxiety, disillusionment and frustrations as ourselves. It is individuals, not 'masses' who are affected by the failure of men to appreciate their solidarity and interdependence.

Against this somewhat depressing background, the Christian must face the problem of racial discrimination. He must face it constructively and optimistically, aware of the immense and exciting possibilities which would be opened up if the world at large were to embrace in practice as well as in theory the truth of the common brotherhood shared by all men with Christ and each other under the fatherhood of God.

To the Christian, the central fact of the history of the world and the basis for any adequate appreciation of the dignity and unity of man is the fact of the coming of Christ. 'God wanted', St. Paul tells us, 'all perfection to be found in Him and all things to be reconciled through Him and for Him, everything in heaven and everything on earth, when He made peace by His death on the Cross'. (Colossians 19:20)

To be a Christian means more than to be a member of an organisation or Church which Christ founded some 2,000 years ago. It means to
be caught up in an eternal plan of God which began with the first act of
creation and which will culminate in the Second Coming of Christ, a
plan of which the Church of the New Testament is but one phase. It
means to belong to a community which includes the whole of mankind
and to have responsibilities towards the whole of mankind.

God's purpose in creating us was to reflect and to communicate His
own glory and His own life of love. He knew full well that the human
race was going to reject His offer of adoption and to cut itself off from
the source of divine life. In order then to make it possible for us to be
rescued from this predicament, God included in His eternal plan the
Redemption—the winning-back—of the human race through Christ.

Christ's coming was therefore to be the central fact of the world's
history. He was the redeemer of the whole human family, of those who
went before Him as well as those who were to come after Him. All men
who had believed in the promises of God's first Covenant with His chosen
People—that He would send them a Redeemer—were saved by Christ. For
the people of the Old Testament, it was faith in the Christ Who was to
come which saved them; for us it is our faith in the Christ Who has come.
We no longer have the promise of a Saviour, but the reality of His
Presence in the Church.

With the coming of Christ into the World, God's plan entered its
second phase, its present phase. The notion of the Church, the People of
God, became more precise in the Church of the New Testament. Yet it is
important to keep in mind that the family of the people of God, the
community of which we are a part, extends beyond the present stage of
history, that all who from the beginning of the world were, or are, or
will be justified, make up one Church in the sense that they are made
holy by one faith in Christ.

The Church of the New Testament in which we now find ourselves
is therefore neither a beginning nor an end. It lies between the Old
Testament which it fulfils and the Heavenly Church for which it prepares
and which it already anticipates in its life of grace. It is the present
expression of God's eternal plan for all men. Each member is personally a
child of God, but is not an isolated individual; he is a member of the
family of God, the body of Christ, united with all those who live in
Christ.

This extension of the notion of what it is to be a member of the
Church should make us realise the dignity and importance of the role
each of us has been given by God. Christ did not want to save the world
without me; but He calls on me to collaborate, to work with Him, in the
plan which began with the beginning of the world and will be completed
only at the end of time. We are invited to develop the gifts which we
have received and to contribute to the growth of the body of which we
are living, free and conscious members.

Each one of us has been placed by God in a given location, for a
particular vocation, with a personal and irreplaceable contribution to
make in the plan of God to restore the whole of creation in Christ and
we should be haunted by this thought of the total growth of the
community of Christ for which we are called upon to work in every way
possible.

In the first Christian community, St. Luke tells us in Acts 2:44-45, 'the faithful all lived together and owned everything in common; they sold their goods and possessions and shared out the proceeds among themselves according to what each one needed'. These people appreciated the fact that the gifts that they had received had not been given to be hoarded but to be shared. They realised that to be a Christian meant to be involved, in a personal manner and as a brother of Christ, in an undertaking so vast that it sweeps aside all his own little plans and transforms the whole meaning of his life. The Christian can no longer be taken up with himself, with his egoism, introspection or narrow, parochial outlook. He can no longer refuse to give himself to Christ and co-operate with Him in the redemption of the world. He will be conscious of a vocation to membership in a great body, a living community, profoundly united through common sonship and, consequently, common brotherhood.

Christ had spoken of the vine and branches, but it was only after the Spirit came that the real meaning of His simile became clear to His disciples. It was then that the life sap was felt in the branches and the inescapable fact that this life united all of the branches and made them inter-dependent came home.

Christ's command to love our neighbour was not new. In Leviticus we read: 'You must love your neighbour as yourself' (Lev. 19:18). Yet Christ did bring a new commandment or, if we prefer, a new dimension to the love which the Old Testament had tried to instil. Henceforth God Himself is to be found in every man and waits there to be loved. The man who had been only a neighbour has now become a brother. If we are sons of the same Father, infused with His life, then we are brothers. Our fellow men are, as it were, God on our door-step.

Pope Paul hammered this theme in his recent message for the 1971 World Day of Peace. 'True peace must be founded upon justice, upon a sense of the intangible dignity of man, upon the recognition of an abiding and happy equality between men, upon the basic principle of human brotherhood, that is, of the respect and love due to each man, because he is man. The victorious word springs forth, because he is a brother. My brother, our brother'. Again he says: 'Whoever works to educate the rising generations in the conviction that every man is our brother, is building from the foundation the edifice of peace. Whoever implants in public opinion the sentiment of human brotherhood without reserve, is preparing better days for the world ... A true brotherhood, among men, to be authentic and binding, presupposes and demands a transcendental Fatherhood .... We can teach human brotherhood, that is peace, by teaching men to acknowledge, to love, to invoke our Father in heaven.'

In Africa, in America, in Asia, in Europe and in Australia, people— not masses, but individuals like you and the person next to you—are being affected by their environment, an environment which will be affected to some extent by the manner in which we correspond to God's invitation to work with Him for the salvation of the world. It is important, and not always easy, to recall that God thought enough of each individual Asian and African and European and Australian and American to create his human soul by a direct, personal act of love. Christ thought enough of each individual to suffer and to die and to rise again in order that he might be given the opportunity to fulfil the destiny for which he was made. We must surely think enough of our brothers to respect them as at least equals, to treat them as persons, to make their hopes and fears ours.

The Christian is often told that he should see Christ in other people. In addition to this—or perhaps simply another way of facing the same truth—it is desirable to see Christ in ourselves. A realisation of the fact that Christ is in him and wants to love the world through him will hopefully lead the Christian to adopt Christ's standards, will make him less self-centred, more sensitive to the needs of others. The miracle Christ wants to work through Christians is a miracle of love, so that the world will in fact see that they love one another and will be drawn together into that love. It is interesting to reflect that, in the description of the Last Judgment given by St. Matthew (ch. 25, vv. 31-46), even the virtuous will ask the questions: 'Lord, when did we see you hungry and feed you?' etc. This implies that even those who go through the motions of loving God and their fellow men can be missing out on the real thrill of doing this for their Father and their brothers in the family of God.

It would be much easier for the Christian to live according to this basic philosophy, to act as Christ would have him act, if other people appreciated and acknowledged his good intentions. Unfortunately, prejudice built up over centuries and the betrayal of their trust and heritage by predators who have carried the name 'Christian' with dishonour have created an atmosphere of distrust and suspicion even amongst the most sincere. On the other hand, there is a great deal of good-will to be found amongst individuals and groups the world over, as is witnessed by the many World Development and Aid programmes currently flourishing and even by the production of such volumes as the present series. Though the task seems a formidable one, each Christian can make a definite contribution towards the establishment of an environment in which the good-will to be found amongst individuals the world over will be shared by the world's leaders and will triumph over suspicion, an environment in which the hopes and aspirations of individuals—people and not statistics —may be realised in an atmosphere which respects the dignity of each person, whatever his race or colour.

The project is vast. Here, as in other human enterprises, it is surely better to light one candle than to curse the darkness.